Building J2EE™ Applications with the Rational Unified Process

The Addison-Wesley Object Technology Series

Grady Booch, Ivar Jacobson, and James Rumbaugh, Series Editors

For more information, check out the series web site at www.awprofessional.com/otseries.

Ahmed/Umrysh, *Developing Enterprise Java Applications with J2EE™ and UML*

Arlow/Neustadt, *Enterprise Patterns and MDA: Building Better Software with Archetype Patterns and UML*

Arlow/Neustadt, *UML and the Unified Process: Practical Object-Oriented Analysis and Design*

Armour/Miller, *Advanced Use Case Modeling: Software Systems*

Bellin/Simone, *The CRC Card Book*

Bergström/Råberg, *Adopting the Rational Unified Process: Success with the RUP*

Binder, *Testing Object-Oriented Systems: Models, Patterns, and Tools*

Bittner/Spence, *Use Case Modeling*

Booch, *Object Solutions: Managing the Object-Oriented Project*

Booch, *Object-Oriented Analysis and Design with Applications, 2E*

Booch/Bryan, *Software Engineering with ADA, 3E*

Booch/Rumbaugh/Jacobson, *The Unified Modeling Language User Guide*

Box/Brown/Ewald/Sells, *Effective COM: 50 Ways to Improve Your COM and MTS-based Applications*

Carlson, *Modeling XML Applications with UML: Practical e-Business Applications*

Collins, *Designing Object-Oriented User Interfaces*

Conallen, *Building Web Applications with UML, 2E*

D'Souza/Wills, *Objects, Components, and Frameworks with UML: The Catalysis(SM) Approach*

Douglass, *Doing Hard Time: Developing Real-Time Systems with UML, Objects, Frameworks, and Patterns*

Douglass, *Real-Time Design Patterns: Robust Scalable Architecture for Real-Time Systems*

Douglass, *Real Time UML, 3E: Advances in The UML for Real-Time Systems*

Eeles/Houston/Kozaczynski, *Building J2EE™ Applications with the Rational Unified Process*

Fontoura/Pree/Rumpe, *The UML Profile for Framework Architectures*

Fowler, *Analysis Patterns: Reusable Object Models*

Fowler et al., *Refactoring: Improving the Design of Existing Code*

Fowler, *UML Distilled, 3E: A Brief Guide to the Standard Object Modeling Language*

Gomaa, *Designing Concurrent, Distributed, and Real-Time Applications with UML*

Gomaa, *Designing Software Product Lines with UML*

Graham, *Object-Oriented Methods, 3E: Principles and Practice*

Heinckiens, *Building Scalable Database Applications: Object-Oriented Design, Architectures, and Implementations*

Hofmeister/Nord/Dilip, *Applied Software Architecture*

Jacobson/Booch/Rumbaugh, *The Unified Software Development Process*

Jordan, *C++ Object Databases: Programming with the ODMG Standard*

Kleppe/Warmer/Bast, *MDA Explained: The Model Driven Architecture™: Practice and Promise*

Kroll/Kruchten, *The Rational Unified Process Made Easy: A Practitioner's Guide to the RUP*

Kruchten, *The Rational Unified Process, 3E: An Introduction*

Lau, *The Art of Objects: Object-Oriented Design and Architecture*

Leffingwell/Widrig, *Managing Software Requirements, 2E: A Use Case Approach*

Manassis, *Practical Software Engineering: Analysis and Design for the .NET Platform*

Marshall, *Enterprise Modeling with UML: Designing Successful Software through Business Analysis*

McGregor/Sykes, *A Practical Guide to Testing Object-Oriented Software*

Mellor/Balcer, *Executable UML: A Foundation for Model-Driven Architecture*

Mellor et al., *MDA Distilled: Principles of Model-Driven Architecture*

Naiburg/Maksimchuk, *UML for Database Design*

Oestereich, *Developing Software with UML, 2E: Object-Oriented Analysis and Design in Practice*

Page-Jones, *Fundamentals of Object-Oriented Design in UML*

Pohl, *Object-Oriented Programming Using C++, 2E*

Pollice et al. *Software Development for Small Teams: A RUP-Centric Approach*

Quatrani, *Visual Modeling with Rational Rose 2002 and UML*

Rector/Sells, *ATL Internals*

Reed, *Developing Applications with Visual Basic and UML*

Rosenberg/Scott, *Applying Use Case Driven Object Modeling with UML: An Annotated e-Commerce Example*

Rosenberg/Scott, *Use Case Driven Object Modeling with UML: A Practical Approach*

Royce, *Software Project Management: A Unified Framework*

Rumbaugh/Jacobson/Booch, *The Unified Modeling Language Reference Manual*

Schneider/Winters, *Applying Use Cases, 2E: A Practical Guide*

Smith/Williams, *Performance Solutions: A Practical Guide to Creating Responsive, Scalable Software*

Stevens/Pooley, *Using UML, Updated Edition: Software Engineering with Objects and Components*

Unhelkar, *Process Quality Assurance for UML-Based Projects*

van Harmelen, *Object Modeling and User Interface Design: Designing Interactive Systems*

Wake, *Refactoring Workbook*

Warmer/Kleppe, *The Object Constraint Language, 2E: Getting Your Models Ready for MDA*

White, *Software Configuration Management Strategies and Rational ClearCase®: A Practical Introduction*

The Component Software Series

Clemens Szyperski, Series Editor

For more information, check out the series web site at www.awprofessional.com/csseries.

Allen, *Realizing eBusiness with Components*

Apperly et al., *Service- and Component-based Development: Using the Select Perspective™ and UML*

Atkinson et al., *Component-Based Product Line Engineering with UML*

Cheesman/Daniels, *UML Components: A Simple Process for Specifying Component-Based Software*

Szyperski, *Component Software, 2E: Beyond Object-Oriented Programming*

Whitehead, *Component-Based Development: Principles and Planning for Business Systems*

Building J2EE™ Applications with the Rational Unified Process

Peter Eeles

Kelli Houston

Wojtek Kozaczynski

✦Addison-Wesley

Boston • San Francisco • New York • Toronto • Montreal
London • Munich • Paris • Madrid
Capetown • Sydney • Tokyo • Singapore • Mexico City

Many of the designations used by manufacturers and sellers to distinguish their products are claimed as trademarks. Where those designations appear in this book, and Addison-Wesley, Inc. was aware of a trademark claim, the designations have been printed with initial capital letters or in all capitals.

The authors and publisher have taken care in the preparation of this book, but make no expressed or implied warranty of any kind and assume no responsibility for errors or omissions. No liability is assumed for incidental or consequential damages in connection with or arising out of the use of the information or programs contained herein.

The publisher offers discounts on this book when ordered in quantity for special sales. For more information, please contact:

Pearson Education Corporate Sales Division
201 W. 103rd Street
Indianapolis, IN 46290
(800) 428-5331
corpsales@pearsoned.com

Visit Addison-Wesley on the Web: www.awprofessional.com

Library of Congress Cataloging-in-Publication Data

Eeles, Peter, 1962-
  Building J2EE applications with the rational unified process / Peter
Eeles, Kelli Houston, Wojtek Kozaczynski.
        p. cm.
Includes bibliographical references and index.
    ISBN 0-201-79166-8
  1. Java (Computer program language) 2. Computer
software–Development. 3. Software engineering. I. Houston, Kelli.
II. Kozaczynski, Wojtek. III. Title.
    QA76.73.J38 E355 2002
    005.13'3–dc21

                                                    2002007332

ISBN 0-201-79166-8
Text printed on recycled paper
2 3 4 5 6 7 8 9 10 11—PH—0807060504
Second printing, May 2004

Contents

Foreword

by Philippe Kruchten

For a long time, I've wanted a book that clearly describes a new technology, a process, and a related project so that I can understand the practical relationships between these essential ingredients that all software development organizations juggle with. But I also understand how difficult it can be to combine all these elements in one book.

Describing a new technology is hard. Well, sort of. If you are an expert, you can indeed describe it to any level of detail, enumerate all the parts, and produce yet another one of those massive 1,500-page volumes that seem to be the craze in the IT world lately. But then it reads like a catalog of integrated circuits—very dry and boring, with few "why's" and "how's" to relate the parts. In fact, you want easy access to this information, but you do not want to read it as a book. It is hard to understand how to effectively use a new technology without putting it in the context of a project and a process, that is, without giving examples of recipes for how to actually use it.

Describing a software development process is hard. I know. This is what I have tried to do for the last six years. Either the process is too generic, painted in broad strokes, and the reader is left to fill in the methods, recipes, templates, and heuristics required to make project decisions. Or, the process is overly precise and specific, and gives in great detail the methods, recipes, templates, and heuristics for specific domains and technologies, and then the process becomes huge, unwieldy, and cumbersome—a straightjacket. A process only has value in as much as it helps the practitioners develop software. Without ties to specific examples, it remains abstract and mysterious. Without ties to technologies, too much is left for the practitioner to invent. It is a classic double-bind: cursed if you do, cursed if you don't.

Describing the inner workings of one specific software project is moderately interesting in itself, unless you are its developing or maintaining organization. After all, the likelihood that your project will use exactly the same solutions as someone else's is low. Giving an example alone, without the reasoning for the choices behind it, is of little value. Also, many textbook examples are so small that their illustrative value is limited, which sometimes even turns against the features that they want to illustrate.

But if we could combine the essence of a *technology*, illustrate its use on an actual, full-size *example project*, and at the same time communicate the *development process* that was used to design this project, we would win on all three fronts. We put the technology to practical use: the parts of the catalog now make sense. By going through the process, we understand how and why the decisions were made to pick this or that part, which is more important than the decision itself because you want to replicate the process, not just copy the solutions. By using a single, nontrivial example, you expose some of the harder problems, the ones related to the complexity of the system, its architecture, rather than the shortsighted details of one single feature of the technology.

Combining in one single book these three aspects:

- **Technologies.** The UML, Java, J2EE
- **Process.** The Rational Unified Process (RUP)
- **Example.** The Online Auction application

is precisely what my friends and colleagues Kelli, Peter, and Wojtek have successfully attempted here, without creating yet another monster of paper. I am personally delighted that they have picked the RUP as the basis for the process aspect. Like the puppets in *The Nutcracker* ballet, the RUP in this book suddenly comes to life. And, the book gives a new perspective to RUP and a rationale (no pun intended) for all the RUP activities, templates, and heuristics that they have selected. The book also helps the reader understand that the RUP is very accessible and flexible, and not a heavyweight bureaucratic monster.

This is a book that a J2EE developer can use as a compass for direction and as a jump-off point to go elsewhere for details. Inside I learned quite a few things about J2EE—a technology that I have never used on an actual project; I learned a lot through the example of the auction system. And at the same time, although I am deeply familiar with the RUP, I now see it in a different light. I am sure you will enjoy and learn a lot from this book, and that it will help you understand not only the technology that you will want to use on your next software endeavor, but also the "how's" and the "why's" to put it to work. Kelli, Peter, Wojtek: you've added 1 + 1 + 1, and got a 10. Bravo! And thank you.

Philippe Kruchten
Rational Fellow
Director, RUP Development

Foreword

by John Crupi

I did a search on Amazon.com for all books with Java in their title and came up with almost 1,700 books. That is pretty amazing for a technology that isn't even a decade old. So I took a look at some of the titles and not surprisingly, most of the books were "how to" learn some Java technology. Very few were actually about "how to" design and architect with Java technology. This makes sense, because just as you first must learn how to walk before you can run, you (in my opinion) must first learn the technology before you can even think about designing with the technology.

When writing *Core J2EE Patterns*, Deepak Alur, Dan Malks, and I added an epilogue on pattern-driven design ("J2EE Patterns Applied"). Our original intent was to show how to go from a business problem to an application design that was based on the patterns. We began documenting a prescriptive process for selecting the appropriate J2EE patterns. But, as we got further into documenting this process, we realized that this chapter was growing to the size of all the previous chapters. Also, based on early feedback from reviewers, we were told that for the context of a patterns book, developers did not want to see a lot of process, they wanted more of a learn-by-example approach. This was fine for us, because we weren't methodologists and were happy to leave that to the experts.

Lucky for us, this book was written. Kelli, Peter, and Wojtek have done a great job of providing process understanding in the context of J2EE. The authors provide a prescriptive model with input artifacts, activities, and resulting artifacts. Using a "learn-by-example" approach, they show in an easily understandable and digestible way how process is applied to build J2EE applications. Once you start getting the hang of things and become comfortable with RUP, it is no longer necessary to constantly refer to it for guidance—it has become "second nature." In this case, we can treat the process as being descriptive in that it is a rich source of knowledge should we need it.

Since the same process can be treated as being either "prescriptive" or "descriptive," this book can be used by both novices and experts, and anyone in between.

Technology is not getting any easier; actually, I think it is getting more sophisticated and complex. The end result is that new technology does more for you and essentially lets you create much more complex systems. J2EE can therefore be viewed as a set of technologies and APIs, which essentially gives you a platform on which to design and build sophisticated business applications—but how? In the typical cycle of new technologies, you end up spending the early part of the cycle learning the technology. Then, you move on to learning how to best apply the technology and how not to apply the technology. This part of the cycle can take a few years to really figure out. Unfortunately, early adopters have little or no guidance in the form of best practices, patterns, and so on—basically because it hasn't been practiced much.

From the success of our *Core J2EE Patterns* book, we know that developers like J2EE patterns. Patterns seem to be the "sweet spot" of design reuse and at the right abstraction for developers. But, there is great opportunity to take patterns beyond the cataloging in a book. There is the opportunity to automate the application of the patterns and to introduce patterns into a process. And that is exactly what the authors have done with RUP and J2EE. RUP is a very powerful process and has been well defined and streamlined for J2EE in this book. What I really like about this book is how the authors introduce J2EE patterns into the RUP design process. The authors have also recognized that patterns by themselves are of modest value. The real value appears when the patterns are combined to address a larger problem. This is what the authors refer to as "reference architectures" and, in my opinion, really help you jumpstart and accelerate J2EE design and development.

I think this book is a great asset to all J2EE developers who want to take advantage of RUP and learn how to apply a proven methodology to the J2EE design and development process.

John Crupi
Coauthor *Core J2EE Patterns*
Distinguished Engineer
Sun Microsystems

Preface

About This Book

This book is about developing Java 2 Platform, Enterprise Edition (J2EE) applications with the Rational Unified Process (RUP) and the Unified Modeling Language (UML). There are a number of books describing the J2EE platform and its associated technologies. There are also books about software development processes and about RUP, in particular. However, we could not find a book that described and exemplified how to use a subset of RUP that contains only the most relevant parts of an otherwise large and comprehensive process, to build J2EE applications. The book bridges this gap between the RUP and J2EE technologies.

A world that combines J2EE, RUP and UML is complex. This world requires a good map if you are to successfully navigate your way through it. This book provides such a map both metaphorically and literally. It is metaphorical because the very objective of the book is to provide a description of a "safe path" through the J2EE application development activities. It is also literal because we define a "J2EE Developer Roadmap," which is a process map, to guide us. We describe the content of the book in more detail in Chapter 1, Introduction.

Who This Book Is For

While writing the book we kept three audiences in mind. The first audience is software architects, designers and developers familiar with the J2EE platform and its technologies, wanting to understand how to apply them in the context of a software development process. The second audience is development team members familiar with RUP, looking for help in applying the process to J2EE development. The third audience is software professionals who are neither familiar with J2EE nor with RUP, and are looking for an example of how to use RUP in the development of a J2EE application.

Conventions Used in This Book

The book is roughly divided into two parts. The first part, Chapters 2–5, summarizes the J2EE technologies, introduces RUP and the J2EE Developer Roadmap, and briefly describes our sample application. The rest of the book is what we refer to as the "process chapters" and contains a guided tour through a J2EE application development project.

We structured the process chapters to make them easy to read "at a glance," and to make it easy to refer to specific topics of interest. Each process chapter is organized primarily by activities. We provide diagrams that indicate the overall flow between the activities and the key artifacts that are consumed and produced by the activities. For each activity, we provide an overview table that summarizes the purpose of the activity, its input and output artifacts, and a summary of the steps performed within the activity. Following the table, we then describe the details of each of these steps, using the sample application.

In the process chapters, we use only one simple editing convention: we emphasize all references to process elements such as activities, steps, and artifacts.

Acknowledgments

We would first like to thank Rational Software Corporation, who has allowed us to incorporate various aspects of Rational's intellectual property in this book (specifically, the elements of the Rational Unified Process). We would also like to express our thanks to the founders and employees of Rational for building a company whose mission, core values, and culture encourage the writing of books such as this.

A special thanks goes to our team of reviewers. The breadth and depth of their collective experience has helped us immensely in ensuring that this book provides the right focus and, more importantly, is of enduring value. We would like to thank Kevin Benner, Grady Booch, John Cheesman, Jim Conallen, John Crupi, Kevin Kelly, Philippe Kruchten, Boris Lublinsky, Bruce MacIsaac, Jim Ning, Davyd Norris, Oliver Sims, Dave West, and Andy Winskill.

Grady, by the way, is also responsible for sowing the seed from which this book has grown. Should Grady ever see a presentation of yours and suggest you "write a book," then know that he's serious. Grady—thanks for the support and encouragement from start to finish.

This book has benefited from the experiences of, and support given by, customers, Rational partners, colleagues, and peers alike. In this respect, we would like to thank Alan Brown, Christina Cooper-Bland, Ian Forsythe, Manjinder Gahir, Bob Houston, Russell Norlund, Alan Perkins, and Jim Thario.

We would also like to thank everyone at Addison-Wesley involved in the production of this book. In particular, we would like to thank our editor, Paul Becker, for his guidance and advice.

Finally, and most importantly, we would like to thank our families. Without *their* weekends and *their* evenings, this book would simply not exist.

To my wife Karen and our children, Daniel, Thomas, and Christopher, for your constant support and understanding. I would like to dedicate this book to my mother Nancy and my father Bob.—PE

To my husband Bob, a respected colleague and friend, for his unwavering support and encouragement; and to our children, Katherine and Ryan, whose enthusiasm and zest for life inspire me every day.—KH

I would like to dedicate this book to my wife Jola and my children Tommy and Natasza. Thank you for your understanding and support.—WK

Chapter 1

Introduction

Developing a J2EE application can be a very complex undertaking, and many questions must be answered. How do we articulate the requirements of the application to be developed? What J2EE components, such as servlets, Java-Server Pages, and Enterprise JavaBeans, are needed to satisfy these requirements? How is the complexity of developing a large J2EE application managed? And so on.

As we worked with Rational customers, we found ourselves writing papers, giving presentations, and producing examples that showed how the Rational Unified Process (RUP) can be successfully applied to develop J2EE applications. We identified the RUP activities and artifacts most relevant to the J2EE developer, recommended a specific sequencing of these activities, provided J2EE-specific guidance on how to produce these artifacts, and so on. This book brings all of this material, and our experiences, together.

In this book we describe a subset of RUP that we refer to as the J2EE Developer Roadmap. This roadmap contains relevant extracts from RUP itself, which we have simplified and specialized to meet the needs of the J2EE application developer. We have also included a number of extensions to RUP, such as a process for modeling the user experience of a J2EE application. The result is a process that is both lightweight and focused. Its purpose is obvious—to help you build higher quality J2EE applications faster.

If you are like us (and we consider ourselves to be software engineers), then you learn best through studying examples (rather than having to read volumes before you can apply what you have learned). With that in mind, we have structured and written the book following a few simple principles: (1) minimize the necessary introductions and get to the essence of the "RUP for J2EE" content as soon as possible, (2) support all discussions with examples and (3) avoid the temptation to discuss everything we know and instead only discuss what is necessary and useful.

How This Book Is Organized

True to our principles, let us briefly describe the structure of the book to provide a map of what's ahead.

Chapters 2 and 3 provide a brief overview of J2EE and RUP, respectively, and therefore provide the technology and process context for the rest of the book.

Chapter 2, An Introduction to the Java 2 Platform, Enterprise Edition, is our attempt at "interpreting" J2EE through the eyes of the architect and the designer who use the J2EE platform as the technical foundation of their applications. In particular, we describe the J2EE platform in terms of the architectural and design concerns it addresses.

Chapter 3, An Introduction to the Rational Unified Process, has two objectives. The first and most obvious is to introduce the key concepts underpinning the RUP and its overall organization. The second objective, which is equally important, is to introduce RUP as a process framework. Over the years RUP has grown to incorporate process guidelines in many different disciplines and domains. No single project will make use of all RUP content and hence RUP should be looked at as a base from which one derives a project, company or domain-specific process. This book provides an example of such a customized process that addresses the needs of the J2EE developer.

The remaining chapters address the primary subject of the book: how to develop J2EE applications. We start by introducing our J2EE-specific process, the J2EE Developer Roadmap.

Chapter 4, An Introduction to the J2EE Developer Roadmap, provides an overview of the customized subset of RUP we have tailored to meet the needs of the J2EE developer. This chapter presents the roadmap that we use throughout the rest of the book. The roadmap shows the RUP activities and artifacts that we consider the "must haves" of J2EE application development as well as the rationale for our selection. Chapter 4 also provides an overview of the J2EE-specific content in the J2EE Developer Roadmap, the details of which are described in Chapters 6–9. Our intention in creating the J2EE Developer Roadmap was not only to visualize the activities and artifacts of the process, but also to use it as a navigational device for a "guided tour" through the development of a J2EE application. However, to follow one of our principles, we needed a comprehensive example. It is the role of the next chapter to introduce such an example. Chapter 5 describes the application that we selected for that example, and Chapters 6–9 walk you through the development of that example.

Chapter 5, An Introduction to the Sample Application, provides an overview of a reference application that we use throughout the book. The application is an Online Auction. Although it implements only selected aspects of a typical auction system, it is complete from the development point of view; that is, it contains a complete set of artifacts from requirements to code. Chapter 5 discusses the scope of the Online Auction application, the business context in which it operates, and the key constraints under which it was designed.

Chapters 6–9 are the guided tour of the process (the process chapters). The tour has been divided along the lines of the RUP "disciplines" of Requirements, Analysis and Design, and Implementation. Although RUP considers Analysis and Design as a single discipline, we have chosen to discuss the analysis and design activities in two separate chapters to ensure that we cover each of them at the necessary level of detail.

Chapter 6, Requirements, follows the requirements activities of the J2EE Developer Roadmap to define the requirements of the Online Auction application. The requirements are captured in a Glossary, a Use-Case Model, and a Supplementary Specification. We pay special attention to use-case modeling and to the gathering of architecturally significant requirements.

Chapter 7, Analysis, describes the transformation of the requirements into two primary analysis artifacts: a first-cut Design Model and a User-Experience Model, as well as an initial Deployment Model and Software Architecture Document. One characteristic of our J2EE Developer Roadmap is that it eliminates the need for a separate Analysis Model, and shows how to perform the analysis activities within the context of the Design Model.

Chapter 8, Design, describes the activities of developing and refining the following design artifacts in preparation for implementation: the Design Model (including Interfaces, Design Subsystems, Framework Components, Design Classes, and Use-Case Realizations), Software Architecture Document, a Deployment Model, and a Data Model. This chapter describes how key design decisions are made and how they are captured in the design artifacts. In particular we spend considerable time discussing the application of J2EE technologies, the use of patterns (including the Sun J2EE patterns) and architectural mechanisms, and the use of UML to model J2EE technologies (such as Enterprise JavaBeans).

Chapter 9, Implementation, discusses the implementation activities that transform the design artifacts into implementation artifacts, such as source code and executable code. In this chapter, we also discuss the production of various J2EE modules (Java archive files) that are required to deploy a J2EE application.

Chapter 9 completes our guided tour through the J2EE Developer Roadmap as it describes activities that result in a working application. It is certainly our expectation that at this point you should be able to repeat the process for any other J2EE application.

Chapter 10, Additional Topics, discusses aspects of RUP that are not covered in the preceding chapters. Since the J2EE Developer Roadmap includes only those parts of the process that we selected as the "must haves" of J2EE development, parts of RUP have been only mentioned or treated very lightly. In particular, we do not discuss business modeling, testing (other than unit testing), configuration management, and project management to any significant depth. We therefore conclude with a brief discussion of the parts of RUP that you may want to examine in more detail on your own.

We also include two appendices that supplement the primary process information provided in the process chapters. Appendix A, Describing a Software Architecture, briefly discusses how to describe software architecture and the different perspectives that are commonly used to construct architecture descriptions. Appendix B, Modeling Conventions, summarizes the conventions used throughout the book for modeling a J2EE application. In particular, we summarize the UML stereotypes that we used, as well as our recommendations for structuring the application models. Finally, in Appendix C, the Glossary provides a summary of the terms and acronyms used in the book.

Chapter 2

An Introduction to the Java 2 Platform, Enterprise Edition

This chapter provides an introduction to the Java 2 Platform, Enterprise Edition (J2EE platform). When describing a new technology, it is always useful to provide a familiar context within which that technology is explained. To provide such a context, we start by discussing the concerns that commonly arise when building enterprise systems, and then describe the architectural solutions that have been proven to address these concerns. It is these general architectural solutions that are implemented by the J2EE platform. Following an overview of the J2EE platform, we discuss each of the J2EE technologies in detail.

Enterprise Concerns

Some development concerns are common to every project. For example, system attributes such as performance, scalability, reliability, maintainability, security, ease of incorporating new functionality, and the ability to integrate the system with existing systems are always on the list. There are also other concerns that are not directly related to the solution's properties, but have everything to do with the project's overall success. Examples include product quality, time to market, cost of development, team productivity, dependence on unique or hard-to-find skills, and dependence on a single technology or vendor.

Although we could discuss the J2EE platform in terms of satisfying such general concerns, we have chosen to concentrate on the concerns that are built on this platform. In particular, the J2EE platform has been designed to support the development and execution of a specific type of software system that

5

we call *enterprise systems*. Enterprise systems exhibit a number of common concerns, which are described in this section.

Business Concerns

Enterprise systems implement business processes. Thus, they must contain some representation of the "business reality" that they work within. In fact, enterprise systems are an essential element of many businesses (and in some cases, the software *is* the business) and therefore contain a rich representation of domain concepts. For example, even a simple order-processing system must keep track of products, customers, orders, inventory, and so on.

Enterprise systems, therefore, collect and process large amounts of structured information. They may manage thousands of business data types and structures, and millions of instances of these types (and associations between them). Consider an order-processing system that has thousands of customers, tens of thousands of products, and hundreds of thousands of orders (both in progress and fulfilled).

Although enterprise systems usually perform only a small number of complex computations, they do perform complex data manipulation. For example, an order-processing system doesn't extrapolate trajectories of flying objects, switch mobile phones from cell to cell, or analyze images. However, such a system is very strict about the integrity of the data it maintains and imposes specific rules about how the data is changed.

On a similar note, an enterprise system does manage complex interactions with its many concurrent users. For example, the process of placing an order requires that a customer make him- or herself known to the system, select one or more products, specify appropriate quantities, provide relevant shipping details, and so on. This complexity is made manageable by ensuring that the system imposes very specific interactions with its users.

Integration Concerns

A fundamental aspect of many enterprise systems is their integration with other systems. Even the apparently simple task of placing an order can result in electronic interactions with a warehouse system (to request delivery of the purchased products) and a bank system (to ensure that payment is made). As a result, enterprise systems often run on complex, distributed technical infrastructures that reflect the physical distribution of the organizations participating in the business processes supported by them.

Moreover, even though an enterprise system may interact with similar systems, these systems may have been implemented at different times and may use different technologies. This is simply a consequence of the rapid pace at which business systems change in today's environment. This constant change must therefore be acknowledged and planned for.

The Internet revolution has lead many organizations to make their valuable information available to third parties through a variety of means, including the electronic exchange of information between businesses. This information often represents an organization's most valuable asset. An emphasis must therefore be placed on the security of the enterprise systems providing that information.

Development Concerns

We should also acknowledge that the development and maintenance of enterprise systems is logistically complex for all sorts of reasons. For example, the development of enterprise systems must keep pace with changing business conditions. Even gathering the requirements of the enterprise system can be a complex task when there are a number of stakeholders involved (including end users and business partners, as well as internal staff).

A related concern is that large enterprise systems are developed over long periods of time (sometimes decades), even though an initial version of the system may be made available quickly to address time-to-market concerns. We must therefore take into account the longevity of the system. Large systems are often implemented through a set of concurrent related projects, leading to systems whose elements are at different levels of articulation and maturity.

Multitier Architectures and the J2EE Platform

It has been known for some time that the best approach to developing systems is to divide their responsibilities across a number of *tiers*[1], resulting in common architectural styles known as *multitier architectures*. An example of a multitier architecture is the 3-tier structure shown in Figure 2.1. The presentation tier is

Figure 2.1   3-Tier Architecture

1 A tier is an architectural layer that has a particular responsibility.

responsible for handling interactions with the end user. The business tier is responsible for performing any business processing. The integration tier is responsible for providing access to backend resources, including databases and external systems. Such division allows the content of each tier to be developed and changed independently.

From a historical perspective, the database technology of the integration tier was the first to mature, resulting in powerful relational databases[2]. The technologies in the presentation tier and business tier matured later, resulting in user interface frameworks and transaction-processing monitors, respectively.

For many years, architects of enterprise systems took the concept of multitier architectures and the available technologies, and produced custom-made platforms for their solutions. This is, of course, a very costly and complex effort. One of the key objectives of the J2EE platform is to provide a standard environment on which to develop enterprise systems.

The J2EE platform has been influenced by many earlier initiatives. One of those was Microsoft's successful integration of technologies for all three tiers: Visual Basic, Microsoft Transaction Server (MTS), and SQL Server. Microsoft also promoted and exemplified the concept of container-based computing with its MTS, which itself was influenced by BEA's Tuxedo and other transaction-processing monitors. The concept of container-based computing is central to the J2EE platform, and allows components to execute in an environment that provides the services they require.

Another major influence on the J2EE platform has been the Internet, which has created a high demand for a class of enterprise system known as *online enterprise systems* and the technology needed to implement them. Internet technology has changed and unified the way that user interactions are supported. For example, the stateless nature of the Hypertext Transfer Protocol (HTTP), whereby a client does not have a permanent connection with the server, has implications on how state is managed between invocations.

Finally, the advent of Java and its "write once, run anywhere" (WORA) philosophy has provided a basis for tying together the many technologies required to develop and deploy enterprise systems.

So, in summary, the J2EE platform is best considered as a set of technologies for developing and deploying multitier enterprise systems. As such, it contains an expected set of services (so expected, in fact, that Microsoft's .NET initiative provides an almost identical set). We introduce these technologies in the next section.

The J2EE platform also has the desirable characteristic of being an open specification. There are many commercial and open-source implementations of

---

2 The foundation of relational database technology was created over two decades ago.

the specification. A free reference implementation of the
available.

We now consider the specific technologies that the J
in supporting a multitier architecture.

J2EE Platform Overview

Let us start from putting the J2EE technologies together to show the context
within which they operate, as well as the relationships between them. Figure 2.2 positions each of the technologies in terms of the tiers discussed earlier. It also shows the physical location of each of the elements in terms of
client and server. The details contained in Figure 2.2[3] are discussed throughout

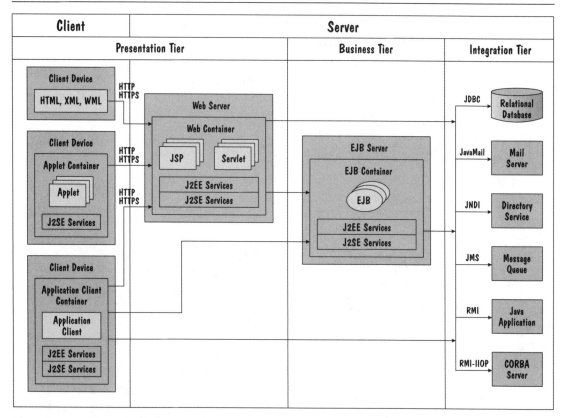

Figure 2.2   The J2EE Platform and Technologies

3 Figure 2.2 shows a multitier deployment configuration that is discussed later in this chapter.

this chapter. Although it is not shown in Figure 2.2, it is also worth mentioning that all containers explicitly use a Java virtual machine (JVM) when executing any compiled Java code.

J2EE Technology Overview

A summary of the various J2EE technologies is shown in Figure 2.3 and described in the following sections.

J2EE Application Component Technologies

The *application component technologies* are those that we use to build the components of the solution. Each of these technologies is discussed in detail later in this chapter. The J2EE application component technologies are described in the following list.

- **Applets**. An applet is primarily used to provide some form of rendering in the user interface, where performance is key.
- **Application clients**. An application client is a standalone Java application that provides an alternate means of accessing a J2EE application, other than through the use of a markup language such as Hypertext Markup Language (HTML).
- **Java Servlets ("servlets")**. A servlet defines how a request from the client is processed and how a response is generated.

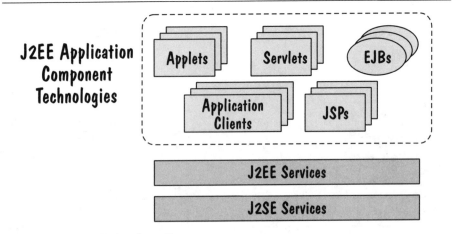

Figure 2.3 J2EE Technology Summary

- **JavaServer Pages (JSPs)**. A JSP is a text document that, like a servlet, describes how a request is processed and a response generated. JSPs provide an alternative to servlets when the generation of statements in a markup language (such as HTML) is required.

- **Enterprise JavaBeans (EJBs)**. An EJB is responsible for implementing an aspect of the business logic of a J2EE application.

J2EE Services

J2EE services, as the name implies, are the services made available by the J2EE platform. They are described in the following list.

- **Java API for XML Parsing (JAXP)**. JAXP provides a standard service that supports the parsing and manipulation of XML documents. JAXP provides a further abstraction when using an external standard such as the Simple API for XML Parsing (SAX), the Document Object Model (DOM) and eXtensible Stylesheet Language Transformations (XSLT).

- **Java DataBase Connectivity (JDBC)**. JDBC provides programmatic access to a relational database.

- **Java Message Service (JMS)**. JMS provides a standard interface to reliable asynchronous messaging implementations (such as IBM's MQSeries or Tibco's Rendezvous).

- **Java Authentication and Authorization Service (JAAS)**. JAAS allows J2EE applications to authenticate users (to reliably and securely determine who is currently executing Java code) and authorize users (to ensure that they have the permissions required to perform the necessary actions).

- **Java Transaction API (JTA)**. In circumstances where programmatic control of transactions is required, JTA provides a standard interface to the transaction services.

- **JavaMail API (JavaMail)**. The JavaMail API allows application components to send mail using a standard interface. Typical implementations of the JavaMail API interface to a number of protocols and specifications, such as the Simple Mail Transfer Protocol (SMTP), Multipurpose Internet Mail Extensions (MIME) and Post Office Protocol 3 (POP3).

- **J2EE Connector Architecture (JCA)**. One of the common requirements of an enterprise application is the ability to connect to enterprise information system (EIS) resources. Some of these resources may be external applications that are accessed using a vendor-specific protocol. JCA provides a standard means for providing resource adapters (more commonly known as "connectors").

J2SE Services

The J2EE platform is dependent upon services provided by the Java 2 Platform, Standard Edition (J2SE)[4]. The J2SE services include support for collections, internationalization (support for multiple human languages), input/output, Java Archive (JAR) files, user interfaces, math, networking, object serialization, Remote Method Invocation (RMI), security, and sound. The J2SE technologies in the following list are considered essential parts of the J2EE platform.

- **Hypertext Transfer Protocol (HTTP) API**. The HTTP API is a client-side API that supports interaction with server-side presentation tier elements using HTTP, the standard protocol for communication on the Web. In many applications, this API is not used since the use of HTTP is handled entirely by the client device and requires no programmatic involvement. For example, the submission of an HTML form to a Web server is handled entirely by the Web browser.

- **HTTPS API**. HTTPS is the use of HTTP over the Secure Socket Layer (SSL). SSL is a security protocol used by Web servers and client devices (such as a Web browser) to establish a secure communication channel over HTTP. This API is the secure equivalent of the HTTP API.

- **Remote Method Invocation over Internet Inter-Orb Protocol (RMI-IIOP)**. RMI is a Java standard for providing distributed object communication between two Java objects. In order to provide maximum interoperability between elements that may not be written in Java (such as an EJB container), the J2EE platform stipulates that the language-independent Internet Inter-Orb Protocol (IIOP) be used. IIOP is an element of the CORBA (Common Object Request Broker Architecture) standard that is defined by the Object Management Group (OMG).

- **Java Naming and Directory Interface (JNDI)**. JNDI provides a uniform interface to a number of directory and naming services, which support the locating of resources on a network. For example, JNDI can be used to obtain a reference to the home interface of a remote EJB.

Containers

The concept of a container is central to the J2EE platform. A container provides runtime support for application components (such as JSPs, servlets, or EJBs) that execute within it. For example, an EJB container provides component life cycle management (the creation and removal of application components, as

---

4 A third Java edition, Java 2 Micro Edition (J2ME), is not a prerequisite of J2EE.

required), transaction management, security, and persistence support to the EJBs that execute within it.

The fact that a component executes inside a container is transparent to its clients. For example, in Figure 2.4 there is a client interacting with an EJB. The client request is handled by the EJB container housing the EJB, rather than directly by the EJB itself. Based upon configuration information held in a deployment descriptor associated with the EJB, the container can interject appropriate transaction characteristics before passing the request on to the EJB for processing.

There is a two-way contract between a container and an application component. From the perspective of the container, the application component must conform to certain interfaces so that the container can manage the component appropriately. For example, an EJB must provide operations to support its removal from memory (known as "passivation"). From the perspective of the application component, the container must make certain services available to the component. For example, an EJB container must provide the Java Data-Base Connectivity (JDBC) API.

As shown in Figure 2.2, there are four types of containers.

- An *applet container,* which provides services required by Java applets
- An *application client container,* which provides services required by Java application clients
- A *Web container,* which provides services to JSPs and servlets
- An *EJB container,* which provides services to EJBs

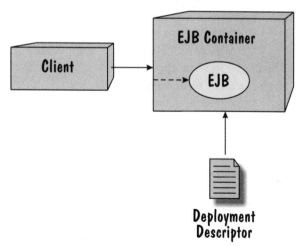

Figure 2.4 An EJB Container

Containers and Servers

In Figure 2.2, we see that a Web container executes inside a Web server, and an EJB container executes inside an EJB server. Some J2EE platform implementations also include the concept of a J2EE application server (or simply "J2EE server"), which includes both a Web container and an EJB container.

Containers and servers are considered to be logical concepts, and the J2EE platform specification does not state how they should be implemented. As a result, a server can be interpreted as the pool of resources, such as operating system processes and memory, which the container implementers can use as they see fit. Therefore, different J2EE platform implementations have taken different approaches to implementing containers, while trying to improve their scalability and reliability properties. For example, load-balancing containers can run in several processes potentially distributed across a number of machines.

Presentation Tier

The presentation tier contains elements that reside on both the client and the server.

The client-side elements are responsible for rendering the user interface and for handling user interactions. In Figure 2.2, we see three clients, each executing in its own device. The first client is processing a markup language. Examples of such a client include a Web browser that processes HTML, an XML-aware device that processes XML, and a Wireless Access Protocol (WAP) device, such as a mobile phone, that processes Wireless Markup Language (WML). The second client houses an applet container that supports the execution of *applets*. An applet (discussed in detail later) is a Java program that typically provides some form of high-performance user interface rendering. The third client houses an application client container that supports the execution of a J2EE application client. A J2EE application client (discussed in detail later) is a standalone Java application that typically provides access to elements in the business tier and integration tier. For example, an application client may be used to provide an administrative interface to the J2EE application.

The server-side elements are responsible for processing client-side requests and providing appropriate responses. A response is typically delivered to the client in the form of a markup language, such as HTML, XML or WML. The response is often dependent on the data held by an EJB or an enterprise information system (EIS), such as a mainframe transaction-processing system or a legacy database. Therefore, the presentation tier application components on the server (the JSPs and the servlets) interact with the components in the business tier or directly with the integration tier. These elements may also be responsible for aspects of user session management, data validation, and application control logic.

Business Tier

The business tier is responsible for an application's business logic. In the most common case, business tier components (EJBs) provide business logic services to the server-side presentation tier application components. However, they can also provide services to standalone Java application clients. EJBs and EJB containers have been designed to simplify communication between the presentation tier and the integration tier.

Integration Tier

The integration tier is responsible for providing access to EIS resources. Figure 2.2 identifies specific types of EIS resources, including a relational database, mail server, directory service, message queue, Java application, and CORBA server. We have labeled each connection to an EIS resource with the technology used to access that resource. For example, JDBC is used to access a relational database.

J2EE Deployment Configurations

A deployment configuration is a mapping of application functionality to application components and then to J2EE containers and services. In other words, it is a way of structuring and distributing the application functionality between tiers, containers, and components. Although there are a number of deployment configurations, there are a few common structures. We briefly look at these common structures in the following sections and discuss the pros and cons of each.

Standalone Deployment Configuration

In the standalone deployment configuration, shown in Figure 2.5, there is not a Web container or an EJB container. The client accesses EIS resources directly and is responsible for handling all presentation logic, business logic, and integration logic.

This configuration may seem like an attractive proposition for applications that provide simple manipulation of data held in the EIS resources. However, this configuration has a number of drawbacks.

Changes to the EIS resource can have a major impact on the implementation of the client, because it is directly dependent on the internal structure of that EIS resource (such as the structure of database tables). In addition, any change to the application itself requires a rollout to every user.

Also, the configuration does not encourage a division of responsibility. For example, often presentation logic and business logic are tightly coupled, making it difficult to support application evolution and maintenance.

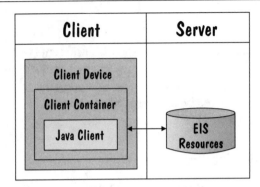

Figure 2.5 Standalone Deployment Configuration

However, the real issues with this deployment configuration start to surface when we want to scale the application to support a large number of concurrent users. When we attempt to provide concurrent client access to an EIS resource, we may find that we are constrained by the EIS resource itself. For example, a database may limit the number of concurrent database connections. However, since there is no coordinated access to the EIS resource, it is not possible to provide an efficient access mechanism (such as a managed pool of database connections).

EJB-Centric Deployment Configuration

In the EJB-centric deployment configuration, shown in Figure 2.6, there is no Web container, and an EJB container sits between the client container and the EIS resources. The presentation logic is in the client, with business logic residing in the EJBs on the server.

Rather than accessing EIS resources directly, all requests from the clients are managed by the appropriate EJBs. Clients are therefore shielded from changes in EIS resources (unless the extent of the change requires additional information to be supplied by the client, for example).

The EJB-centric deployment configuration is designed to address a number of the issues present in the standalone deployment configuration. From a scalability perspective, an EJB container is responsible for ensuring efficient use of limited resources, such as database connections. From an application evolution and maintenance perspective, this configuration also encourages a separation of presentation logic and business logic.

However, one of the drawbacks of the EJB-centric deployment configuration is that any change to the presentation logic requires a rollout to every client.

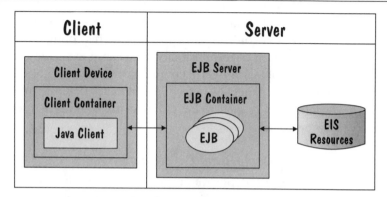

Figure 2.6 EJB-Centric Deployment Configuration

Web-Centric Deployment Configuration

In the Web-centric deployment configuration, shown in Figure 2.7, a Web container sits between the client and the EIS resources, and there is no EJB container. Both presentation logic and business logic are handled by components in the Web container. A Web-centric deployment configuration typically results in an emphasis on the look and feel of the application, with less emphasis on supporting the business logic.

This configuration provides a number of benefits. Clients aren't affected by changes to EIS resources, since clients don't access these resources directly (again, unless the extent of the change requires additional information to be supplied by the client, for example). It is also easier to redeploy the entire application, since all of the application logic resides on the server.

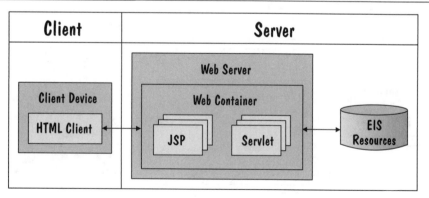

Figure 2.7 Web-Centric Deployment Configuration

However, although the use of EJBs is sometimes considered to be overkill, the omission of EJBs results in some of the same issues raised for the standalone deployment configuration. Specifically, this configuration does not encourage a clear division of responsibility between presentation logic and business logic, often resulting in tightly coupled elements that impede application evolution and maintenance. Also, from a scalability perspective, it is the developer's responsibility to ensure the efficient use of limited resources, such as database connections.

Multitier Deployment Configuration

The multitier deployment configuration is shown in Figure 2.8 and was also shown in Figure 2.2. This configuration includes both a Web container and an EJB container. Presentation logic is handled by elements in the Web container, with business logic handled by EJBs in the EJB container.

In this configuration, clients aren't affected by changes to EIS resources since these resources aren't accessed directly by the clients (again, unless the extent of the change requires additional information to be supplied by the client, for example).

It is also possible to redeploy the entire application without requiring any rollout to clients, since the application resides wholly on the server. From a scalability perspective, the EJB container is responsible for ensuring efficient use of limited resources, such as database connections.

From an application evolution and maintenance perspective, this configuration encourages a clean separation of responsibilities. The presentation logic is decoupled from EIS resources, and the business logic is decoupled from the look and feel. This separation helps when allocating work to developers with

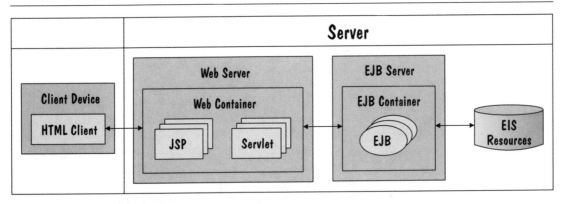

Figure 2.8 Multitier Deployment Configuration

different skills. It also allows for concurrent development, testing, and deployment of presentation logic and business logic elements. The decoupling of presentation logic and business logic also increases the reuse potential of the business logic elements.

The multitier deployment configuration can also ease the migration from one client device (such as a Web browser) to another (such as a PDA). A complete rewrite of the application isn't required since the business logic encapsulated in the EJBs remains unchanged.

To summarize, there are a number of deployment configurations, each with its pros and cons. One of the objectives of the J2EE platform is to be flexible enough to support whatever configuration best fits an organization, while addressing the development concerns we discussed earlier in this chapter.

J2EE Component Technologies

Let's now take a closer look at the J2EE application component technologies.

Applets

A Java applet is a Java program that executes within an applet container that is contained within a client device, such as a Web browser. An applet is primarily used to provide some form of rendering in the user interface where performance is key. For example, supporting graphical manipulation in a Web browser may be best achieved by using an applet. An applet is specified using the OBJECT tag in HTML, as shown in the code fragment below.

```
<html>
  <body>
    <object codetype="application/java" code="TestApplet.class"
width=300 height=100>
    ....
    </object>
  </body>
</html>
```

This tag tells the browser to load the applet whose compiled code is in the file TestApplet.class. The code fragment below is the source code of the applet. This code shows the paint method that is invoked whenever the applet must repaint itself.

```
import java.applet.Applet;
import java.awt.Graphics;
```

```
public class TestApplet extends Applet
{
  public void paint(Graphics g)
  {
    ....
  }
}
```

Application Clients

An application client is a standalone Java application that can contain presentation logic, business logic, and integration logic, and as a result is sometimes referred to as a "fat client". In order to perform its processing, an application client may access the server-side elements of the presentation tier, the elements of the business tier, and the elements of the integration tier. Application clients are often used where a more sophisticated user interface is required than can be provided using a markup language such as HTML. An application client may be used to provide an administration interface to a J2EE application.

Java Servlets

A servlet is a Java class that is used to implement presentation logic on the server. A servlet defines the way in which a request is processed and the way in which a response is generated. Servlets are often accessed directly from a client device, such as a Web browser, either by using a URL or through the use of an HTML form, as shown in the HTML fragment below. When the form represented by this HTML code is submitted to the Web server for processing, the Web server identifies the target servlet, based on the name specified in the form's "action" attribute; identifies the appropriate servlet method, based on the form's "method" attribute; constructs an appropriate request; and invokes the servlet method, passing the request as an argument.

```
<html>
  <body>
    <form method=post action="/auction/main">
      ....
    </form>
  </body>
</html>
```

The code fragment below is the source code of the servlet used in the example above. This code shows aspects of the implementation of the doPost method that is invoked by the Web server when the HTML form is submitted. This method takes two parameters. The first parameter is an HttpServletRequest, which provides the content of the request. The second parameter is an HttpServletResponse, which is used to return the response. In implementing the required presentation logic, a servlet often interacts with other servlets, EJBs, and JSPs. Specific design patterns that describe such interactions are discussed in Chapter 8, Design.

```
package com.pearlcircle;

import java.io.*;
import javax.servlet.*;
import javax.servlet.http.*;

public class PresentationRequestController extends HttpServlet
{
  public void doPost(HttpServletRequest req, HttpServletResponse resp)
                throws ServletException, IOException
  {
    ....
  }
}
```

It is often necessary for a servlet to produce output that can be rendered in the client device, such as HTML (if this is the output expected). This requires writing the doPost method so that it places HTML in the HttpServletResponse object. However, when it comes to Web page layout, the J2EE platform provides an alternative technology, JavaServer Pages (JSP), to render the markup language required.

JavaServer Pages (JSP)

A JSP is a text document that, like a servlet, describes how a request is processed and a response is generated. A JSP is often accessed directly from a client device, such as a Web browser, using a URL. For example, accessing the URL http://www.pearlcircle.com/utils/getServerDate.jsp will result in the Web server executing the getServerData.jsp file and returning the response generated by this JSP. One way to think about JSPs is that they provide an alternative to servlets for generating statements in a markup language. Internally, the Web server automatically compiles JSPs into servlets before they are executed. This does raise the question of when to use servlets and when to use JSPs, since they can provide equivalent functionality. This is a design decision that is touched upon in Chapter 8.

The content of a simple JSP file that returns the date associated with the machine on which the Web server is executing is shown below. We can see that the JSP contains two types of statements. The first type of statement is a markup language to be returned in the response. In the example, the markup language is HTML. The second type of statement is a command language that supports the generation of dynamic content when the JSP file is executed. In the example, the text *new Date().toString()* is a command that will create a new Java Date object, and return its current value as a string. All command statements are enclosed within "<% ... %>" pairs. The statement *@page import="java.util.Date"* is included to declare the location of the Date class.

```
<%@page import="java.util.Date"%>
<html>
  <body>
    <h2>Web server information</h2>
    <table border=1>
      <tr>
        <td>Date:</td>
        <td><%= new Date().toString()%></td>
      </tr>
    </table>
  </body>
</html>
```

When this JSP file is executed by the Web server, it produces output similar to that shown below. All of the HTML statements are placed in the response as-is. However, the command statements in the original JSP file are executed and the result included in the response. In particular, we can see that executing the statement *new Date().toString()* produced the value "Wed Mar 03 17:02:50 GMT+00:00 2002".

```
<html>
  <body>
    <h2>Web server information</h2>
    <table border=1>
      <tr>
        <td>Date:</td>
        <td>Wed Mar 03 17:02:50 GMT+00:00 2002</td>
      </tr>
    </table>
  </body>
</html>
```

When rendered, this HTML produces the result shown in Figure 2.9.

JSP technology encourages an interface-based contract between the provider of the JSP pages and the provider of any application components used by the JSP pages (which may be EJBs, as well as simple Java classes like the Date class used in the above example). This division of responsibility is something that we shall revisit later in this book when we discuss user-experience modeling in Chapter 7, Analysis.

Figure 2.9 The Output from a JSP Rendered in a Browser

Enterprise JavaBeans (EJB)

Enterprise JavaBeans (EJBs) reside in the business tier and are typically responsible for implementing the business logic of J2EE applications. In this section we discuss the different types of EJBs and the interfaces and classes that constitute an EJB.

A client's access to an EJB is provided through interfaces. The interfaces provided by an EJB are dependent on the manner in which the EJB is intended to be invoked. An EJB can offer interfaces that allow the EJB to be invoked remotely (known as the *home interface* and the *remote interface*) or interfaces that allow the EJB to be invoked locally (known as the *local home interface* and the *local interface*)[5].

Figure 2.10 shows a client accessing the home interface and remote interface of an EJB. These interfaces are considered remote from the perspective of the client in that the EJB providing these interfaces may physically reside in a different JVM than the client (possibly on another machine). Figure 2.10 also shows the single bean class that implements the operations defined in the EJB

---

5 Local interfaces were introduced in EJB 2.0, which is part of J2EE 1.3.

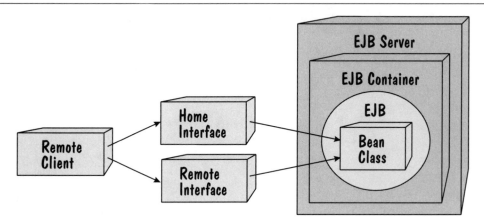

Figure 2.10 An EJB Exposing Home and Remote Interfaces

interfaces (even though an EJB may be implemented by any number of classes). This class is an internal implementation class that is not directly accessed by client objects (it is invoked indirectly by the EJB container).

Figure 2.11 shows a client accessing the local home interface and local interface of an EJB. These interfaces are considered local from the perspective of the client in that the EJB providing these interfaces always resides in the same JVM as the client.

One of the advantages of using remote interfaces is that the application developer need not be concerned with the physical location of the target EJB. However, one of the disadvantages is that, even though the target EJB may reside in the same JVM, there is an overhead in treating it as being *potentially* remote.

Local interfaces are used in situations where *co-location* of source and target is both required and known. Use of these interfaces allows the EJB container to optimize the messaging. One of the disadvantages of local interfaces is that it is the responsibility of the client to determine whether the target EJB should be treated as local or potentially remote.

Some guidance is therefore required in making the decision of whether to use local or remote interfaces. This is briefly discussed in Chapter 8.

Home Interface

The home interface of an EJB declares operations that pertain to the management of the elements represented by the EJB. For example, there are typically operations to create, remove, and find these elements. Consider the code fragment below, where we see the home interface of a UserAccount EJB. The create operation supports the creation of a new UserAccount.

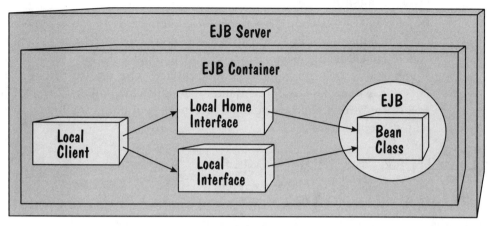

Figure 2.11   An EJB Exposing Local Home and Local Interfaces

```
package com.pearlcircle;

import java.rmi.RemoteException;
import javax.ejb.CreateException;
import javax.ejb.EJBHome;
....

public interface UserAccountHome extends EJBHome
{
  public UserAccount create() throws CreateException, RemoteExcep-
tion;
  ....
}
```

Remote Interface

The remote interface of an EJB declares business operations supported by the EJB. In the code fragment below, we see an operation to set the password of a UserAccount.

```
package com.pearlcircle;

import java.rmi.RemoteException;
import javax.ejb.EJBObject;
....

public interface UserAccount extends EJBObject
{
  public void setPassword(String password) throws RemoteException;
  ....
}
```

Local Home Interface

Should the UserAccount EJB support local interfaces rather than remote interfaces, then the definition of the local home interface would be as shown in the code fragment below. As you can see, the definition of the local home interface is identical to that of a remote home interface, with the exception that the interface extends EJBLocalHome rather than EJBHome, and that RemoteException is not thrown. The convention used here is to prefix the interface name with the word "Local".

```
package com.pearlcircle;

import javax.ejb.CreateException;
import javax.ejb.EJBLocalHome;
....

public interface LocalUserAccountHome extends EJBLocalHome
{
  public LocalUserAccount create() throws CreateException;
  ....
}
```

Local Interface

Likewise, the definition of the local interface is identical to that of the remote interface, with the exception that the interface extends EJBLocalObject rather than EJBObject, and that RemoteException is not thrown. Again, the convention used here is to prefix the interface name with the word "Local".

```
package com.pearlcircle;

import javax.ejb.EJBLocalObject;
....

public interface LocalUserAccount extends EJBLocalObject
{
  public void setPassword(String password);
  ....
}
```

Bean Class

A code fragment of the bean class for the UserAccount EJB (irrespective of whether it supports remote or local interfaces) is shown below.

```
package com.pearlcircle;

import javax.util.*;
import javax.ejb.*;
```

```
....

public abstract class UserAccountBean implements EntityBean
{
  // Instance variables
  private String password;
  ....

  // Business operations
  public void setPassword(String password) { this.password = pass-
word; }
  public String getPassword() { return password; }
  ....

  // Container operations
  public void ejbCreate() throws CreateException { .... }
  public void ejbRemove()                        { .... }
  public void ejbActivate()                      { .... }
  public void ejbPassivate()                     { .... }
  ....
}
```

This example has been kept deliberately simple to help us concentrate on specific EJB features. You can see that the bean class contains instance variables that represent the state of the objects implemented by this EJB. You can also see that the bean class implements the business operations defined in the remote interface (or local interface), such as setPassword. Finally, you can see that the bean class implements operations that are required as part of the two-way contract between the bean and the container. For example, when a client invokes the create operation on the home interface (or local home interface), this eventually results in the container calling the ejbCreate method of the bean class.

There are three distinct "flavors" of EJBs: session beans, entity beans, and message-driven beans.

Session Beans

Session beans, as the name suggests, are beans whose state is valid in the context of a "user session." For example, if you were to access a Web site that provided a "shopping cart" capability then, in most circumstances, the content of the cart would be "lost" were you to exit the site before placing the order. This occurs because the content of the cart is not, in this scenario, maintained beyond the life of the user session[6]. The content of the cart is often referred to as "conversational state," since it is available during the "conversation" the user has

---

6 Depending on the J2EE platform implementation, the state may reside in memory or on disk.

with the Web site. The J2EE platform specifies two types of session beans: stateless session beans and stateful session beans.

A **stateless session bean** is intended to be very lightweight, in that it maintains no conversational state whatsoever. Stateless session beans are often used as "controllers" that coordinate a series of interactions between other EJBs, but don't actually maintain any state of their own. A good example would be a stateless session bean that handles the checkout of the shopping cart we've just mentioned. In implementing the checkout process, the session bean determines the items in the cart, ships the items, debits the bank account of the buyer, credits the bank account of the seller, and then empties the shopping cart. Although the stateless session bean may store intermediate values (in program variables) during the execution of the checkout operation, it does not maintain these values outside of this operation. This is why it is called "stateless."

A **stateful session bean**, on the other hand, does maintain the state between one invocation and the next, within the context of the user session. For example, a shopping cart could be implemented as a stateful session bean[7]. Another common example of conversational state is login information, such as username and password. If this information weren't maintained with the session, then the user would have to log in with every request made. Hence, a stateful session bean could be used in this circumstance also.

Entity Beans

Entity beans represent coarse-grained elements that are considered to be multi-user and generally long-lived. They are, therefore, provided with support for persistence. Examples of entity beans are Customer, Order, and Product.

An entity bean has an associated *primary key class*. This is a Java class that is used to represent the primary key of the entity and may be a user-defined class[8]. For example, if we were implementing a Product entity bean, then we might have a ProductPrimaryKey class that holds the product manufacturer and product model as attributes, since these two attributes are what make a product unique. This class is used, for example, as a parameter to the findByPrimaryKey method on a home interface. The J2EE platform specifies two types of entity beans: container-managed persistence (CMP) entity beans and bean-managed persistence (BMP) entity beans.

---

7 HttpSession objects, available to servlets, provide an alternative mechanism for managing conversational state. The choice is discussed briefly in Chapter 8, Design.

8 Any Java class that implements the Serializable interface can be used as a primary key class.

A **CMP entity bean** is one that delegates the storage and retrieval of its persistent attributes to the EJB container. This is only possible if the container knows which attributes are to be made persistent. This is specified in the deployment descriptor associated with the entity bean (deployment descriptors are discussed later in this chapter). The deployment descriptor can also specify the relationships that a CMP entity bean has with other local CMP entity beans. If specified, the EJB container will manage such relationships. The J2EE platform also defines an *EJB Query Language (EJB QL)* that a developer uses to specify the queries used by a CMP entity bean within its finder methods[9].

A **BMP entity bean** is one that handles its own persistence, rather than delegating this responsibility to the EJB container. BMP entity beans are typically used in situations where the persistence facilities available to CMP entity beans are insufficient. A developer is therefore responsible for writing a certain amount of database access code when creating a BMP entity bean, and will make use of the Java DataBase Connectivity (JDBC) API.

Message-Driven Beans

In addition to session beans and entity beans, the J2EE platform specifies message-driven beans[10]. Message-driven beans are designed to support asynchronous communication. A client sending messages to message-driven beans does not block waiting for a response after sending a message.

A client of a message-driven bean uses the Java Message Service (JMS) to deliver a message to either a queue or a topic. A *queue* represents a list of messages that are processed by a single message-driven bean, whereas a *topic* represents a list of messages that are processed by potentially many message-driven beans. From the perspective of a client, message-driven beans are anonymous and have no client-visible identity (all interactions occur via queues and topics).

A message-driven bean is automatically instantiated by the container within which it resides and consumes messages from a JMS destination (a message queue or topic), as shown in Figure 2.12.

A code fragment of the bean class for a CloseAuction EJB (that e-mails the buyer and seller when an auction closes) is shown below. We can see from this example that the core of the bean implementation is the onMessage operation that is invoked by the EJB container when a message is received on the queue

---

9 EJB QL was introduced in EJB 2.0, which is part of J2EE 1.3.

10 Message-driven beans were introduced in EJB 2.0, which is part of J2EE 1.3.

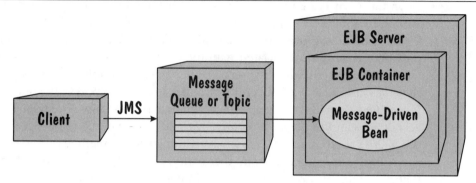

Figure 2.12   Interactions Involving a Message-Driven Bean

or topic associated with this bean (this association is set up when the bean is deployed).

```
package com.pearlcircle;

import javax.ejb.*;
import javax.jms.*;
....

public class CloseAuctionBean implements MessageDrivenBean, Message-
Listener
{
  // Process a message
  public void onMessage(Message msg)
  {
    ....
  }

  // Container operations
  public void ejbCreate() throws CreateException { .... }
  public void ejbRemove()                        { .... }
  ....
}
```

Assembly and Deployment

In this section, we discuss various aspects of J2EE Assembly and Deployment, specifically J2EE Modules.

J2EE Modules

An overview of J2EE modules is provided in Figure 2.13.

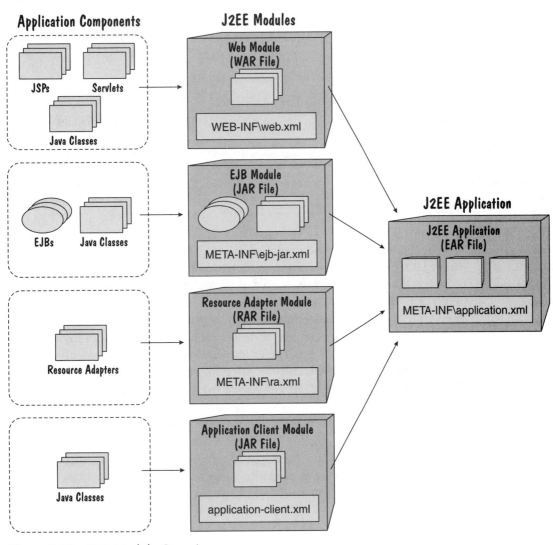

Figure 2.13 J2EE Module Overview

After their initial creation, all application components (such as JSPs, servlets, and EJBs) are packaged within a J2EE module, which is physically represented as a Java Archive (JAR) file. A JAR file contains one or more files, usually in a compressed form (much like ZIP files). The use of JAR files allows related files to be deployed as a unit. For example, a Web module is used to package the presentation tier components of a J2EE application, such as JSP files, servlets, and required Java classes.

Table 2.1 J2EE Modules

J2EE Module	*Content*	*File Type*	*Deployment Descriptor*
Web module	JSPs, servlets, image files, static HTML files, Java classes	Web Archive (WAR)	WEB-INF\web.xml
EJB module	EJBs, Java classes	Java Archive (JAR)	META-INF\ejb-jar.xml
Resource adapter module	Resource adapters	Resource adapter Archive (RAR)	META-INF\ra.xml
Application client module	Java classes	Java Archive (JAR)	application-client.xml
J2EE application module	J2EE modules	Enterprise Archive (EAR)	META-INF\application.xml

A J2EE module can be deployed as is, or it can be assembled, along with other J2EE modules, into a larger module that represents the J2EE application, which is then deployed. A summary of the different J2EE modules is shown in Table 2.1. This table includes the name of the deployment descriptor associated with each J2EE module, and its location within that module.

Every J2EE module includes a description supplied in a deployment descriptor, which is an XML file. The example below shows the elements describing a UserAccount EJB, which is a CMP entity bean. We have chosen to show the description of a single EJB, although a deployment descriptor can describe any number of items.

This descriptor introduces the UserAccount entity EJB to the container in which it will reside. It declares the bean's name, the names of the interfaces supported by this bean (and their type in terms of home, remote, local home, or local), the name of the bean class, the name of the primary key class, the persistence type (container-managed or bean-managed), and the names of all persistent fields.

```
<ejb-jar>
  <description>Online Auction</description>
  <display-name>OnlineAuction</display-name>
  <enterprise-beans>
    <entity>
      <ejb-name>UserAccount</ejb-name>
      <home>com.pearlcircle.UserAccountHome</home>
      <remote>com.pearlcircle.UserAccount</remote>
      <ejb-class>com.pearlcircle.UserAccountBean</ejb-class>
      <prim-key-class>com.pearlcircle.UserAccountPK</prim-key-class>
      <persistence-type>Container</persistence-type>
      <cmp-field><field-name>userId</field-name></cmp-field>
      <cmp-field><field-name>password</field-name></cmp-field>
```

```
            <cmp-field><field-name>firstName</field-name></cmp-field>
            <cmp-field><field-name>lastName</field-name></cmp-field>
            <cmp-field><field-name>address</field-name></cmp-field>
            <cmp-field><field-name>city</field-name></cmp-field>
            <cmp-field><field-name>state</field-name></cmp-field>
            <cmp-field><field-name>zipcode</field-name></cmp-field>
            <cmp-field><field-name>country</field-name></cmp-field>
            <cmp-field><field-name>phone</field-name></cmp-field>
            <cmp-field><field-name>email</field-name></cmp-field>
            ....
        </entity>
        ....
    </enterprise-beans>
</ejb-jar>
```

Summary

In this chapter, we have provided a brief introduction to the Java 2 Platform, Enterprise Edition.

Although the J2EE platform provides a good starting point for developing enterprise systems, it only provides a part of the solution required. In particular, the J2EE platform does not provide a complete solution since we still need to define the application logic that executes using the J2EE platform. J2EE is also a complex platform, and we need to look for ways to simplify the developers' perception of these complexities.

Both of these concerns can be addressed by following the process described in this book. Before introducing this process in Chapter 4, An Introduction to the J2EE Developer Roadmap, we discuss the foundation upon which this roadmap is based in Chapter 3, An Introduction to the Rational Unified Process.

Chapter 3

An Introduction to the Rational Unified Process

The purpose of this chapter is to introduce the Rational Unified Process (RUP), the process framework on which this book is based. We start with a discussion of the software best practices that form the foundation of RUP. We then discuss the key concepts and overall organization of RUP (the RUP "architecture"), and then close with a discussion of the use of RUP as a process framework for developing a customized process.

This chapter is important because it sets the context for the next chapter, Chapter 4, An Introduction to the J2EE Developer Roadmap, which provides an overview of our customized view of RUP that has been explicitly tailored to meet the needs of the J2EE developer. The J2EE Developer Roadmap is the process we use in this book to describe the development of the Online Auction application described in Chapter 5, An Introduction to the Sample Application.

Best Practices—The Foundation of RUP

The Rational Unified Process is a software development process framework that provides a disciplined approach to assigning tasks and responsibilities within a development organization. Its goal is to ensure the production of high-quality software that meets the needs of its end users within a predictable schedule and budget ("better software faster").

Best practices are a set of commercially proven approaches to software development. When used in combination, best practices ensure the success of a software development project by striking at the root causes of typical software development problems. RUP was explicitly designed to support the implementation of six best practices[1].

- **Develop iteratively**. Deliver the functionality of the system in a successive series of releases of increasing completeness, where each release is the result of an iteration. The selection of which requirements are addressed within each iteration is driven by the mitigation of project risks, with the most critical risks being addressed first.

- **Manage requirements**. Use a systematic approach to elicit and document the system requirements, and then manage changes to those requirements, including assessing the impact of those changes on the rest of the system. Effective requirements management involves maintaining a clear statement of the requirements, as well as maintaining traceability from these requirements to the other project artifacts.

- **Use component architectures**. Structure the software architecture using components[2]. A component-based development approach to architecture tends to reduce the complexity of the solution, and results in an architecture that is more robust and resilient, and which enables more effective reuse.

- **Model visually**. Produce a set of visual models of the system, each of which emphasizes specific details, and "ignores" (abstracts, filters away) others. These models promote a better understanding of the system being developed and provide a mechanism for unambiguous communication among team members ("a picture is worth a thousand words").

- **Continuously verify quality**. Continuously assess the quality of the system with respect to its functional and nonfunctional requirements. Perform testing as part of every iteration. It is a lot less expensive to correct defects found early in the software development life cycle than it is to fix defects found later.

- **Manage change**. Establish a disciplined and controlled approach for managing change (changing requirements, technology, resources, products, platforms, and so on). Control how changes are introduced into the project artifacts, who introduces the changes, and when those changes are

---

1 There are additional best practices in RUP. These are just the ones we chose to highlight.

2 *Components* are cohesive parts of a system with well-defined interfaces that provide strong encapsulation of their contents. Because their contents are "hidden," components may be replaced by other components that offer compatible interfaces.

introduced. Provide a means to efficiently synchronize those changes across the different development teams, releases, products, platforms, and so forth.

These best practices are the result of Rational's experiences in developing its software products together with the experiences of Rational's many customers. Implementing these best practices puts a software development organization in a much better position to deliver high-quality software in a repeatable and predictable fashion.

RUP Key Concepts

RUP can be described in terms of two dimensions: *time* and *content*. Figure 3.1 provides a graphical representation of these dimensions. The horizontal axis represents *time* and shows the life cycle aspects of the process. This dimension is described in terms of phases and iterations. The vertical axis represents *content* and shows the disciplines, which logically group the process content.

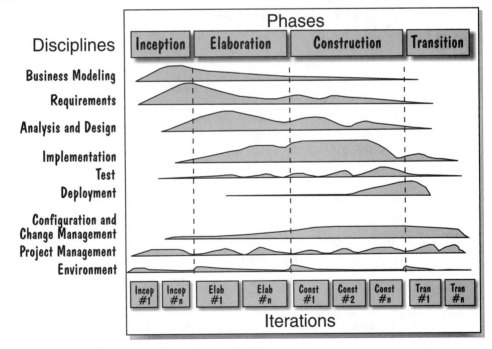

Figure 3.1   Time and Content Dimensions of RUP

As the "humps" in Figure 3.1 illustrate, the relative emphases of the disciplines change over the life of the project. For example, in early iterations more time is spent on Requirements, and in later iterations more time is spent on Implementation. Configuration and Change Management, Environment, and Project Management activities are performed throughout the project. Keep in mind, however, that all disciplines are considered within every iteration. We discuss the iterative nature of the disciplines in more detail within each of the process chapters (Chapters 6–9).

An effective software development process should describe *who* does *what*, *how*, and *when*. RUP does exactly that in terms of the following key concepts:

- Roles: The *who*
- Artifacts: The *what*
- Activities: The *how*
- Phases, iterations, disciplines and workflow details: The *when*

The RUP key concepts and their relationships are shown in Figure 3.2.

A software development project moves through a number of *phases* each of which is divided into a number of *iterations*. Within each iteration, we consider the various *disciplines*. The activities within a discipline are described in terms of *workflow details*. Workflow details describe *activities* that are usually performed together, the *roles* that perform those activities, and the resulting *artifacts*.

Artifacts

An *artifact*[3] is a piece of information that is produced and/or used during the execution of the process. Artifacts are the tangible by-products of the process. The deliverables that end up in the hands of the customers and end users are only a subset of the artifacts that are produced on a project.

Artifacts may take various shapes or forms.

- A model, such as a **Use-Case Model** or **Design Model**[4], which contains model elements
- A model element, such as a **Use Case**, **Design Class**, or **Design Subsystem**, which is part of a model
- A document, such as a **Software Architecture Document**

---

3 Other common terms that have the same meaning as "artifact" include work product, work unit, deliverable, and so on.

4 Throughout this book, we emphasize artifact, role, activity, and workflow-detail names using bold-faced text.

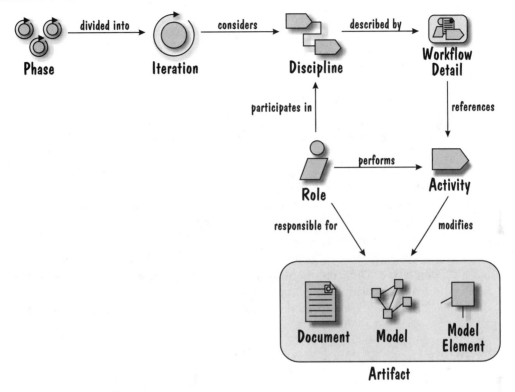

Figure 3.2 RUP Key Concepts

- Source code
- An executable
- A project plan

Artifacts are the responsibility of a single role. Roles use artifacts as input to activities, and roles produce or modify artifacts in the course of performing activities.

Artifacts are represented in RUP (and in the J2EE Developer Roadmap) using graphical symbols. Some examples of RUP artifacts are shown in Figure 3.3.

Roles

A *role* defines the behavior and responsibilities of an individual, or a set of individuals working together as a team, within the context of a software development organization. A role is responsible for one or more artifacts and performs

Software Architecture Document   Implementation Model   Implementation File

Figure 3.3   Examples of RUP Artifacts

a set of activities. For example, the designer role defines the responsibilities, operations, attributes, and relationships of one or several **Design Classes**, and determines how they will be implemented.

It is important to emphasize that roles are not individuals. Individuals may play multiple roles ("wear multiple hats") and multiple individuals may play a single role. The **Project Manager** performs the assignment of individuals to roles when planning and staffing the project.

Roles are also represented in RUP graphically as shown in Figure 3.4.

Activities

An *activity* is a unit of work that provides a meaningful result in the context of the project. It has a clear purpose, which usually involves creating or updating artifacts. Every activity is assigned to a specific role. Activities may be repeated several times, especially when executed in different iterations.

Activities are composed of one or more steps. For example, the activity **Implement Design Elements** of the Implementation discipline in the J2EE Developer Roadmap has the following steps:

- Implement Design Subsystems
- Implement Framework Components

Software Architect   Designer   Implementer

Figure 3.4   Examples of RUP Roles

Figure 3.5   Examples of RUP Activities

- Implement Design Classes and Interfaces
- Implement Deployment Elements

An activity is displayed in RUP as shown in Figure 3.5.

Disciplines

A *discipline* is a collection of activities that are related to a major "area of concern" within the overall project. Disciplines group activities logically. As we show in Figure 3.1, RUP is organized around nine disciplines. Table 3.1 provides a brief description of each of these disciplines.

Table 3.1   RUP Disciplines

RUP Discipline	*Brief Description*
Business Modeling	The purpose of the Business Modeling discipline is to: ♦ Understand the structure and the dynamics of the organization in which a system is to be deployed (the target organization) ♦ Understand current problems in the target organization and identify improvement potential ♦ Ensure that customers, end users, and developers have a common understanding of the target organization ♦ Derive the system requirements needed to support the target organization
Requirements	The purpose of the Requirements discipline is to: ♦ Establish and maintain agreement with the customers and other stakeholders on what the system should do ♦ Provide system developers with a better understanding of the system requirements ♦ Define the boundaries of (delimit) the system ♦ Provide a basis for planning the technical contents of iterations ♦ Provide a basis for estimating the cost and time to develop the system
Analysis and Design	The purpose of the Analysis and Design discipline is to: ♦ Transform the requirements into a design of the system-to-be ♦ Evolve a robust architecture for the system ♦ Adapt the design to match the implementation environment *continued*

Table 3.1 RUP Disciplines *continued*

RUP Discipline	*Brief Description*
Implementation	The purpose of the Implementation discipline is to: ◆ Define the organization of the implementation ◆ Implement the design elements ◆ Unit test the implementation ◆ Integrate the results produced by individual implementers (or teams), resulting in an executable system
Test	The purpose of the Test discipline is to: ◆ Find and document defects in software quality ◆ Provide general advice about perceived software quality ◆ Prove the validity of the assumptions made in design and requirement specifications through concrete demonstration ◆ Validate that the software product functions as designed ◆ Validate that the software product functions as required (that is, the requirements have been implemented appropriately)
Deployment	The purpose of the Deployment discipline is to: ◆ Ensure that the software product is available for its end users
Configuration and Change Management	The purpose of the Configuration and Change Management discipline is to: ◆ Identify configuration items[5] ◆ Restrict changes to those items ◆ Audit changes made to those items ◆ Define and manage configurations[6] of those items
Project Management	The purpose of the Project Management discipline is to: ◆ Manage a software-intensive project ◆ Plan, staff, execute, and monitor a project ◆ Manage risk
Environment	The purpose of the Environment discipline is to: ◆ Provide the software development organization with the software development environment—both processes and tools—that will support the development team. This includes configuring the process for a particular project, as well as developing guidelines in support of the project.

---

5 *Configuration items* are elements that are placed under configuration management control. Configuration items are individually versioned and thus can be uniquely identified at a given point in time. Configuration items are part of a configuration.

6 A *configuration* is the set of configuration items that define a particular version of a system or part of a system.

Workflow Details

It is not enough to describe the artifacts produced by a process and the roles that perform the activities that produce these artifacts. A process also needs to provide guidance on what activities are performed together and the order in which the activities are performed. Such guidance can be expressed in a set of workflows. A *workflow* is a sequence of activities that produces a result of observable value.

In RUP, the process is described at two levels: the discipline level and the workflow detail level. A *workflow detail* is a grouping of activities that are often performed together to produce a specific result. In particular, workflow details describe groups of activities performed together in a discipline.

The workflows for the RUP disciplines and workflow details are described using Unified Modeling Language (UML) activity diagrams. Discipline diagrams contain the workflow details of the discipline. The diagram for the Implementation discipline, as configured in the J2EE Developer Roadmap, is shown in Figure 3.6. This discipline consists of two workflow details: **Structure the Implementation Model** and **Implement Design Elements**.

Within a workflow detail, activities may be performed in parallel, and each activity may affect more than one artifact. Workflow detail diagrams show the key artifacts, activities, and roles involved in the workflow detail. The content

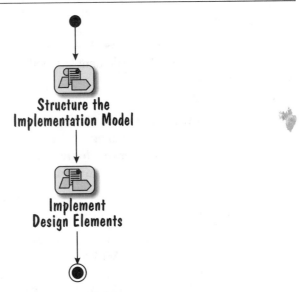

Figure 3.6   Implementation Discipline Workflow

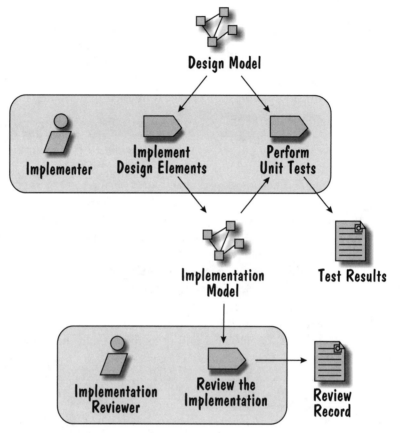

Figure 3.7   Implement Design Elements Workflow Detail

of the **Implement Design Elements** workflow detail, as tailored in the J2EE Developer Roadmap, is shown in Figure 3.7. This workflow detail consists of three activities: **Implement Design Elements**, **Perform Unit Tests**, and **Review the Implementation**.

Iterations

Iterative development is a key characteristic of successful software development projects. Within an iterative software development life cycle, several passes are made through each of the disciplines. Each pass is called an iteration. An *iteration* is a distinct, time-boxed sequence of activities that results in a release (internal or external) of an executable product. As the project progresses, releases evolve from a subset of the final product to the final system.

An iterative development process is similar to "growing" software, where the end product matures over time. Each iteration results in a better understanding of the requirements, a more robust architecture, a more experienced development organization, and a more complete implementation.

Figure 3.8 illustrates how the focus of a project shifts across successive iterations. The size of the boxes within each of the disciplines illustrates the relative time spent performing the activities within that discipline. Each discipline is addressed during every iteration, but the relative emphasis shifts as the project progresses from Requirements to Analysis and Design to Implementation to Test, and finally to Deployment.

The following list provides some important characteristics of a successful iteration.

- The iteration has clear evaluation criteria.
- The iteration has a planned capability that is demonstrable.
- The iteration is concluded by a minor milestone, where the result of the iteration is assessed relative to the objective success criteria of that particular iteration.

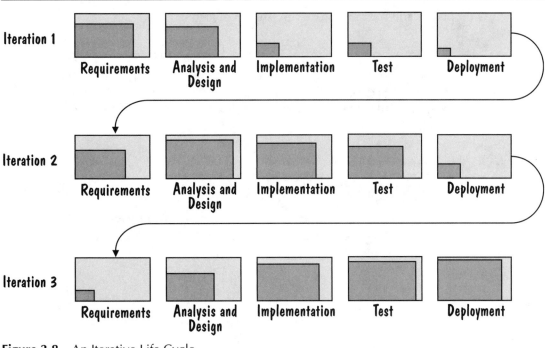

Figure 3.8 An Iterative Life Cycle

- During the iteration, artifacts are updated (artifacts evolve with the system).
- During the iteration, the system is integrated and tested.

Phases

There is more to an iterative development process than a stream of iterations. There must be an overall framework in which the iterations are performed that represents the strategic plan for the project and drives the goals and objectives of each of the iterations. Such a framework is provided by phases. *Phases* provide well-defined business milestones that ensure that the iterations make progress and converge on a solution, rather than just iterating indefinitely.

Phases and iterations together provide the foundation for iterative development. The objectives of each phase are achieved by executing one or more iterations within the phase. Each phase concludes with a major milestone and an assessment to determine whether the objectives of the phase have been met. A satisfactory assessment allows the project to move to the next phase. Iterations are time-based (they are of a fixed duration), whereas phases are goal-based. A phase cannot be time-boxed since the completion of a phase is assessed based on the state of the project.

In RUP, the software development life cycle is decomposed into four sequential phases: *Inception, Elaboration, Construction,* and *Transition*. These phases and their milestones are shown in Figure 3.9.

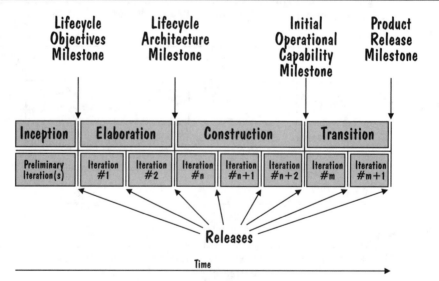

Figure 3.9 RUP Phases and Milestones

Inception

The Inception phase is where the "business case" for the project is established, and where concurrence among all stakeholders on the objectives for the project is also established. Inception is where we focus is on ensuring that the project is both valuable and feasible. The primary objectives and milestone criteria of the Inception phase are summarized in Table 3.2.

Elaboration

The Elaboration phase is where the software architecture is established that provides a stable foundation for the design and implementation that is performed during the Construction phase. The primary objectives and milestone criteria of the Elaboration phase are summarized in Table 3.3.

Table 3.2 Inception Phase Objectives and Evaluation Criteria

Primary Objectives	*Milestone Evaluation Criteria*
Establish the project's scope.	Stakeholders concur with the scope definition.
Establish the project's acceptance criteria.	Stakeholders concur with the project acceptance criteria.
Identify the features of the system, and select those that are critical.	Stakeholders concur that the right set of requirements has been captured and there is a shared understanding of the requirements. All requirements are prioritized.
Estimate the overall cost and schedule for the entire project (more detailed estimates for the Elaboration phase that will immediately follow).	Stakeholders concur that the cost/schedule estimates, priorities, risks, and development process are appropriate.
Estimate potential risks.	All known risks have been recorded and assessed, and a risk mitigation strategy has been defined.
Set up the supporting environment for the project (for example, hardware, software, process, resources).	The supporting environment is in place.

Table 3.3   Elaboration Phase Objectives and Evaluation Criteria

Primary Objectives	*Milestone Evaluation Criteria*
Ensure that the architecture, requirements and plans are stable. Establish a baselined architecture.	The product vision, requirements and baselined architecture are stable.
Ensure that the risks are sufficiently mitigated to be able to predictably determine the cost and schedule for the completion of the development.	The major risk elements have been addressed and have been credibly resolved.
Demonstrate that the baselined architecture will support the requirements of the system at an acceptable cost and within an acceptable timeframe.	All architecturally significant aspects of the system, and selected areas of functionality, have been evaluated in an evolutionary prototype[7].

Construction

The Construction phase is where the remaining requirements are clarified and where development of the system is completed based on the baselined architecture established during the Elaboration phase. Between the Elaboration and Construction phases, the focus shifts from understanding the problem and identifying key elements of the solution, to the development of a deployable product. The primary objectives and milestone criteria of the Construction phase are summarized in Table 3.4.

Transition

The Transition phase is where we ensure that the software is available to, and accepted by, its end users. This is where the system is deployed into the user's environment for evaluation and testing. The focus is on fine-tuning the prod-

Table 3.4   Construction Phase Objectives and Evaluation Criteria

Primary Objectives	*Milestone Evaluation Criteria*
Achieve useful versions (alpha, beta, and other test releases) in a timely fashion.	The system has been developed in line with the expectations specified in the phase plan and iteration plans.
Complete the analysis, design, implementation and testing of all required functionality.	All required functionality has been incorporated into the system.
Make sure the system is ready to be deployed into the end user's environment.	The system has met all acceptance criteria when tested in the development environment.

---

7 An *evolutionary prototype* gradually evolves to become the real system, as opposed to an *exploratory prototype*, which is thrown away when it has served its purpose.

Table 3.5 Transition Phase Objectives and Evaluation Criteria

Primary Objectives	*Milestone Evaluation Criteria*
Successfully roll out the system to the delivery channels.	The system has passed the formal acceptance criteria in the end user's environment.

uct, and on addressing configuration, installation, and usability issues. All the major structural issues should have been worked out much earlier in the project's life cycle. By the end of the Transition phase, the project should be in a position to be closed out. The primary objectives and milestone criteria of the Transition phase are summarized in Table 3.5.

RUP as a Process Framework

RUP is comprehensive and complete. It provides detailed activity steps, artifact templates, guidelines, checkpoints, and examples. However, a "one size fits all" perspective does not apply to a software development process. Thus, RUP was designed to be a process framework from which customized processes could be derived. In fact, in addition to *software development* guidance, RUP contains *process customization* guidance. In other words, RUP contains detailed information on how to tailor RUP for a specific project, type of solution, or organization. The process customization guidance is provided in the RUP Environment discipline, and we have used it to tailor RUP for the needs of the J2EE developer. The resulting roadmap, which we describe in Chapter 4, contains the process elements that we feel are most applicable to J2EE application development.

Summary

In this chapter we provided a brief introduction to the Rational Unified Process (RUP), including the software engineering best practices from which it originates, the key concepts used to describe it, and the support provided for tailoring it. In summary, RUP captures software development best practices in a form that can be adapted for a wide range of purposes.

This chapter sets the context for the next chapter, Chapter 4, which describes the J2EE Developer Roadmap, the RUP customization that is used as the foundation of this book. A basic understanding of RUP is important because, from this point on, we concentrate on the details of the J2EE Developer Roadmap and its use in developing a sample J2EE Online Auction application, which is described in Chapter 5.

Chapter 4

An Introduction to the J2EE Developer Roadmap

In this chapter we introduce the J2EE Developer Roadmap. As we described in Chapter 3, An Introduction to the Rational Unified Process, RUP has been designed as a process framework from which customized processes can be developed. The J2EE Developer Roadmap is such a customization. The process chapters of this book (Chapters 6–9) provide a guided tour of the roadmap, and exemplify how it has been used to develop the sample J2EE Online Auction application described in Chapter 5, An Introduction to the Sample Application.

We begin this chapter by defining what a RUP roadmap is. We then describe what RUP activities and artifacts have been included in the J2EE Developer Roadmap, and provide a brief explanation as to why these particular process elements were selected. We end with an overview of the roadmap, demonstrating how the roadmap has been tailored to include specific J2EE process guidance.

What Is a RUP Roadmap?

RUP is a comprehensive and detailed process framework. It addresses almost every aspect of software development and can be intimidating to the first-time user. A question we often hear is "Where do I start?" RUP roadmaps provide the answer.

A RUP roadmap provides a starting point because it provides a tour through RUP with some viewpoint in mind. That viewpoint may be a specific development context (for example, J2EE online enterprise systems) or a specific role (for example, software developer). A roadmap describes the elements of the process that are relevant to that viewpoint, and ignores the elements that are not relevant. A roadmap is intended to be a directed reading and learning aid and can be thought of as a customized view of the process.

J2EE Developer Roadmap–Scope and Rationale

The J2EE Developer Roadmap provides a customized view of RUP that has been tailored to meet the needs of the J2EE developer. It concentrates on providing guidance on the essential requirements, analysis, design, and implementation activities and artifacts from the developer's perspective. The RUP elements considered relevant to the J2EE developer are described in detail, while those considered less relevant are treated lightly or skipped altogether.

Before identifying the J2EE developer-relevant process elements, we should define what we mean by "developer." We use the term "developer" to encompass multiple RUP-defined roles, which we describe in Table 4.1. All of these RUP roles correspond to one role in the J2EE platform specification—the *application component provider*. In other words, what we call J2EE developer in the book closely approximates to the application component provider role in the J2EE platform specification. The J2EE developer is responsible for taking a **Vision** of a system (possibly just a problem statement) through to an implementation of the system using the J2EE platform.

The J2EE Developer Roadmap includes activities from the Requirements, Analysis and Design, and Implementation disciplines of RUP and focuses on the development of the following models[1]: **Use-Case Model**, **User-Experience Model**, **Design Model**, **Data Model**, **Implementation Model**, and **Deployment Model**. The software architecture is another important product of the development process that represents the architecturally significant aspects of these models. Software architecture is described in more detail in Appendix A, Describing a Software Architecture. We discuss other artifacts, but they are either contained within, or directly support the development of, one of these models.

Figure 4.1 provides an overview of these models and illustrates the relationships that exist between them. These models and their relationships are

---

1 A *model* is a complete description of a system from a particular perspective ("complete" meaning you don't need any additional information to understand the system from that perspective). A model contains a set of model elements. Two models cannot overlap.

Table 4.1 RUP Roles Included in the J2EE Developer Roadmap

RUP Role	*Brief Description*
Architecture Reviewer	The Architecture Reviewer plans and conducts the formal reviews of the overall software architecture.
Database Designer	The Database Designer defines the tables, indexes, views, constraints, triggers, stored procedures, tablespaces or storage parameters, and other database-specific constructs needed to store, retrieve, and delete persistent data.
Designer	The Designer defines the responsibilities, operations, attributes, and relationships of one or several design elements, and determines how they should be implemented.
Design Reviewer	The Design Reviewer plans and conducts the formal reviews of the design.
Implementer	The Implementer is responsible for implementing and testing design elements, in accordance with the project's adopted standards.
Implementation Reviewer	The Implementation Reviewer plans and conducts the formal reviews of the implementation.
Requirements Reviewer	The Requirements Reviewer plans and conducts the formal review of the requirements.
Requirements Specifier	The Requirements Specifier details the requirements.
Software Architect	The Software Architect leads and coordinates technical activities that establish the overall structure of the system, the key system elements, and the interfaces between these elements.
System Analyst	The System Analyst leads and coordinates requirements elicitation by outlining the system's functionality and by scoping the system.
User-Experience Designer[2]	The User-Experience Designer defines the user actions, dynamic content, and navigation paths of one or several Screens, and determines how they should be implemented.
User-Experience Reviewer	The User-Experience Reviewer plans and conducts the formal reviews of the system's user experience.

described briefly in the section below, and will be discussed in detail within their respective process chapters.

The **Use-Case Model** describes the intended behavior of the system as seen through its interaction with its environment, and serves as a contract between the customer and the developers. The **Use-Case Model** is the foundation of the other models, as it contains a complete specification of the observable system behavior. It is used as an essential input to activities in analysis, design, and test.

---

2 The user-experience process elements (for example, the **User-Experience Designer** role, the **User-Experience Reviewer** role, and the **User-Experience Model** artifact, which includes **Screens**, **Use-Case Storyboards**, and **Navigation Maps**) are not part of classic RUP, but are described in the User-Experience Modeling plug-in to RUP.

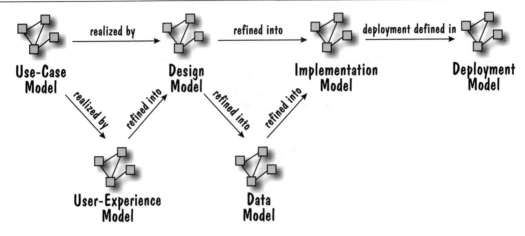

Figure 4.1   J2EE Roadmap System Models

The **User-Experience Model** describes what the user will see when interacting with the system. It describes the **Screens**, the dynamic content that appears on the **Screens**, and how the user navigates through the **Screens** to perform the system **Use Cases**. It provides the contract between the presentation and the business elements of the system and describes how the content provided by the business elements is presented to the user.

The **Design Model** describes the realization of the system **Use Cases**, and serves as an abstraction of the **Implementation Model**. It is a comprehensive, composite artifact encompassing **Analysis Classes**[3], **Design Classes**, **Framework Components**, **Design Subsystems**, **Design Packages**, and **Use-Case Realizations**. The **Design Model** is as an essential input to the implementation activities.

The **Data Model** describes the persistent data in the system, including any behavior defined in the database, such as stored procedures, triggers, constraints, and so forth. The **Data Model** contains a set of model elements, which represent the physical storage of the persistent **Design Model** elements. It defines the mapping between the persistent **Design Classes** and the persistent data structures, and also defines the persistent data structures themselves. The **Data Model** is needed when the persistent data structures cannot be inferred from the structure of persistent classes in the **Design Model** and a mapping from the **Design Model** to the persistence storage mechanism must be explicitly defined.

---

3 In the J2EE Development Roadmap, **Analysis Classes** are initially created in the **Design Model**, and then evolve into design elements. An analysis view of the system is not maintained in a separate **Analysis Model**.

The **Implementation Model** is a UML model of the implementation of the **Design Model** and **Data Model** elements. It describes the **Implementation Directories** and **Implementation Files** needed to build and manage the system in the development environment. These files include both the operational files, such as executables, deployment descriptors, and so on, as well as the source code files from which the operational files are derived. The **Implementation Model** can be a very useful visualization of the relationships (for example, traceability) between the **Implementation Model** elements that represent the implementation and the elements in the other system models. Given the right toolset, the consistency between the visual representation of the **Implementation Model** and the physical files and directories of the **Implementation Model** can be maintained using roundtrip engineering.

The **Deployment Model** shows the configuration of processing nodes at runtime, the communication links between them, and the **Implementation Model** elements that are deployed on them. It describes the distribution of behavior across nodes.

When deciding on the scope J2EE Developer Roadmap, our goal was to only include those artifacts that are directly relevant to the J2EE developer. It was our intention that the selected artifacts would serve as "stepping stones" from the **Vision** of the system to its implementation. Once the artifacts were selected, we only included activities that supported the production of these artifacts. The results are shown in Table 4.2, which summarizes the RUP activities and artifacts included in the J2EE Developer Roadmap. The table is organized by book chapter and is meant to provide an overview of the roadmap. The artifacts listed in parentheses represent "subartifacts" of the preceding artifact (subartifacts are artifacts that are contained within another artifact). Some of the artifacts are referenced in the roadmap, but their development is considered outside of its scope. These artifacts are considered to be provided to the roadmap and are indicated in the table with "[provided]" following their name.

Some may question the inclusion of the requirements activities and artifacts in a process that is focused on the developer. We have chosen to include them since the requirements artifacts, especially the **Use Cases**, drive all other aspects of the process.

The fact that we excluded some of the RUP process elements from the J2EE Developer Roadmap does not mean that those elements are not important. They

Table 4.2 J2EE Developer Roadmap Activities and Artifacts

Chapter	Workflow Details	Activities	Artifacts
6—Requirements	Define the System	◆ Capture a Common Vocabulary ◆ Find Actors and Use Cases ◆ Prioritize Use Cases ◆ Review the Requirements	◆ Change Request[4] ◆ Glossary ◆ Iteration Plan [provided] ◆ Risk List [provided] ◆ Review Record ◆ Supplementary Specification ◆ Use-Case Model (Actor, Use Case, Use-Case Package) ◆ Use-Case Modeling Guidelines [provided] ◆ Use-Case Priority List ◆ Vision [provided]
	Refine the System Definition	◆ Detail a Use Case ◆ Structure the Use-Case Model ◆ Review the Requirements	
7—Analysis	Define an Initial Architecture	◆ Architectural Analysis ◆ Review the Architecture	◆ Change Request ◆ Data Model ◆ Deployment Model ◆ Design Guidelines[5] [provided] ◆ Design Model (Analysis Class, Design Class, Framework Component, Design Package, Design Subsystem, Interface, Use-Case Realization) ◆ Reference Architecture [provided] ◆ Review Record ◆ Software Architecture Document ◆ User-Experience Guidelines [provided] ◆ User-Experience Model (Navigation Map, Screen, Use-Case Storyboard)
	Analyze Behavior	◆ Model the User Experience ◆ Use-Case Analysis ◆ Review the Analysis	
8—Design	Refine the Architecture	◆ Identify Design Mechanisms ◆ Identify Design Elements ◆ Incorporate Existing Design Elements ◆ Describe Concurrency and Distribution ◆ Review the Architecture	
	Detail the Design	◆ Use-Case Design ◆ Subsystem Design ◆ Component Design ◆ Class Design ◆ Database Design ◆ Review the Design	
9—Implementation	Structure the Implementation Model	◆ Structure the Implementation Model	◆ Change Request ◆ Implementation Guidelines [provided] ◆ Implementation Model (Implementation File, Implementation Directory) ◆ Programming Guidelines [provided] ◆ Review Record ◆ Test Guidelines [provided] ◆ Test Results ◆ Test Script
	Implement Design Elements	◆ Implement Design Elements ◆ Perform Unit Tests ◆ Review the Implementation	

4 **Change Requests** can be produced during any of the J2EE Developer Roadmap activities. However, they are only explicitly listed as output artifacts from the review activities. The processing of **Change Requests** is not in the scope of the roadmap.

5 The provided **Design Guidelines** are refined to include design mechanism details.

are just not the primary focus of the J2EE developer. We will briefly discuss some of these elements in Chapter 10, Additional Topics. For additional information on the process elements that are not included in the J2EE Developer Roadmap, see RUP.

In addition to the detailed process element descriptions provided in the process chapters (Chapters 6–9), we have provided additional information in the appendices that summarizes some key aspects of the elements in the J2EE Developer Roadmap. Specifically, we have provided the following appendices:

- Appendix A, Describing a Software Architecture, which describes what should be considered when documenting the software architecture
- Appendix B, Modeling Conventions, which summarizes the modeling conventions we use throughout the book, including modeling element stereotypes and recommended model structures
- Appendix C, Glossary, which provides brief descriptions of all J2EE Developer Roadmap elements, including artifacts and roles

RUP is an iterative process. Thus, the J2EE Developer Roadmap activities should be interpreted as occurring in the context of phases and iterations. This means that the described activities may be performed multiple times with different emphases and varying levels of effort throughout the software development process. The iterative nature of the disciplines is discussed in more detail in the individual process chapters (Chapters 6–9). For more information on phases and iterations, see Chapter 3.

J2EE Developer Roadmap–J2EE-Specific Content

In this section, we provide a glimpse into the J2EE-specific content provided in the J2EE Developer Roadmap. Table 4.3 summarizes this content by chapter, workflow detail, and activity. In addition to demonstrating the breadth of the J2EE coverage provided in the roadmap, this table can be used to access those parts of the book that address a specific J2EE process area.

Throughout this book, discipline and workflow detail diagrams are used as the visual representation of the J2EE Developer Roadmap. Examples of these diagrams are provided in Chapter 3. These diagrams serve several important purposes.

- They provide a graphical overview of the process described in the text.

Table 4.3 J2EE-Specific Content of the J2EE Developer Roadmap

Chapter	Workflow Detail	Activity[6]	J2EE-Specific Content
6—Requirements	Define the System	Capture a Common Vocabulary	None
		Find Actors and Use Cases	None
		Prioritize Use Cases	None
	Refine the System Definition	Detail a Use Case	None
		Structure the Use-Case Model	None
7—Analysis	Define an Initial Architecture	Architectural Analysis	Select a J2EE deployment configuration. Identify possible J2EE technologies that may be used.
	Analyze Behavior	Model the User Experience	None
		Use-Case Analysis	None
8—Design	Refine the Architecture	Identify Design Mechanisms	Identify what J2EE patterns are going to be used. Identify what J2EE technologies are going to be used.
		Identify Design Elements	Identify JSPs, servlets, EJBs, and other J2EE elements.
		Incorporate Existing Design Elements	None
		Describe Concurrency and Distribution	Describe the use of Java threads and message-driven EJBs. Map J2EE modules to nodes.
	Detail the Design	Use-Case Design	Describe the interactions between collaborating J2EE elements.
		Subsystem Design	Describe subsystems in terms of their internal J2EE elements.
		Component Design	Produce a detailed design of EJBs.
		Class Design	Produce a detailed design of JSPs, servlets, and other Java classes.
		Database Design	Define the mapping between entity EJBs and the underlying database.
9—Implementation	Structure the Implementation Model	Structure the Implementation Model	Decide on the organization of virtual directory elements (such as JSPs) and Java elements (such as servlets, EJBs, and Java classes), and also the content of J2EE modules.
	Implement Design Elements	Implement Design Elements	Implement EJBs, JSPs, servlets and other Java classes. Create the J2EE modules and their associated deployment descriptors.
		Perform Unit Tests	Test the J2EE elements.

6 Review activities are not shown since all review activities are the same, irrespective of the technology used.

- They establish the context of the process chapters, providing "you are here" reference points.

- They describe the overall flow between activities and highlight the key artifacts that are consumed and produced by the activities.

Summary

In this chapter we provided an introduction to the J2EE Developer Roadmap, which is the process we use in this book to guide you through the development of a J2EE application. The process details are provided in the process chapters (Chapters 6-9). The roadmap serves as the organizational guide through the content of these chapters.

Before leaving this chapter, let us emphasize that the J2EE Development Roadmap is a role-based view of RUP that focuses on providing guidance to the J2EE developer. Since its intent is not to cover all aspects of the software development process, we encourage you to refer to RUP for more complete coverage. However, for J2EE developers who want to understand how to apply RUP's best practices in the context of a J2EE software development project, the J2EE Developer Roadmap offers an excellent place to start.

Chapter 5

An Introduction to the Sample Application

The purpose of this chapter is to introduce the sample application used as an example in Chapters 6–9. This chapter sets the context and high-level requirements for the application and contains information commonly found in a **Vision** document. Development of a **Vision** document is outside the scope of the J2EE Developer Roadmap. However, the document itself is an input artifact to a number of activities in the Requirements discipline (see Chapter 6, Requirements).

Application Overview

Our sample application is an online auction. An online auction is a subcategory of a larger family of enterprise applications called *e-commerce systems*. An e-commerce system enables buyers and suppliers of products and services to conduct business-to-business transactions in a virtual marketplace. The three concepts underlying auctions are auction, bid, and exchange.

The term *auction* can be used both as a verb ("to auction an item") and as a noun ("the auction has closed"). When used as a verb, an auction represents the process of offering an item for sale and the corresponding transaction between a buyer and a seller. When used as a noun, an auction represents a system entity, which stores information about the offered item and any bids. An auction has a number of interesting characteristics, which we describe in the following list.

- An auction item is usually specialized (it is one-of-a-kind item, rather than a commodity).

- There are only a few buyers or sellers.
- Sellers and buyers are often anonymous.
- An auction is often used when there is a single supplier for a product and potentially many customers.

In an auction, a buyer expresses his readiness to purchase an item by placing a *bid*. There are usually multiple bids for the same item, and later bids are higher than earlier bids. When the auction closes, at a predefined time, the highest bid becomes the purchase price.

An *exchange* occurs when the seller accepts a bid, delivers the item to the buyer, and receives the payment. In our example, the transaction between the buyer and seller is outside the scope of the system. The Online Auction application we use as an example in the following chapters simply provides the buyer and seller with each other's information.

Online auctions are a virtual place where sellers can present their items or services to potential buyers. Auctions also provide buyers with access to a potentially large selection of items. For both buyers and sellers, they provide an option of staying anonymous until the very end of the transaction and, even then, the disclosure of identities occurs only between the specific buyer and seller.

The popularity of online auctions is growing because of their simple business models. Usually the auction site owner charges the sellers for completed transactions. The charge is either a flat fee or a percentage of the sale value. The profitability of an auction site depends on (1) the volume of transactions and (2) the cost of running the site. Both of these can be greatly influenced by a well-designed and well-implemented online auction system. If a system is easy to access and use, is reliable and performs well, it is likely that it will attract both sellers and buyers. If the system is easy to install, administer, and maintain, its cost of operation will be lower.

Problem Statement

Our Online Auction application must address the needs of its stakeholders and users, which are described in the following list.

- The sellers need to reach the largest possible number of potential buyers to obtain competitive purchase offers for their items or services.
- The buyers require access to a large and diverse catalog of items and want control over the amount of money they are willing to pay for those items.
- Both the buyers and sellers want the option of remaining anonymous until they decide to complete the exchange transaction.

- The auction site owner wants to provide an environment in which sellers and buyers meet frequently and anonymously and complete frequent exchanges, and wants to make a profit by charging a fee to the seller for completed exchanges.
- The Online Auction application must provide a secure, virtual environment in which sellers can advertise their items, buyers can bid on them, and the administrator can effectively support this e-commerce solution.

Stakeholders and Users

The term "stakeholders" refers to people or organizations directly involved in making or influencing key decisions about the functionality and properties of the Online Auction application. The term "users" represents individuals or legal entities who use the Online Auction application and support its operation.

Stakeholders: Their Concerns and Responsibilities

The key stakeholders of the Online Auction application are the Auction Site Owner and Auction System Provider, both of whom are briefly described in Table 5.1.

Table 5.1   Stakeholders

Name	Description	Concerns and Responsibilities
Auction Site Owner	An individual or organization who owns the auction site	◆ Define, review, and prioritize key requirements for the Online Auction application ◆ Define the rules of using the site including fees, rules of conduct, types of traded items, and so on ◆ Receive statistics of site usage, performance, and so on ◆ Assume financial responsibility for the management and development of the Online Auction application
Auction System Provider	An individual or organization who provides the Online Auction application	◆ Understand the requirements of the system and satisfy the needs of the Auction Site Owner ◆ Develop an elegant, well-architected, maintainable, and extensible system ◆ Reuse known solutions during the development of the system ◆ Reuse system designs and parts in the subsequent development of similar systems

Users: Their Concerns and Responsibilities

The key users are Seller, Buyer, Casual Visitor and Auction Administrator. These are briefly described in Table 5.2.

Functional Features and Constraints

The functional features of the Online Auction application should address the concerns of its stakeholders and users. The following are descriptions of typical features of an auction system that should be realized by our Online Auction.

Management of user accounts. Auction site users (the Sellers and Buyers) are able to create accounts with the system and update account information if it is incorrect or when it changes. The Auction Administrator is able to browse user accounts, update user information, and archive or delete information.

Placing items for auction. The Seller is able to create an auction by describing the auction item to be sold and by defining the initial starting price and minimum bid increment.

Table 5.2 Users

Name	Description	Concerns and Responsibilities
Seller	An individual or an organization who puts an item up for auction	◆ Provide a proof of credit ◆ Describe the auction item ◆ Define the starting price and bid increment ◆ Monitor bids and reject unwanted bids ◆ Deliver the auction item to the buyer ◆ Pay the transaction fee to the auction site owner
Buyer	An individual or an organization who places a bid on an auction item	◆ Browse the catalog of auctions ◆ Place a bid on an auction item ◆ Remove (cancel) one of his or her own bids (before the auction closes) ◆ Pay for the auction item if the bid is accepted
Casual Visitor	A person who visits the auction site just to browse the catalog. Such a visitor may become a Buyer or a Seller	◆ Browse the auction catalog without any commitment to placing a bid (the "just looking" attitude) ◆ Register with the Auction Site Owner
Auction Administrator	An individual who administers the auction site	◆ Maintain the classification of auctions ◆ Maintain Seller and Buyer registrations ◆ Monitor auction site activities and collect statistics ◆ Track violations of rules of conduct, and prevent violators from participating in trading

Browsing a structured catalog of open auctions and placing bids. Any user (defined as a Casual Visitor above) is able to browse a catalog of open auctions, view the description of auction items, and see the bid history of auctions.

Managing auctions. The system supports the operations performed by Sellers, Buyers and the Auction Administrator. A Seller may reject bids (for any reason) associated with any auction that he or she has created. A Buyer is able to enter a bid on an auction item. A Buyer is able to cancel his or her own bids before the auction closes. An Auction Administrator is able to close auctions without accepting any bids (for example because of unpaid seller fees), remove bids of certain Buyers (who, for example, violate rules of conduct) and archive auctions.

Maintaining system security. The application supports system security and in particular, authenticates users and ensures that users perform only the operations for which they have been authorized. For example, a Buyer must not be able to cancel a bid of another Buyer, and only the Auction Administrator may see all completed transactions.

There is also one particularly important constraining assumption that the Online Auction application must address. When a Seller accepts a bid and his or her auction is closed, the following exchanges take place:

- The Seller receives payment for the auction item from the Buyer.
- The Buyer receives the purchased items.
- The Seller pays the transaction fee to the Auction Site Owner.

The assumption is that the Auction Site Owner does not get involved in the exchange of the auction item, or the payment from Buyer to Seller. The Online Auction application discloses the Buyer's and Seller's information to each other, but they (the Buyer and the Seller) decide how to complete the exchange (not the Online Auction application). From the system's point of view, this disclosure of information indicates the end of the application's participation in a given auction.

As a result of the above constraint, the online auction application does not support features that are present in some auction systems such as placing an item "on hold" with the Auction Administrator or providing an escrow account.

Other Requirements and Properties

Nonfunctional Properties

The important nonfunctional properties of the system must address the key concerns of the stakeholders. These concerns include: usability, reliability, ease of maintenance, ease of extending system functionality, and security.

It is anticipated that these concerns will be addressed by following software development best practices such as requirements management and visual modeling, and also by the reuse of proven designs. The Online Auction application does not have specific performance requirements beyond those commonly expected from an online system, such as acceptable response times.

User Environment

Sellers, Buyers and Casual Visitors will access the system via Internet connections and will use commonly available Web browsers. It is anticipated that the Auction Administrator will primarily use a Web browser interface to the system, but will also have access within a local area network that is "behind the firewall."

Deployment Environment

The Online Auction application will run on a reference implementation of the J2EE specification. This choice of words here is deliberate, in that an application that deploys and runs in this environment should also deploy and run using commercial implementations of the J2EE platform.

Summary

As we mentioned in the introduction to the chapter, the presented information is commonly found in a **Vision** document. A **Vision** is the first "approximation" of what a system should provide and is used as a major input to the project go/no-go decision. If the project goes ahead then the **Vision** becomes the basis for the development of more detailed requirements as described in the next chapter (Chapter 6).

One thing that has not been discussed in this chapter, but that is often a part of a **Vision** document, is a business analysis of the return-on-investment (ROI) and buy-versus-build alternatives. These concerns have been deliberately skipped. Had we decided to purchase rather than build our Online Auction application, then there would be no reason to look at the development process and the book would stop here!

Chapter 6
Requirements

In this chapter we discuss requirements[1]. Some may question whether a developer-focused process should include requirements at all, since many developers are not responsible for defining them. We have chosen to include a discussion on this topic because some requirements artifacts have a significant impact on the development effort. In particular, we discuss the specification of **Use Cases**, which then drive the rest of the development process.

A key concern of any software development project is not only building the system right, but also building the right system, where the "right system" is one that meets the requirements as specified by the end users and other key stakeholders[2]. Implementing a requirements management process ensures that the system delivered to the end users meets their expectations.

Requirements management is a systematic approach to:

- Eliciting, organizing, and documenting the requirements of the system in such a way that all stakeholders (including the developers) understand them

- Establishing and maintaining agreement between the customer and the project team on the system's changing requirements

---

1 A *requirement* describes a condition or capability to which a system must conform; it is either derived directly from user needs, or stated in a contract, standard, specification, or other formally imposed document.

2 A *stakeholder* is someone who is materially affected by the outcome of the project. This includes, among others, the customer, the end user, and the developers.

We have found **Use Cases** to be a very effective technique for achieving both objectives. In fact, one of RUP's characteristics is that it is use-case-driven, which means that **Use Cases** are not only used for documenting the requirements, but are also used to drive iteration planning, analysis, design, implementation, and testing. As we will demonstrate in subsequent chapters, **Use Cases** provide the unifying thread through the software development process and its artifacts. This thread starts with the **Use Cases** themselves (discussed in this chapter), continues with the **Use-Case Storyboards** and the analysis-level **Use-Case Realizations** (both discussed in Chapter 7, Analysis) and culminates with the design-level **Use-Case Realizations** (discussed in Chapter 8, Design), which describe how the **Use Cases** are performed by collaborations of system elements.

For the purpose of this book, we assume that a **Vision** of what needs to be built already exists. A **Vision** defines the stakeholders' view of the system to be developed, and is specified in terms of the stakeholders' key needs and desired features. A **Vision** outlines the envisioned core requirements and may be as simple as a problem statement.

In this chapter, we describe the process for developing the following requirements artifacts:

- **Use-Case Model**. The **Use-Case Model** defines the behavior of the system from an external perspective. It includes the **Actors** that interact with the system (such as the end user), and the **Use Cases** that describe these interactions (such as "Place Bid" in an auction system).

- **Supplementary Specification**. The **Supplementary Specification** captures system-wide requirements that are not readily captured in the **Use-Case Model**. Such requirements include legal and regulatory requirements, application standards, quality attributes (such as usability, reliability, scalability, performance), operating systems and environment requirements, compatibility requirements, and other design and implementation constraints.

- **Glossary**. The **Glossary** defines important terms used by a project. It provides a set of definitions, which promotes consistency of the terminology used on the project.

These artifacts serve as a contract between the customer, the end users and the system developers. They allow customers and end users to verify that the system will become what they expected, and enable system developers to build what is expected.

Requirements and Iterative Development

As described in Chapter 3, An Introduction to the Rational Unified Process, the requirements activities vary throughout the development life cycle as shown in Figure 6.1.

The definition of the system requirements is not something that happens once, at the beginning of the project. It would be unrealistic to assume that we could fully understand and document all of the requirements of the system up front. The requirements must be refined throughout the life cycle of the project (hence the need for an effective requirements management process). The requirements activities are most visible late in the Inception phase, where the scope of the system is established and the **Use Cases** are prioritized, and during the early Elaboration phase, where the architecturally significant requirements are detailed as part of the development of the architectural baseline. However, some requirements activities are performed in the Construction phase, as the remaining requirements are detailed, and even in the Transition phase, as requirements are refined based on feedback received as a result of transitioning the system to the end user.

Requirements Overview

The Requirements discipline in the J2EE Developer Roadmap is described using two workflow details (1) **Define the System** and (2) **Refine the System Definition** as shown in Figure 6.2.

The **Define the System** workflow detail is where the scope of the system is established and documented in the **Use-Case Model**. It concentrates on the requirements "big picture" and is usually performed very early in the project.

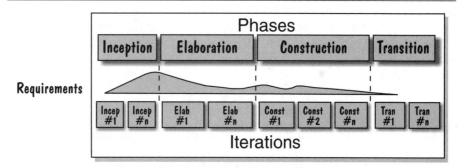

Figure 6.1   Requirements and Iterative Development

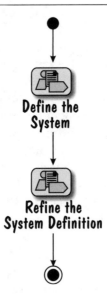

Figure 6.2 Requirements Discipline Overview Diagram

However, since the system definition is rarely (if ever) known completely, the system definition resulting from this workflow detail evolves over time as we gain a better understanding of what is expected of the system.

The **Refine the System Definition** workflow detail concentrates on the details of the **Use Cases** being addressed in the current iteration, and on refining the overall system definition, where necessary. Thus, the **Refine the System Definition** activities are performed multiple times in a project, usually once per iteration.

Throughout the requirements activities, system-wide requirements that are not applicable to specific **Use Cases** are captured in the **Supplementary Specification** and common terms and concepts are captured in the **Glossary**.

We look at the activities performed in each of these workflow details in subsequent sections.

Workflow Detail: Define the System

One of the first things that must be done on a project is to initially define what is to be included in the system, and what is not. Establishing this system scope is the purpose of this workflow detail, whose activities and key artifacts are shown in Figure 6.3.

In early iterations we establish the common terms and concepts to be used throughout the project. This is done in the activity **Capture a Common Vocabulary**. The use of a single **Glossary** eliminates the need to document the same concept in multiple places and ensures that the same term is used consistently. The **Glossary** is continually refined throughout the project, as new terms and concepts are identified and existing ones are better understood.

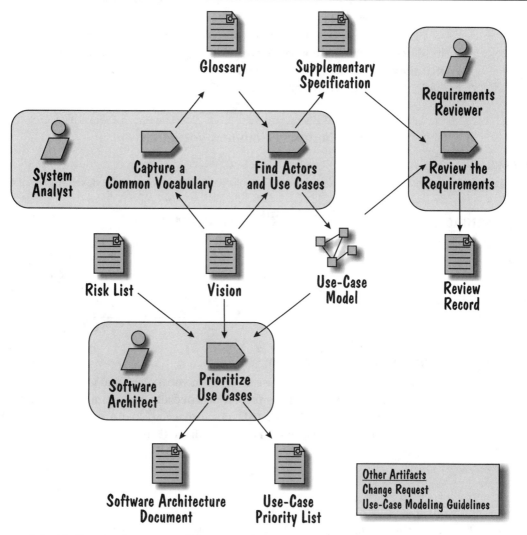

Figure 6.3   Define the System Workflow Detail Overview Diagram

A critical aspect of the system definition is its scope and therefore, its boundaries. In the activity **Find Actors and Use Cases**, we identify the **Actors** and **Use Cases** and document them in the **Use-Case Model**. We do not describe the **Use Cases** in detail at this point. Instead, we concentrate on defining their intent and purpose and possibly on outlining their content in order to allocate requirements to them. We document the requirements that we cannot associate with a particular **Use Case** in the **Supplementary Specification**.

Once the scope of the system is understood, we prioritize the identified **Use Cases** in the activity **Prioritize Use Cases**. We can then use the resulting **Use-Case Priority List** to plan the iterations, scheduling the work on the highest priority **Use Cases** first[3].

The workflow detail concludes with the **Review the Requirements** activity where, as the name implies, we review the requirements artifacts to verify that they reflect the customer's view of the system and we make sure that we understand what we are building.

Activity: Capture a Common Vocabulary

OVERVIEW
The purpose of this activity is to define a common vocabulary that is used during the development of the system.

INPUT ARTIFACTS
◆ Use-Case Model (Use Case)[4]

◆ Vision

RESULTING ARTIFACTS
◆ Glossary

STEPS
◆ Identify Common Terms

Step: Identify Common Terms

A project should consistently use a common vocabulary that is aligned with the terminology of the problem domain. It is especially important that the use-case descriptions consistently use that vocabulary to avoid misunderstandings among the project members. The vocabulary terms are documented in the **Glossary**.

---

3 Iteration planning is not in the scope of the J2EE Developer Roadmap. For more information, see RUP.

4 In the activity tables, artifacts shown within parentheses are "subartifacts" of the preceding artifact.

Table 6.1   Online Auction Application Glossary Terms

Name	Description
Auction	A sale in which an item is sold to the highest bidder
Auction Information	Information about an auction, which includes the start time and duration of the auction, product information (title, description, image), starting price (minimum initial bid price), minimum bid increment, and auction category (the category in which the auction is listed)
Credit Card Information	Information about a credit card, which includes the credit card number, billing address, and the card's expiration date
Pending Payment Notice	Information about a payment that the user still owes to the system
User Information	Information about a user, which includes the user's name, password, and e-mail address

Common terms are typically those that frequently come up when describing the system and what it does. Each term should have a clear and concise definition, and all stakeholders should agree on these definitions. In Table 6.1, we show a few terms from the **Glossary** of the Online Auction application.

Activity: Find Actors and Use Cases

OVERVIEW

The purpose of this activity is to define the scope of the system by describing what will be handled by the system, what will be handled outside the system, and who and what will interact with the system.

INPUT ARTIFACTS

◆ Glossary

◆ Use-Case Modeling Guidelines

◆ Vision

RESULTING ARTIFACTS

◆ Supplementary Specification

◆ Use-Case Model (Actor, Use Case, Use-Case Package)

STEPS

◆ Find Actors

◆ Find Use Cases

◆ Collect Supplementary Requirements

◆ Describe How Actors and Use Cases Interact

◆ Package Use Cases and Actors

The **Actors** and **Use Cases** that we identify during this activity are considered preliminary. We will refine them as we examine the use-case flows of events in more detail in the **Refine the System Definition** workflow detail, and as we gain a better understanding of the requirements. Also, even though we present the identification of the **Actors** and **Use Cases** as a series of discrete and sequential steps, in reality the **Actors** and **Use Cases** are usually identified at the same time—defining a **Use Case** may result in the identification of additional **Actors**, defining an **Actor** may result in the identification of additional **Use Cases**, and the cycle continues.

Step: Find Actors

When defining the system, one of the first things we identify is the system **Actors**. An **Actor** is someone or something *outside* the system that interacts with the system. An **Actor** can be a person, an external system, or an external device (such as a printer).

Finding **Actors** helps establish the boundaries of the system since **Actors**, by definition, are external to the system. It also assists us in understanding the purpose and extent of the system. Only **Actors** that communicate directly with the system are considered.

The **Actors** we identified for the Online Auction application are shown in Figure 6.4. As you can see, we have defined a generalization relationship between the Buyer and Seller **Actors**, and the User **Actor**. We use generalization to express the commonality of these roles. The benefits of defining a separate User **Actor** will become clearer once we identify the **Use Cases** in the next step and see how the individual roles interact with the system. We discuss generalization among **Actors** in more detail in the **Structure the Use-Case Model** activity.

In Table 6.2, we show our descriptions of the **Actors** for the Online Auction application.

In the Online Auction application, we put the **Actors** in the "Actors" package of the **Use-Case Model**, as shown in Figure 6.5. Figure 6.5 represents a

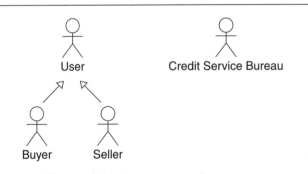

Figure 6.4 Online Auction Application Actors

Table 6.2 Online Auction Application Actors' Descriptions

Actor	*Description*
User	The User represents the general, casual user of the Auction system who has not yet committed to either buying or selling anything. It is the role that performs a basic set of system features that may be performed by all roles derived from this role.
Buyer	The Buyer represents a User who has registered with the system and is interested in purchasing an item that is available for auction.
Credit Service Bureau	The Credit Service Bureau is an external system that validates a User's credit card information and assists in handling credit card payments.
Seller	The Seller represents a User who has registered with the system and is interested in selling an item in an auction.

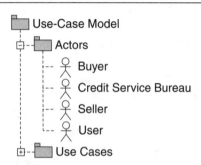

Figure 6.5 "Actors" Package in the Use-Case Model Structure

"model explorer view" of the model elements. Model explorer views are not UML, but are a graphical notation we use throughout this book to represent the organization of the models in an "outline form."

Step: Find Use Cases

Now that we have a candidate list of **Actors**, the next step is to look for the system's **Use Cases**. A **Use Case** is a description of a complete flow of events that results in something of value to an **Actor**. The best way to find **Use Cases** is to consider what each **Actor** requires of the system. This is because the system only exists in order to service the requests of the **Actors** that interact with it.

The following is a set of questions that we have found useful when identifying **Use Cases**.

- For each **Actor**, what are the tasks in which the system would be involved?

- Does the **Actor** need to be informed about certain occurrences in the system?
- Will the **Actor** need to inform the system about external changes?
- Can the identified **Use Cases** provide all the system features described in the **Vision**?
- What information must be modified or created in the system, and what **Actors** must participate in those changes?
- What **Use Cases** will support administration and maintenance of the system (for example, adding new users)?

In the Online Auction application, we put the **Use Cases** in the "Use Cases" package of the **Use-Case Model**, as shown in Figure 6.6.

When we identify a **Use Case**, we need to name it and give it a brief description. The name of the **Use Case** should indicate what is achieved through the interactions between the **Actors** and the **Use Case**, and may consist of several words, of which one should be a verb. The brief description of a **Use Case** should reflect its goal and purpose, should refer to the **Actors** involved, and should use the terms defined in the **Glossary**. We have found that a name and brief description is usually all that is needed for the **Use Case** at this point in the process. We will expand on this information when we flesh out the details of the **Use Case** in the **Detail a Use Case** activity.

In Table 6.3, we show the **Use Cases** we have identified for the Online Auction application, as well as their brief descriptions.

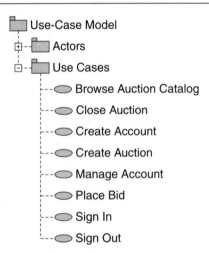

Figure 6.6 "Use Cases" Package in the Use-Case Model Structure

Table 6.3   Online Auction Application Use Cases

Use Case	*Description*
Browse Auction Catalog	The Browse Auction Catalog use case allows the User to browse items currently available for auction. The User may search for a specific item, or look at all of the items currently available for auction, sorted by category.
	The User has the option to place a bid on an item available for auction (see the Place Bid use case).
	The User does not have to be signed in to browse the auction catalog.
Close Auction	The Close Auction use case describes what occurs when an auction is closed. This use case is executed when an auction's end time is reached.
	When an auction is closed, the current highest bid becomes the purchase price for the item. The Buyer and Seller are notified that the auction has closed, what the final purchase price is, and information on how to contact each other in order to complete the transaction. The transaction fee is charged to the Seller's credit card. If the Seller's credit card cannot be charged, a pending payment is recorded for the Seller and the Seller will not be able to participate in any auctions until the pending payment is made.
Create Account	The Create Account use case allows the User to create and activate a user account, using entered user information, which optionally includes credit card information. Once the account has been created and activated, the User is considered to be signed in.
Create Auction	The Create Auction use case allows a Seller to create an online auction by specifying auction information (including the start and end times) and, if it was not provided when the Seller created his or her user account, credit card information (see the Create Account use case). Once the auction has been created, Buyers can then place a bid on the item (see the Place Bid use case).
	To create an auction, the Seller must be signed in (see the Sign In use case) and must not have any pending payments (see the Close Auction use case).
Manage Account	The Manage Account use case allows a User to update the information maintained in his or her account. If new credit card information is entered, the system attempts to pay any pending payment notices via the Credit Service Bureau using the entered information.
	The User may also deactivate his or her account. If there are any auctions in progress for the account, or the User has any pending payments, the account cannot be deactivated. A deactivated account is not deleted from the system (it may be needed later for auditing purposes), but the User cannot access it.
Place Bid	The Place Bid use case allows a Buyer to place a bid on an item when browsing the auction catalog (see the Browse Auction Catalog use case).
	To place a bid on an item, the Buyer must be signed in (see the Sign In use case) and must not have any pending payments (see the Close Auction use case).

continued

Table 6.3 Online Auction Application Use Cases *(continued)*

Use Case	Description
Sign In	The Sign In use case allows the User to identify him- or herself to the system. If the User already has an account in the system, the User supplies a username and password for authentication purposes. If the User does not have an account in the system, the system gives the User the opportunity to create one (see the Create Account use case).
	All sign in attempts, whether successful or not, are logged.
	If the User has pending payment notices, the system informs the User that payment for the notices must be made before the User can participate in any auction (as either the Buyer or the Seller).
Sign Out	The Sign Out use case allows the User to indicate that he or she no longer wants to use the system. The User's account remains unchanged (that is, it is not removed).
	Sign out events are not logged. The User must be signed in to sign out (see the Sign In use case.)

Step: Collect Supplementary Requirements

As we examine the system requirements to identify **Actors** and **Use Cases**, we may find that some of the requirements cannot be allocated to specific **Use Cases**, but instead apply to the system as a whole. We document such requirements in the **Supplementary Specification**.

In Table 6.4, we show a few entries from the **Supplementary Specification** of the Online Auction application.

Step: Describe How Actors and Use Cases Interact

Now that we have identified the preliminary set of **Actors** and **Use Cases**, we model the relationships between them. A relationship between an **Actor** and a **Use Case** is represented in UML as an association. A **Use Case** has at most one association to a specific **Actor**, and an **Actor** has at most one association to a specific **Use Case**, no matter how many interactions there are between them. The complete network of such associations is a static picture of the communication between the system and its environment.

A **Use Case** is usually initiated by a single **Actor**, but may interact with multiple **Actors**. There are exceptions to this rule. One is **Use Cases** that have relationships with other **Use Cases**, which we will discuss later in the activity **Structure the Use-Case Model**. Another exception is **Use Cases** that are initiated by an internal system event, such as a timer. In such cases, the use of an

Table 6.4 An Extract from the Supplementary Specification of the Online Auction Application

Category	Description
Usability	The system shall provide online help.
Availability	The system shall be continuously available (often referred to as 24 x 7 operation)[5]. Backup and maintenance operations shall not require a system shutdown.
Performance	The response time for any query shall be less than three seconds when measured on a 100Mb/sec local area connection. The response time for all transactions, such as creation of an auction, shall be less than five seconds from the time that transaction data is submitted to the time that transaction results are reported to the User.
Supportability	All errors shall be time stamped and logged in the system error file. Exception messages should identify the system element that threw the caught exceptions.
Development and Deployment Environment	The application should be developed and deployed on the J2EE platform.

Actor may be considered inappropriate since the **Use Case** is not initiated by something *external* to the system.

In Figure 6.7, we show a subset of the interactions between the **Actors** and **Use Cases** identified for the Online Auction application. The interpretation of the model is straightforward and goes like this. A Seller can put an item up for sale by creating an auction ("Create Auction" **Use Case**), and a Buyer can request that a bid be entered for a particular item ("Place Bid" **Use Case**). In both of these cases, the **Actor** initiates the communication with the system, so the navigation is from the **Actor** to the **Use Case**. Periodically, the system closes auctions ("Close Auction" **Use Case**). Since the **Use Case** is initiated by the system itself, no initiating **Actor** is shown. When an auction is closed, the system notifies the Buyer and the Seller, as well as the Credit Service Bureau (to charge a fee to the Seller's credit card). In this case, the system initiates communication to the **Actors**, so the navigation is from the **Use Case** to the **Actors**.

Figure 6.7 also demonstrates the specific interactions that the individual roles have with the system in terms of the **Use Cases** they initiate. For example,

---

5 This is a simplification. In reality, a more detailed service level agreement is produced, which provides a much clearer guide as to the level of failure that is deemed "acceptable." A blanket "24 x 7" availability requirement often results in an overengineered application.

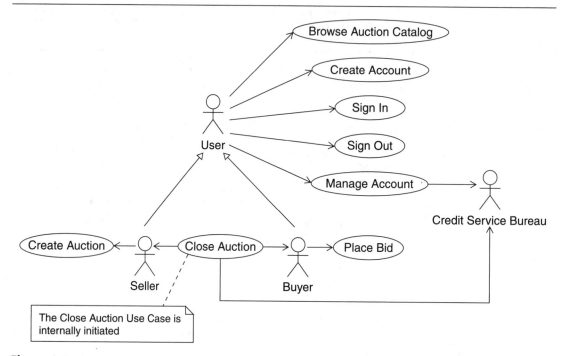

Figure 6.7 Interactions Between Initial Actors and Use Cases in the Online Auction Application

a casual User can browse the auction catalog, sign in and out of the system, create a user account, and manage his or her account information. However, only Buyers can place bids and only Sellers can create auctions.

Step: Package Use Cases and Actors

The purpose of the **Use-Case Model** is to serve as the contract between the development team and the system stakeholders. It is therefore important that the complexity of the model be kept to a minimum. If the number of **Actors** or **Use Cases** becomes too great, then we group them and put them into separate packages in the **Use-Case Model**. This additional packaging can help with the communication, development and maintenance of the model. In our example, there are a small number of **Actors** and **Use Cases**, so no further packaging is required.

Activity: Prioritize Use Cases

OVERVIEW

The purpose of this activity is to define the relative priority of the **Use Cases**, which then drives the content and planning of the iterations.

INPUT ARTIFACTS	**RESULTING ARTIFACTS**
◆ Risk List	◆ Use-Case Priority List
◆ Software Architecture Document	◆ Software Architecture Document
◆ Use-Case Model	
◆ Vision	

STEPS

◆ Prioritize the Use Cases

◆ Update the Software Architecture Document

A critical input to this activity is the **Vision**, which identifies the key things the stakeholders require of the system, and the **Risk List**, which identifies the known and open risks to the project. Both the risks and the key requirements should have been prioritized in order of importance.

Step: Prioritize the Use Cases

As we discussed in Chapter 3, a system is built in a series of iterations where a portion of the system's functionality is delivered incrementally. The sequence in which the functionality is developed is chosen in order to address and mitigate the most critical project risks as early as possible.

In this step, we order the **Use Cases**[6] according to established project-specific criteria. This criteria may include the benefit to stakeholders (for example, how important the **Use Case** is to the end user, or how important it is to demonstrate a consistent part of the system functionality to the project's sponsor), the architectural impact and coverage (for example, performing the **Use Case** involves key aspects of the architecture such as access to databases, integration with legacy systems, and so on), and the risks mitigated by addressing the **Use Case** (for example, the **Use Case** includes access to an external system whose interface is not well understood).

---

6 In practice, entire **Use Cases** are usually not developed in a single iteration. In most cases, specific flows, or specific scenarios, are delivered. Thus, the prioritization may need to be done at a granularity that is smaller than an entire **Use Case**. The granularity should reflect whatever granularity the iteration planning is based on.

We document the results in the **Use-Case Priority List**, which is used during iteration planning. The content and order of successive iterations is determined by selecting the **Use Cases** to be analyzed, designed, and implemented in the iterations, selecting the highest priority ones first. It is quite possible that in order to meet the specified project end date, the lower priority **Use Cases** may not be implemented before the release of the system.

It is important to note that the **Use Cases** are not just prioritized once. We examine their relative priorities in every iteration and, where necessary, adjust those priorities based on the current project status, including new requirements, discovery of new risks, and mitigation of existing risks.

In our Online Auction example application, we prioritized the **Use Cases** as follows:

1. Create Auction
2. Place Bid
3. Close Auction
4. Browse Auction Catalog
5. Create Account
6. Sign In
7. Manage Account
8. Sign Out

The first two **Use Cases** (Create Auction and Place Bid) are at the heart of the Online Auction application, so we put them at the top of the list. The third **Use Case** (Close Auction) may have some interesting performance requirements if we want to close a large number of auctions at the same time, so we put it next on the list. The fourth **Use Case** (Browse Auction Catalog) places more emphasis on the user interface than the other **Use Cases** and may best be experimented with after the core auction management capabilities are in place. The remaining **Use Cases** have to do with typical user account management that is expected to be straightforward to implement, so we put them last on the list.

Step: Update the Software Architecture Document

Related to the prioritization of **Use Cases** is the identification of which **Use Cases** are architecturally significant. Architecturally significant **Use Cases** are those that represent some significant, central functionality, that have substantial architectural coverage, or that stress or illustrate a specific, delicate point of the architecture. There will always be overlap between the priority of a **Use Case** and its architectural significance. For example, early iterations focus on technical risks, so the **Use Cases** are primarily ordered by architectural significance. Later iterations focus on business risks, so the **Use Cases** are primarily ordered by critical business functionality.

In the case of our Online Auction application, the highest priority **Use Cases** are also the **Use Cases** that exercise the architecturally significant parts of the system.

The architecturally significant **Use Cases** are documented in the **Software Architecture Document**. For more information on documenting the software architecture, see Appendix A, Describing a Software Architecture.

Activity: Review the Requirements

OVERVIEW

The purpose of this activity is to review the common terms, system scope, and relative priorities before detailing the system requirements. This review is important because this is where the system scope is accepted, so that resources are not spent detailing incorrect requirements.

INPUT ARTIFACTS

- Glossary
- Risk List
- Supplementary Specification
- Use-Case Model (Use Case, Use-Case Package)
- Use-Case Modeling Guidelines
- Use-Case Priority List
- Vision

RESULTING ARTIFACTS

- Change Request
- Review Record

STEPS

- Conduct the Review

Step: Conduct the Review

In this step, we review the "big picture" requirements artifacts (those artifacts whose scope is the system as a whole). These are the artifacts that define the common terms to be used throughout the system (the **Glossary**), specify the scope of the system (the **Use-Case Model**), describe any system-wide requirements (the **Supplementary Specification**), and recommend the order in which the **Use-Cases** should be developed (the **Use-Case Priority List**).

This review serves as a "quality gate" where we make sure that the requirements artifacts are mature enough to support the next set of activities—

detailed requirements definition. It is important that people outside the development team (for example, end users and customers) approve the requirements artifacts at this stage. They need to verify that the artifacts capture the intended scope of the system and the required system behavior. It is also important that the development team be involved to make sure they understand what needs to be built, as well as to identify areas where more information is needed.

We document any discovered problems in the artifacts in **Change Requests**. Once the review is complete, we briefly capture the results of the review, including any action items, in a **Review Record**.

The following checkpoints describe things that should be kept in mind when reviewing the requirements artifacts at this stage.

- The **Use Cases** and **Actors** should capture the required system behavior and interactions. Each functional requirement should be mapped to at least one **Use Case**. All use-case-specific nonfunctional requirements should be mapped to the appropriate **Use Cases**.

- All requirements that do not map to a specific **Use Case** should be captured in the **Supplementary Specification**.

- There should be no unnecessary **Use Cases**. The **Use-Case Model** should not contain any superfluous behaviors; it should be possible to trace all **Use Cases** back to a functional feature in the **Vision**.

- The **Use-Case Model** should adhere to the **Use-Case Modeling Guidelines**.

- Each term in the **Glossary** should have a clear, concise, and unambiguous definition.

- The **Use-Case Model** and the **Glossary** should be consistent. Terms defined in the **Glossary** should be used consistently within the **Use Cases**, and any terms that appear in multiple use-case specifications should be included in the **Glossary**.

- The relative priorities of the **Use Cases** should be captured accurately in the **Use-Case Priority List**. These priorities should reflect the **Vision** and the current **Risk List**.

Workflow Detail: Refine the System Definition

At this point, we have an initial specification of what the system is required to do and what its scope is. The specification has been captured in the **Use-Case Model** and the **Supplementary Specification**. Now, we turn our attention to refining this initial system definition to gain a deeper understanding of the requirements. The primary output of this workflow detail is a detailed set of **Use Cases**, a refined **Supplementary Specification**, and (possibly) a restructured **Use-Case Model**. The activities performed in this workflow detail are shown in Figure 6.8.

In the activity **Detail a Use Case**, the flows of events of a previously identified **Use Case** are described. Any requirements that are not specific to the **Use Case** are documented in the **Supplementary Specification**. The **Detail a Use Case** activity is performed once for each **Use Case** in the current iteration. The detailing of the individual **Use Cases** can occur in parallel, but it is a good idea to hold frequent informal walkthroughs to ensure consistency among the **Use Cases**.

Once a more detailed understanding of the use-case flows of events is reached, some refactoring may be done in the **Structure the Use-Case Model**

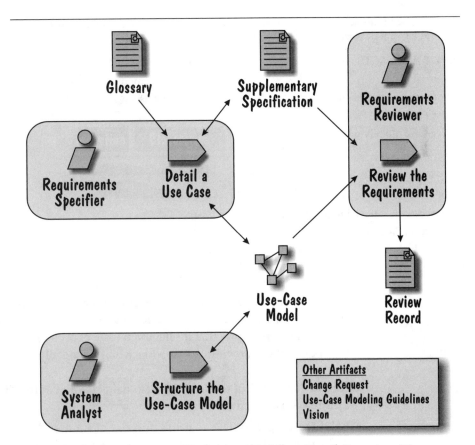

Figure 6.8   Refine the System Definition Workflow Detail Overview Diagram

activity to eliminate redundancy and to reduce the complexity of the **Use-Case Model**. We recommended that such refactoring be deferred until this activity (as opposed to being done during the activities of the **Define the System** work-flow detail) because an effective and appropriate restructuring effort cannot be undertaken until you have a more in-depth knowledge of the requirements. Before we move on to the analysis and design activities, the requirements arti-facts are reviewed in the **Review the Requirements** activity to verify that they capture the customer's view of the system.

Use Cases are detailed incrementally, with a subset of the **Use Cases** being detailed in a particular iteration. Thus, the **Refine the System Definition** activities are performed multiple times in a project.

Activity: Detail a Use Case

OVERVIEW

The purpose of this activity is to add detailed content to the use-case description. It is performed for each **Use Case** being developed in the current iteration.

INPUT ARTIFACTS

- Glossary
- Supplementary Specification
- Use-Case Model (Use Case)
- Use-Case Modeling Guidelines
- Vision

RESULTING ARTIFACTS

- Supplementary Specification
- Use-Case Model (Use Case)

STEPS

- Detail the Flows of Events of the Use Case
- Describe the Special Requirements of the Use Case
- Describe Preconditions of the Use Case (optional)
- Describe Postconditions of the Use Case (optional)

In this activity, we start with the use-case description produced in the **Find Actors and Use Cases** activity, and gradually make it more detailed until all of the stakeholders are happy that it unambiguously expresses their requirements. We specify the following information when we detail a **Use Case**:

- **Name.** The name of the **Use Case** (initially defined in the **Find Actors and Use Cases** activity)

- **Brief Description**. The goal and purpose of the **Use Case** (initially defined in the **Find Actors and Use Cases** activity)

- **Flows of Events**. A textual description of what the system does; it is expressed in terms of interactions between the **Actors** and the system

- **Special Requirements**. A textual description of requirements not considered in the use-case flows of events, but that need to be taken care of during design or implementation; in other words, nonfunctional requirements specific to the **Use Case**

- **Preconditions**. The required state of the system in order to execute the **Use Case**

- **Postconditions.** A list of possible states the system must be in immediately after the **Use Case** has finished

We capture the detailed textual description of the **Use Case** in a separate document known as a use-case specification and associate it with the **Use Case**, as shown in Figure 6.9.

Step: Detail the Flows of Events of the Use Case

A **Use Case** may have a number of potential flows through it, as shown symbolically in Figure 6.10. A **Use Case** has an expected flow, usually referred to as the "basic flow," as well as a number of alternative flows that may arise due to, for example, exceptional conditions. All of these flows must be captured.

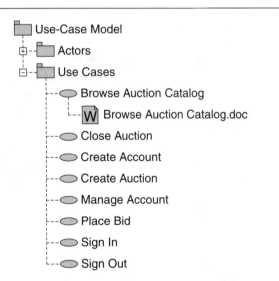

Figure 6.9   Use Case Specification in the Use-Case Model Structure

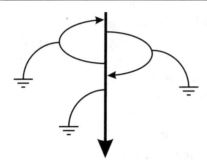

Figure 6.10 The Flows of Events of a Use Case

The following information should be included in the detailed use-case flows of events:

- How and when the **Use Case** starts
- When the **Use Case** interacts with the **Actors**, and what information is exchanged
- How and when the **Use Case** uses information stored in the system, or stores information in the system
- How and when the **Use Case** ends

When describing the flows of events of a **Use Case**, it is important to consider the context of the **Use Case**. The context of the **Use Case** is described by the relationships that the **Use Case** has with **Actors** and other **Use Cases** (for more information on relationships between **Use Cases**, see the **Structure the Use-Case Model** activity described later). This context can be expressed using a "local" use-case diagram that only contains the **Use Case**, its **Actors**, and other **Use Cases** with which the **Use Case** interacts. The local use-case diagram for the "Close Auction" **Use Case** is shown in Figure 6.11.

The use-case specification should refer to the **Glossary** to ensure that consistent terms are used. Also, all of the **Actors** that interact with the **Use Case** (as shown in Figure 6.11) should be explicitly mentioned in the use-case specification.

In Table 6.5, we describe the flows of events for the "Close Auction" **Use Case**.

Step: Describe the Special Requirements of the Use Case

We sometimes come across requirements that are associated with a **Use Case** but that are not associated with any flow of events in particular. Such require-

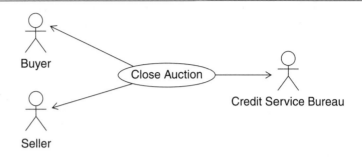

Figure 6.11 "Close Auction" Use Case Local Use Case Diagram

Table 6.5 "Close Auction" Use-Case Flows of Events

Name	*"Close Auction" Use-Case Flow of Events*
Basic Flow	1. This use case starts when the time for an auction to close has been reached. 2. The system marks the auction as closed, so that no more bids will be accepted. 3. The system collects the transaction fee from the Seller's account by submitting a payment request to the Credit Service Bureau. 4. The system sends an e-mail to the Buyer, notifying the Buyer that he or she is the auction winner. 5. The system sends an e-mail to the Seller, notifying the Seller that the auction has been closed and that a transaction fee has been debited from his or her account. 6. The use case ends.
Alternative Flow 1— No Bids Posted for Auction	After marking the auction as closed, if no bids have been posted for this auction, the following steps are performed. 1. The system sends an e-mail to the Seller to inform the Seller that the auction has been closed, but that there were no bids posted for it. 2. The use case ends.
Alternative Flow 2— Transaction Fee Not Collected	After the system marks the auction as closed, if the system is unable to collect the transaction fee from the Seller's credit card account (for example, the Credit Service Bureau responds to the request with a message such as "insufficient credit"), the following steps are performed. 1. The system adds a pending payment notice to the Seller's account. Such pending notices will be checked each time the Seller signs in (see the "Sign In" use case). When the Seller enters new credit card information, the System will attempt to pay the pending notices (see the "Manage Account" use case). 2. The system sends an e-mail to the Seller notifying the Seller that the transaction fee could not be collected from his or her credit card account. The Seller is requested to update the on-file credit card information (see the "Manage Account" use case). Until that occurs, the system will prohibit the Seller from participating in any auctions, either as the Seller or the Buyer. 3. The use case ends.

ments are often nonfunctional in nature, and are described in the "Special Requirements" section of the use-case specification.

For example, the following are the special requirements of the "Place Bid" **Use Case** of the Online Auction application:

- The system must guarantee that the order of bids processed is strictly the same as the order in which they came in. It must not be possible for two identical bids arriving closely together to be accepted out of order, regardless of network service delays, processing delays or the like.
- The Buyer should be able to place a bid on an item within three mouse clicks after accessing the auction catalog.
- The Buyer should be able to scroll a list of auction items by pressing a single keyboard button.

Step: Describe Preconditions of the Use Case

Sometimes it is necessary for the system to be in a particular state before the **Use Case** can start. A common example is the "user is signed in" state. This step ensures that all such preconditions are specified and documented with the **Use Case**. For example, the "Place Bid" **Use Case** of our Online Auction application specifies the preconditions shown in Table 6.6.

Step: Describe Postconditions of the Use Case

It may also be necessary to describe what must be true after the **Use Case** completes. The "Close Auction" **Use Case** has the postcondition shown in Table 6.7.

Table 6.6 "Place Bid" Use-Case Preconditions

Precondition	Description
Buyer is signed in	The Buyer must be signed in before the Buyer can place a bid.
Buyer has displayed the item	The Buyer has identified the item that the Buyer is interested in placing a bid on.

Table 6.7 "Close Auction" Use-Case Postconditions

Postcondition	Description
Auction is deactivated	After the auction has been closed, its status is set to "closed" and the auction no longer can be browsed or its item information changed.

Activity: Structure the Use-Case Model

OVERVIEW

The purpose of this activity is to extract common, optional, and exceptional behavior from existing **Use Cases** and create new **Use Cases**. Additional **Actors** may also be identified to define roles shared by several **Actors**.

When performed correctly, the introduction of the additional **Use Cases** and **Actors** eliminate redundant requirements and identify reusable **Use-Case Model** elements.

This activity is optional.

INPUT ARTIFACTS

- Glossary
- Supplementary Specification
- Use-Case Model (Actor, Use Case, Use-Case Package)
- Use-Case Modeling Guidelines

RESULTING ARTIFACTS

- Use-Case Model (Actor, Use Case, Use-Case Package)

STEPS

- Structure the Use Cases
- Structure the Actors

Step: Structure the Use Cases

Now that we have detailed the **Use Cases**, we will take another look at the **Use-Case Model** and refine its structure to eliminate redundant requirements and improve its overall maintainability. This must be done carefully because there is the potential that such restructuring can decrease the overall understandability of the **Use-Case Model**, since we are spreading flows across multiple **Use Cases**. Structuring the **Use-Case Model** should not significantly degrade the comprehension of the requirements. If it does, do not restructure.

Refining the structure of the **Use-Case Model** involves identifying new elements and relationships or modifying existing ones. With regard to **Use Cases**, we will focus our discussion on two relationships—include and extend.

The *include* relationship is where common flows of events are extracted and placed in a separate **Use Case**. The **Use Case** containing the common flows of events is "included" in those **Use Cases** that require the common flows of events. In the UML, the include relationship is modeled as a dependency association with the stereotype «include». It is drawn from the **Use Case** requiring the common flows of events to the **Use Case** containing the common flows of events.

An example of the includes relationship from our Online Auction application is shown in Figure 6.12, where the "Create Account" **Use Case** includes the "Sign In" **Use Case**. This means that when a new User creates and activates his or her account, the User is automatically signed in to the system.

Figure 6.12 An Include Relationship Between Use Cases

The *extend* relationship is where optional or exceptional flows of events are extracted and placed in a separate **Use Case**. The **Use Case** containing the optional or exceptional flows of events then "extends" the original **Use Case**. In the UML, the extend relationship is modeled as a dependency association with the stereotype «extend». It is drawn from the **Use Case** containing the optional or exceptional flows of events to the **Use Case** being extended.

An example of the extends relationship from the Online Auction application is shown in Figure 6.13, where the "Place Bid" **Use Case** extends the "Browse Auction Catalog" **Use Case**. What this means is, as the Buyer browses the auction catalog, the Buyer has the option to place a bid on an auction item.

Step: Structure the Actors

As mentioned earlier, we use generalization relationships to model **Actors** that have common characteristics. Now that we understand the roles a little better and how they interact with the system, we further refine the initial **Actor** generalization hierarchy shown in Figure 6.7 to include another generalized **Actor**, "Registered User." A Registered User is a User that has an account with the Online Auction application. As we show in Figure 6.14, each **Actor** has a different interaction with the system in terms of the **Use Cases** he or she is able to initiate.

A general User can browse the auction catalog or create an account (which then makes him or her a Registered User). A Registered User can sign in or out of the system, or make changes to his or her account. A Seller can create auctions, and a Buyer can place bids on those auctions.

Figure 6.13 An Extend Relationship Between Use Cases

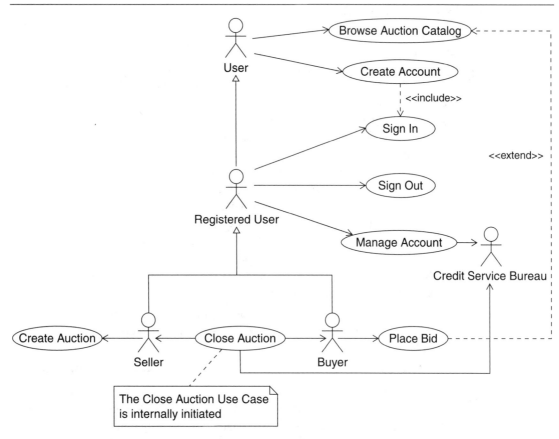

Figure 6.14   Generalized Actors in the Online Auction Application

---

Activity: Review the Requirements

OVERVIEW

The purpose of this activity is to review the detailed requirements before moving on to the analysis of these requirements. This review ensures that resources are not spent analyzing incorrect requirements.

INPUT ARTIFACTS

- ◆ Glossary
- ◆ Supplementary Specification
- ◆ Use-Case Model (Actor, Use Case, Use-Case Package)
- ◆ Use-Case Modeling Guidelines
- ◆ Vision

RESULTING ARTIFACTS

- ◆ Change Request
- ◆ Review Record

STEPS

- ◆ Conduct the Review

Step: Conduct the Review

In this step, we review the detailed requirements artifacts, especially the detailed descriptions of the **Use Cases** being considered in the current iteration. We also review the **Supplementary Specification**.

This review serves as a "quality gate" that ensures that the requirements artifacts are mature enough to support the analysis activities. It is important that people outside the development team (for example, end users and customers) approve the requirements artifacts at this stage. They should verify that the artifacts capture the detailed requirements accurately.

We document any discovered problems in the artifacts in **Change Requests**. Once the review is complete, we capture the results of the review, including any action items, in a **Review Record**.

The following checkpoints describe things that should be kept in mind when reviewing the requirements artifacts at this stage.

- The use-case specifications should accurately capture the functional and use-case-specific nonfunctional requirements.

- The **Supplementary Specification** should accurately capture the requirements not specifically tied to a **Use Case**, as well as any design or implementation constraints.

- The use-case specifications should adhere to the **Use-Case Modeling Guidelines**.

- The use-case specifications and the **Glossary** should be consistent. Terms defined in the **Glossary** should be used consistently within the **Use-Case** specifications, and any terms that appear in multiple **Use-Case** specifications should be included in the **Glossary**.

- If the **Use-Case Model** was restructured, all the original relationships between **Actors** and **Use Cases** should still hold and should be consistent with the refined relationships.

- The descriptions of the **Actors** and **Use Cases** should be consistent with their relationships.

- All relationships between **Use Cases** and **Actors** should be required (that is, there is justification for all include-, extend-, and generalization-relationships).

- The readability of the **Use-Case Model** should not be reduced as a result of any restructuring.

Summary

In this chapter, we described the process for documenting the requirements of the system, resulting in the following key artifacts: **Use-Case Model**, **Supplementary Specification**, and **Glossary**. These artifacts, most notably the **Use Cases** in the **Use-Case Model**, drive the development activities in Chapter 7, Analysis, Chapter 8, Design, and Chapter 9, Implementation.

Chapter 7

Analysis

The objective of analysis is to produce the first approximation of the shape of the solution and to lay the groundwork for design. Similarly, the objective of design is to lay the groundwork for implementation. Analysis, design and implementation are parts of a continuum of system refinements from requirements to working code.

In this chapter, we describe the activities that produce this "first approximation" of a solution that realizes the requirements defined in Chapter 6, Requirements. This solution will then be refined in Chapter 8, Design and ultimately implemented in Chapter 9, Implementation.

Analysis is sometimes overdone, resulting in "analysis paralysis" and a result that is overengineered. The goal of the analysis activities described in this chapter is to get you to a design and an architecture as quickly as possible, producing "just enough" to demonstrate that you understand the current set of requirements and that those requirements have been appropriately allocated to parts of the solution.

The primary analysis artifacts we describe in this chapter are the **Design Model** and the **User-Experience Model**.

- The **Design Model** contains the key elements of the software solution and their organization, as well as the **Use-Case Realizations** that describe how the **Use Cases** are realized in terms of these elements. During analysis, we concentrate on **Analysis Classes** and **Use-Case Realizations** expressed in terms of those **Analysis Classes**. Consistent with our view of analysis and design as a continuum, we do not maintain a separate **Analysis Model**.

- The **User-Experience Model** provides an abstraction of the user interface elements and the user's interaction with the system. It contains **Screens**, **Use-Case Storyboards**, and a **Navigation Map**. The **Use-Case Storyboards** show how the **Use Cases** are realized in terms of **Screens**, and the **Navigation Map** shows the legal navigation paths between those **Screens**. We use the **User-Experience Model** as a contract between the presentation and business aspects of the system. A separate **User-Experience Model** is not needed if the system does not have a user-experience aspect (for example, no user interface), or if that aspect is very well known, or of minor importance. In such cases, the relevant aspects of the user-experience can be captured in the **Design Model** (specifically, in the boundary **Analysis Classes**).

An "outline" of the proposed architecture is also defined and documented in the **Software Architecture Document**. However, this architecture is not truly defined until design (see Chapter 8).

Analysis and Iterative Development

As discussed in Chapter 3, An Introduction to the Rational Unified Process, the analysis and design activities vary throughout the development life cycle as shown in Figure 7.1.

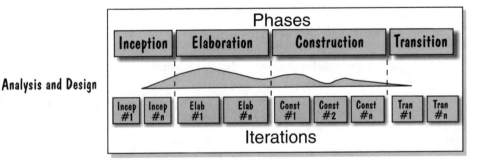

Figure 7.1   Analysis and Design Iterative Development

The analysis activities are most visible during the Elaboration phase where we are focused on establishing the software architecture. During this phase, we concentrate on analyzing those requirements that are considered architecturally significant. During the Construction phase, we analyze any remaining requirements, but this analysis is not as extensive as that performed during the Elaboration phase because most of the major system elements have already been discovered. The time we spend on analysis continues to taper off throughout the Construction phase, as the number of requirements that we have not analyzed decreases and the focus shifts to implementation. We may need to perform some minimal analysis activities even into the Transition phase, as changes to the requirements are introduced based on feedback received when transitioning the system to the user.

Analysis Overview

The analysis portion of the Analysis and Design discipline in the J2EE Developer Roadmap is described using two workflow details, as shown in Figure 7.2. These are (1) **Define an Initial Architecture** and (2) **Analyze Behavior.**

Analysis concentrates on two aspects of the system (1) an initial architecture and (2) a first approximation of the system elements and how they interact to realize the system functional behavior. Each of these aspects is reflected in the roadmap.

- The activities of the **Define an Initial Architecture** workflow detail focus on sketching out the software architecture, which is further refined in design (see Chapter 8).
- The activities of the **Analyze Behavior** workflow detail focus on:
  - Identifying the elements of the user interface (**Screens**) and detailing the user interactions with the system (**Use-Case Storyboards**).
  - Identifying the **Analysis Classes**, their responsibilities and their interactions (**Use-Case Realizations**), where the **Analysis Classes** represent the first approximation of the system elements that are then used during design to identify the design elements.

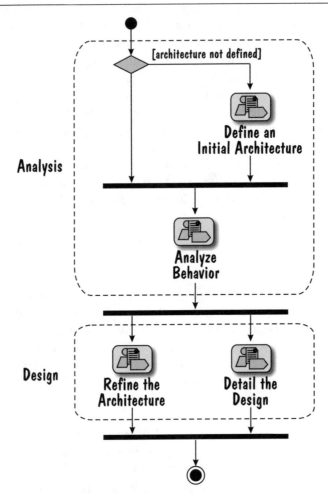

Figure 7.2   Analysis and Design Overview Diagram

Workflow Detail: Define an Initial Architecture

The purpose of the **Define an Initial Architecture** workflow detail is to create an initial "sketch" of the system architecture that leverages any existing **Reference Architectures**[1] or architectural frameworks. This "sketch" includes the

---

1 A **Reference Architecture** is a predefined architectural pattern, or set of patterns, possibly partially or completely instantiated, designed and proven for use in particular business and technical contexts, together with
supporting artifacts to enable their use. Often, these artifacts are harvested from previous projects.

overall structure of the system, its key abstractions, and its mechanisms. The identified key abstractions are then used to jump-start the analysis activities in the **Analyze Behavior** workflow detail.

The **Define an Initial Architecture** workflow detail is where we start to think about how to best leverage the technologies provided by the J2EE platform to meet both the functional and nonfunctional requirements of the system.

Figure 7.3 provides an overview of this workflow detail. As we show in the diagram, the **Architectural Analysis** activity results in an initial architecture that is reflected in initial versions of the **Design Model** and **Deployment Model**, and is documented in the **Software Architecture Document** (see Appendix A, Describing a Software Architecture). The initial architecture is then reviewed in the **Review the Initial Architecture** activity before the analysis of the **Use Cases** starts in the **Analyze Behavior** workflow detail, which is described later.

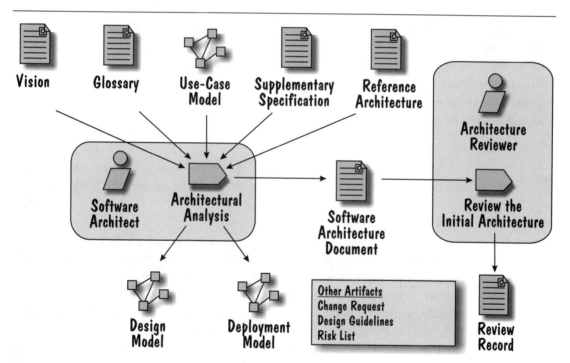

Figure 7.3 Define an Initial Architecture Workflow Detail Overview Diagram

Activity: Architectural Analysis

OVERVIEW

The purpose of this activity is to propose an initial architecture for the system, based on experience gained from similar systems or similar problem domains. This candidate architecture is developed in detail during design.

In cases where there is already a well-defined architecture, **Architectural Analysis** may be omitted since it is primarily of benefit when developing new and unprecedented systems.

INPUT ARTIFACTS

- Design Guidelines
- Glossary
- Reference Architecture
- Supplementary Specification
- Use-Case Model
- Vision

RESULTING ARTIFACTS

- Deployment Model
- Design Guidelines
- Design Model (Analysis Class, Design Package)
- Software Architecture Document

STEPS

- Develop Architecture Overview
- Survey Available Assets
- Define the Initial Deployment Model
- Structure the Design Model
- Identify Key Abstractions
- Identify Analysis Mechanisms

In this activity, we make sure that the initial architecture takes into account the technologies and mechanisms that are provided by the J2EE platform.

Step: Develop Architecture Overview

In this step, we create an overview of the architecture based on experiences developing similar systems, or systems in similar domains, or possibly by reusing an existing **Reference Architecture**. This is typically a simple step to perform when developing with J2EE technologies, since there are a number of standard deployment configurations on which we can base our initial architecture (see Chapter 2, An Introduction to the Java 2 Platform, Enterprise Edition). Each of these deployment configurations exhibits different characteristics, so here we select one based upon a number of factors. Some factors that should be considered when selecting a deployment configuration include: maintainability (how do you isolate changes in one tier so they don't affect other tiers, how easy is it to deploy upgrades?), performance and scalability (how easy is it to add additional computing resources?), and reliability (what happens if one of the resources goes down?). For more information on how the different J2EE deployment configurations address these concerns, see Chapter 2).

An architecture overview can take many forms. It can be a single "rich" picture, or several UML diagrams. The overview is documented in the **Software Architecture Document**. In Figure 7.4, we show the architecture overview for the Online Auction application.

This diagram depicts the initial architectural decisions made for the Online Auction application. Specifically, we selected a multitier J2EE deployment configuration, with separate Web and EJB servers. Elements in the Web container will handle the user's requests, while elements in the EJB container will handle the business logic (auction and user account management). We also show the connection of the system to the external "XYZ Credit Authorization System" (remember the "Credit Service Bureau" **Actor** from requirements?), as well as the existence of a "Corporate Database" that supports the back up and archival of business data.

The architecture overview is typically created in an early iteration of the project to explore different architectural options and to identify the constraints imposed by each option. For example, if we choose a multitier deployment configuration, then we know that the client does not connect directly to the database. The architecture overview then allows us to convey an early understanding of the architecture of the system to the customer, the development team, and other stakeholders.

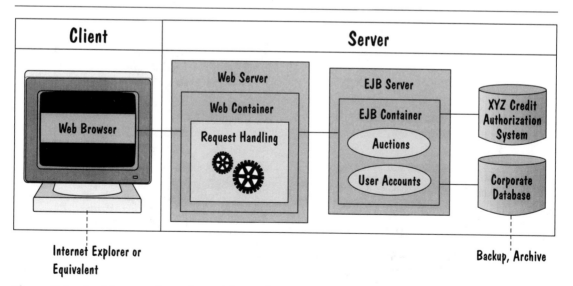

Figure 7.4 Architecture Overview of the Online Auction Application

Step: Survey Available Assets

An important part of **Architectural Analysis** is to identify assets that could be used as the building blocks of the system. For example, in the Online Auction application, we may choose to use a third-party credit authorization capability rather than writing this ourselves. The decision to use an existing asset is based upon a number of factors, including the fit of the asset with our needs, and the costs involved. There are several types of assets that can be considered, such as (but not limited to) industry models, frameworks, components and class libraries. If a **Reference Architecture** is being used as the basis for the software architecture, then any assets associated with the **Reference Architecture** are considered as well.

Step: Define the Initial Deployment Model

Using the architecture overview and the identified assets, we develop a high-level **Deployment Model** that shows the physical nodes of the system and the connections between the nodes. This allows us to gain an understanding of the physical distribution and operational complexity of the system.

In Figure 7.5, we show an example of the initial **Deployment Model** for the Online Auction application. This diagram reflects the architecture overview shown in Figure 7.4. In particular, the Web container(s) will run on separate nodes than the EJB container(s), and we model separate nodes for the external Credit Authorization System and the Corporate Database.

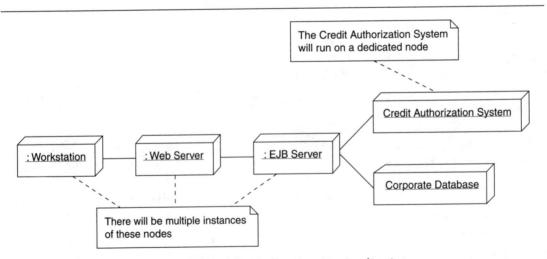

Figure 7.5   Initial Deployment Model of the Online Auction Application

The initial **Deployment Model** is documented in the **Software Architecture Document**.

Step: Structure the Design Model

The **Design Model** is a key artifact that is used to communicate the logical structure of the system, which organizes the analysis and design model elements. In this step we decide on the structure of the **Design Model** (that is, we define the **Design Packages** that are used to partition the **Design Model** elements).

Rather than discussing a number of equally valid structures of the **Design Model**, we discuss a specific structure[2] that we adopted for the Online Auction application. This structure is shown in Figure 7.6.

The "Analysis Elements" package represents the "analysis sandbox." This package is where the analysis elements (**Analysis Classes** and analysis-level **Use-Case Realizations**) reside. An analysis-level **Use-Case Realization** describes how a **Use Case** is performed by a collaboration of **Analysis Classes**. All analysis-level **Use-Case Realizations** exist in the "Use-Case Realizations" sub-package of the "Analysis Elements" package. **Analysis Classes** and analysis-level **Use-Case Realizations** are used as a basis for design, but are not maintained (as discussed in Chapter 4, Introduction to the J2EE Developer Roadmap, we do not maintain a separate **Analysis Model**). For more information on how these analysis elements are used in design, see Chapter 8, specifically, the **Identify Design Elements** activity and the **Use-Case Design** activity.

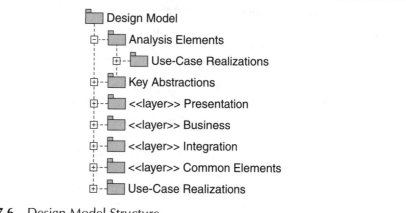

Figure 7.6 Design Model Structure

---

2 For a summary of the model structures we used for the Online Auction application, see Appendix B, Modeling Guidelines.

The "Key Abstractions" package is where we maintain an analysis-level view of the key abstractions (key business concepts) of the system. For more information on key abstractions and why they are important, see the next step, **Identify Key Abstractions**.

The «layer» packages represent the separate areas of concern within the system, specifically handling interactions with the end user (Presentation layer), performing business functionality (Business layer), and providing access to backend resources, including databases and external systems (Integration layer). There is also a Common Elements layer that contains the design elements that are common across layers. The relationship among these packages is shown in Figure 7.7.

The "Use-Case Realizations" package contains a design-level **Use-Case Realization** for each **Use Case**. A design-level **Use-Case Realization** describes how a **Use Case** is performed by a collaboration of design elements.

Step: Identify Key Abstractions

The purpose of this step is to identify the key abstractions of the system and their attributes, as well as any semantic relationships[3] between the key abstractions. Key abstractions are system-wide concepts derived primarily from the requirements artifacts (such as the **Vision, Glossary, Supplementary Specification** and **Use-Case Model**), as well as knowledge of the system's business domain. Key abstractions are represented in the UML as classes with the stereotype «entity».

For the Online Auction application, we identified the key abstractions by looking at the **Glossary** and reading through the use-case descriptions and identifying those terms repeatedly used to describe the functionality of the system. We spent some time understanding what each of the key abstractions

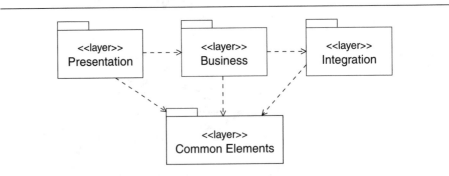

Figure 7.7 The Design Model Layers

---

3 The key abstraction relationships that exist at this point are those that are immediately obvious from the key abstraction definition.

meant in the context of our system and its domain. We then identified attributes and relationships between the key abstractions, which helped us to express their overall semantics. The results are shown in Figure 7.8.

Figure 7.8 captures important semantics of the key abstractions in our application. An *Auction* consists of a single *Auction Item* for which there can be

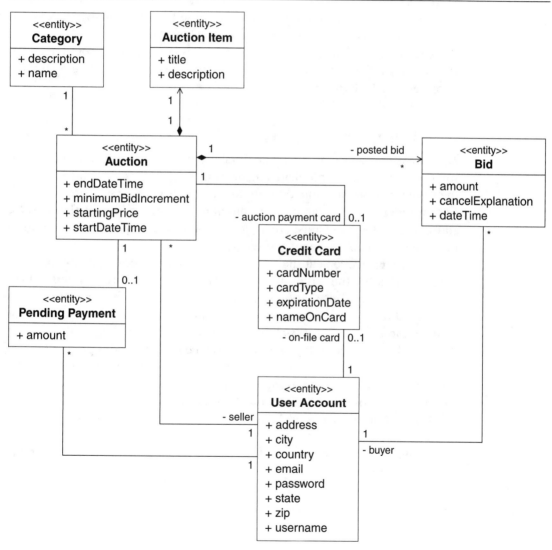

Figure 7.8 Key Abstractions of the Online Auction Application

any number of *Bids* posted. Every *Auction* belongs to a specific *Category* and there can be any number of *Auctions* within the same *Category*. A user (represented by a *User Account*) can place any number of *Bids* as a Buyer, or can participate in an *Auction* as the Seller. A user can optionally have a *Credit Card* on file that can be used to pay the transaction fee for a closed *Auction*. If the fee for an *Auction* cannot be collected using that *Credit Card*, a *Pending Payment* is recorded against the *User Account* for the *Auction*.

We will use these key abstractions as a starting point when we identify **Analysis Classes** during the **Use-Case Analysis** activity. Using this approach, we significantly reduce the possibility that these key concepts will be defined in conflicting ways when we analyze the individual **Use Cases**.

The key abstractions are placed in the "Key Abstractions" package of the **Design Model**, and are documented in the Logical View of the **Software Architecture Document**.

Step: Identify Analysis Mechanisms

An analysis mechanism is an architectural capability that represents a common solution to a common problem. Mechanisms represent general capabilities of the system that provide functionality that interacts with, or supports, the basic system functionality. Examples of common architectural needs that may be addressed with a mechanism include persistency, inter-process communication, transaction management and security.

In this step, we look at the key services we might need going forward and describe what we think they should do. The **Supplementary Specification** provides excellent "inspiration" for analysis mechanisms, as mechanisms are often used to address system-wide requirements. J2EE provides support for many of these mechanisms "right out of the box," and can help us think about what we should be considering for analysis mechanisms. At this point, all we do is identify the mechanism, provide a name and description. We will describe how these mechanisms are designed and implemented in Chapter 8 (specifically in the **Identify Design Mechanisms** activity).

The analysis mechanisms identified for the Online Auction application are listed in Table 7.1.

We document the mechanism's name and description in the **Software Architecture Document**.

Table 7.1 Analysis Mechanisms

Name	Description
Authentication	Verifies that the user has the credentials to access the system
Authorization	Makes sure that a user requesting specific system services is authorized to access and use those services
Messaging	Sends e-mail messages to the system users
Persistency	Stores system state
Presentation Request Processing	Handles user requests to the system made over the Web interface
System Parameter Management	Handles external parameters

Activity: Review the Initial Architecture

OVERVIEW

The purpose of this activity is to review the initial architecture and supporting guidelines to verify that they accurately reflect the system requirements, are consistent with one another, and can serve as a good basis for analysis and design.

INPUT ARTIFACTS

◆ Design Guidelines

◆ Glossary

◆ Risk List

◆ Software Architecture Document[4]

◆ Supplementary Specification

◆ Use-Case Model

RESULTING ARTIFACTS

◆ Change Request

◆ Review Record

STEPS

◆ Conduct the Review

Step: Conduct the Review

In this step, we review the initial architecture. This review serves as a "quality gate" that ensures that the proposed architecture supports the system requirements and provides an adequate starting point for analysis and design.

---

4 In this review, only the architecturally significant aspects of the models are reviewed, and that information is captured in the **Software Architecture Document**. Thus, the individual models are not listed as input artifacts to this activity.

We document any discovered problems in **Change Requests**. Once the review is complete, we briefly capture the results of the review, including any action items, in a **Review Record**. A **Review Record** is a form filled out for each review that provides an auditable record of the review and its conclusions.

The following checkpoints describe things that should be kept in mind when reviewing the initial architecture.

- The proposed architecture should be realistic, given the requirements captured in the **Use-Case Model** and the **Supplementary Specification**, and the projects risks documented in the **Risk List**. Someone generally knowledgeable in the problem domain should be able to easily understand it.
- The initial structure of each of the models should be defined and should be consistent. The model structures should be consistent with the proposed architecture overview.
- Mechanisms should be identified and described in the **Software Architecture Document**.
- The key abstractions should be identified, along with any attributes, operations, and relationships. They should be consistent with the requirements, especially the **Glossary** entries.

Workflow Detail: Analyze Behavior

The activities in the previous workflow detail, **Define an Initial Architecture**, focused on identifying the overall structure of the system, its key abstractions, and its mechanisms. The **Analyze Behavior** workflow detail concentrates on adding analysis-level system elements that realize the **Use Cases** to this initial structure. The identified key abstractions are used as a starting point for identifying these analysis elements. Figure 7.9 provides an overview of the activities performed and the artifacts produced in this workflow detail.

In the **Analyze Behavior** workflow detail, there are two "streams" of activities. In the first stream, the **Model the User Experience** activity considers how each **Use Case** is realized in terms of **Screens**. The result of this activity is the **User-Experience Model** that has been refined for the current iteration's **Use Cases**, which is then reviewed in the **Review the User Experience** activity.

The **Use-Case Analysis** activity represents the second stream where we consider how each **Use Case** is realized in terms of **Analysis Classes**. The result of this activity is the **Design Model** that has been refined for the current iteration's **Use Cases**, which is then reviewed in the **Review the Analysis** activity.

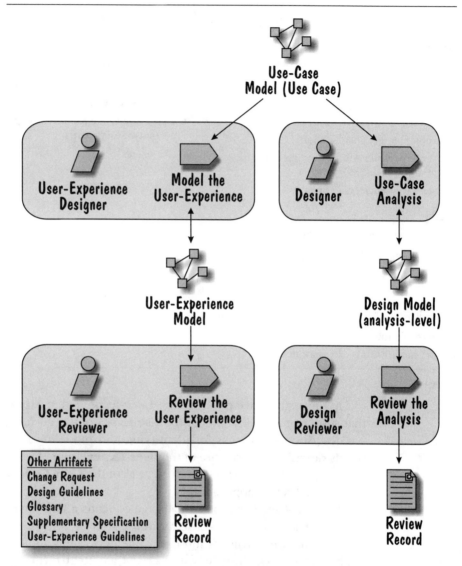

Figure 7.9   Analyze Behavior Workflow Detail Overview Diagram

The activities performed in each stream take **Use Cases** as their primary input and produce appropriate "realizations" of these **Use Cases** in terms of their respective model elements (**Screens** and **Analysis Classes**). We should remember that the nature of these activities is to provide us with an analysis-level perspective of the system, and we should avoid the temptation to design the system at this stage, since this entails additional concerns as discussed in Chapter 8.

Activity: Model the User Experience

OVERVIEW

The purpose of this activity is to define how the behavior of each **Use Case** is provided by the user-experience elements of the system.

INPUT ARTIFACTS

- Use-Case Model (Use Case)
- Supplementary Specification
- User-Experience Model (Navigation Map, Screen, Use-Case Storyboard)
- User-Experience Guidelines

RESULTING ARTIFACTS

- User-Experience Model (Navigation Map, Screen, Use-Case Storyboard)

STEPS

For each **Use Case** in the current iteration[5]:

- Identify the Participating Screens
- Model the Screen Flows
- Define the Screen Navigation Paths

The following are performed once per iteration:

- Reconcile the Use-Case Storyboards
- Document Usability Requirements

In this activity, we populate the **User-Experience Model** with elements that support the realizations of the **Use Cases** of the current iteration. Before we describe the process for identifying and modeling these elements, we briefly describe the structure of the **User-Experience Model**.

In Figure 7.10, we show the structure[6] of the **User-Experience Model** for the Online Auction application.

The "Use-Case Storyboards" package contains a **Use-Case Storyboard** for each **Use Case** in the **Use-Case Model**. **Use-Case Storyboards** describe the **Screens** the user navigates through while performing the **Use Case**. You can think of a **Use-Case Storyboard** as a **Use-Case Realization** that focuses exclusively on the user-interface elements of the **Use Case**.

---

5 In practice, these steps are performed in parallel (for example, the **Screens** are identified and described at the same time the **Screen** flows are modeled). The ability to do this comes with experience. We have chosen to present the modeling of the user experience as a series of "passes" through the use-case flows; however, the number of "passes" can be minimized as you become more experienced at applying the process.

6 For a summary of the structures we used for the models of the Online Auction application, see Appendix B, Modeling Guidelines.

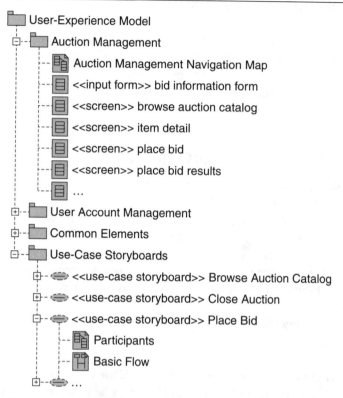

Figure 7.10 User-Experience Model Structure

We represent a **Use-Case Storyboard** as a UML collaboration instance with the stereotype «use-case storyboard». We give the **Use-Case Storyboard** the same name as the **Use Case** it realizes. If explicit traceability is desired from the **Use-Case Storyboard** to its associated **Use Case**, a realization relationship can be modeled as is shown in Figure 7.11. However, in most cases, using the same name for both the **Use Case** and the **Use-Case Storyboard** is probably enough. For more information on traceability, see Chapter 10, Additional Topics.

Each **Use-Case Storyboard** has a structural view and a dynamic view. The structural view describes the **Screens** that participate in the **Use-Case**

Figure 7.11 Traceability Between a Use-Case Storyboard and a Use Case

Storyboard and the navigation paths between them. It is represented on a class diagram called "Participants." The dynamic view describes the flow of **Screens** that occurs during the execution of the **Use Case**. It is represented as a set of interaction diagrams with at least one interaction diagram per use-case flow of events. The location of the diagrams representing these views is shown in Figure 7.10. The development of the structural and dynamic views of the **Use-Case Storyboards** is what we concentrate on in this activity.

Step: Identify the Participating Screens

In this step we identify the **Screens** the user will interact with during the execution of the **Use Case**.

Screens are the major modeling element of the **User-Experience Model**. We use **Screens** to represent what the user interacts with. In a Web application, a **Screen** is a client-side element that represents everything the application generates for the user in a single client window. A **Screen** may contain multiple pages of information. For example, it could be a frameset that renders multiple HTML pages.

The following list describes the information we capture for each identified **Screen**.

- *Dynamic content.* Dynamic content is the content displayed on the **Screen** that is provided by the business logic at runtime. Static content (for example, overall **Screen** structure, field names, titles, text, images, and client-side scripts) is not represented in the **User-Experience Model** since static content is often concerned with "look and feel" and does not affect the contract between the presentation and business aspects of the system (it is constant for each user of the system).
- *User-supplied content.* The content provided by the user via input forms.
- *User actions.* Actions that a user can perform on the **Screen**. For example, clicking on a button or selecting a menu item.

Before describing how to identify the participating **Screens** and the above information, we describe the basics of how to represent the **User-Experience Model** elements in the UML.

A **Screen** is modeled as a UML class with the stereotype «screen». The dynamic content of a **Screen** is modeled as a set of attributes of the **Screen** class as shown in Figure 7.12. The "item detail" screen is used to display information about an item that is available for auction such as the item title, item description, and the current highest bid that has been placed on the item.

Figure 7.12 A Screen with Dynamic Content

The user-supplied content of a **Screen** is modeled using a separate **User-Experience Model** element called an "input form," which is also modeled as a UML class, but has the stereotype «input form», as shown in Figure 7.13. The attributes of the input form are used to represent the user-supplied content. These input form attributes can be specified with an optional data type indicating the type of input element (such as Text, TextArea, Radio, Checkbox, and Select). We use separate «screen» and «input form» classes because their attributes represent different things. **Screen** attributes represent dynamic business content provided by the application, whereas input form attributes represent content provided by the user.

Input forms are always part of a **Screen**. Input forms never exist outside the context of a **Screen** and can never be navigated to directly (all navigation is to a **Screen**). The relationships between a **Screen** and its input forms are modeled as composition relationships from the «screen» class to the contained «input form» class(es). In the example shown in Figure 7.13, the "signin" **Screen**

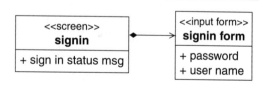

Figure 7.13 A Screen with an Input Form

is displayed when the user requests to sign into the system. It contains an input form ("signin form") where the user enters their user name and password.

User actions are modeled as operations on the **Screen** or input form classes. An example of a **Screen** with user actions is shown in Figure 7.14. In this example, the user can place a bid on the item ("place bid" operation), as well as display the image of the item ("display image" operation), both from the "item detail" **Screen**. The "display" and "navigate to" operations represent screen creation/rendering actions that are invoked by the environment (the Web browser), not the user. **Screen** creation/rendering actions are modeled as static operations on the «screen» or «input form» class (hence the underlined names).

The key input to the process of identifying **Screens** participating in a **Use Case** is the use-case specification developed during requirements, especially the detailed flows of events (see Chapter 6).

The following list describes ideas that we find helpful when identifying **Screens**.

- Identify one central **Screen** to represent the main **Screen** with which a particular **Actor** interacts. The main **Screen** should be the window that is opened when the user launches the application, and is the place where the user spends a considerable part of his or her "use time." If such a **Screen** already exists, reuse it. For example: an application's home **Screen**.

- Look for functions the user will be performing in the system. Identify one **Screen** for each major system function (possibly one **Screen** per **Use Case**). For example, a "browse auction catalog" **Screen**, or a "place bid" **Screen**.

- Look in the use-case specification for information interesting to the user, information that is manipulated by the system, and information that needs to be visible and managed in the user interface. Some of this information may end up being modeled as dynamic content on the same **Screen** or on

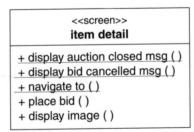

Figure 7.14 A Screen with User Actions

separate **Screens**. For example, the description of the item available for auction is modeled as dynamic content on the "item detail" **Screen** instead of a separate **Screen** (see Figure 7.12).

When identifying **Screens**, try to reuse existing **Screens** wherever possible to eliminate redundancy, enhance consistency, and reduce the consolidation and reconciliation effort that occurs later amongst the individual **Use-Case Storyboards**.

To identify user-supplied content (and thus the need for input forms), look for places in the **Use Case** where the user must supply information to the system.

To identify user actions, examine the **Use Case** for requests the user makes of the system.

The initial set of **Screens** we identified for the "Place Bid" **Use Case** is shown in Figure 7.15. This diagram represents the initial content of the "Participants" diagram shown in Figure 7.10. Additional information (for example, navigation relationships) will be added to this diagram as we perform the remaining steps in this activity (see the **Define the Screen Navigation Paths** step).

The location of these **Screens** and the "Participants" diagram in the **User-Experience Model** is shown in 7.10.

Step: Model the Screen Flows

In this step we take a look at the dynamic aspect of the **Use-Case Storyboard**—the **Screen** flows for the **Use Case**. The **Screen** flows describe how the use-case flows of events are realized in terms of the **Screens** identified in the previous step.

For each use-case flow of events, we create a UML interaction diagram (either a sequence diagram or a collaboration diagram) that describes the **Screens** that are navigated through during the execution of the **Use Case**. In the **Screen** flow

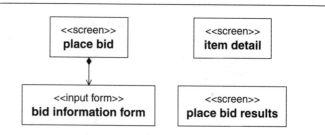

Figure 7.15 "Place Bid" Use-Case Storyboard Participating Screens

diagrams, the objects are the **Screen** instances and the messages are associated with user actions that cause a navigation to occur from one **Screen** to another. A script can be added to the interaction diagram to describe the **Screen** flow, if a more detailed description is needed.

A sequence diagram describing the **Screen** flow of the "Place Bid" **Use Case** (basic flow) is shown in Figure 7.16. This diagram represents the content of the "Basic Flow" diagram shown in Figure 7.10. The objects shown on the diagram represent instances of the **Screens** and input forms identified in the previous step and shown on Figure 7.15. A very important aspect of this dynamic view of the **Use-Case Storyboard** is that it describes the transitions between the **Screens** caused by user-system interactions. In our case, all **Screen** transitions are initiated by some user action.

Step: Define the Screen Navigation Paths

At this point, we have identified the **Screens** participating in the **Use Case** (Figure 7.15), and have modeled the flow between these **Screens** (Figure 7.16). Now we define the navigation paths that must exist between the participating **Screens** to support the **Screen** flows. Navigation paths are the relationships between **Screens** that define the valid transitions between **Screens**.

A transition between **Screens** is modeled as a UML directed association from the source «screen» or «input form» class to the destination «screen» class (the **Screen** being navigated to)[7]. The name of the navigation association should reflect the reason for the navigation (for example, if a "place bid" user action causes the navigation, the navigation association should be named "place bid"). Not all navigation associations need names, only those that add to the understanding of the diagram.

To identify the navigation paths, we examine the **Screen** flow diagrams. For every message, we define a supporting navigation path between the associated «screen» classes. For example, in Figure 7.16, the "place bid" user action on the "item detail" **Screen** causes the "place bid" **Screen** to be displayed. Thus, a navigation association must exist from the "item detail" **Screen** to the "place bid" **Screen**.

We add the **Screen** navigation paths to the **Use-Case Storyboard** "Participants" diagram created in the **Identify the Participating Screens** step (Figure 7.15). The resulting "Participants" diagram for the "Place Bid" **Use Case** is shown in Figure 7.17.

---

7 Remember, input forms never exist outside the context of a **Screen** and thus, can never be navigated to directly.

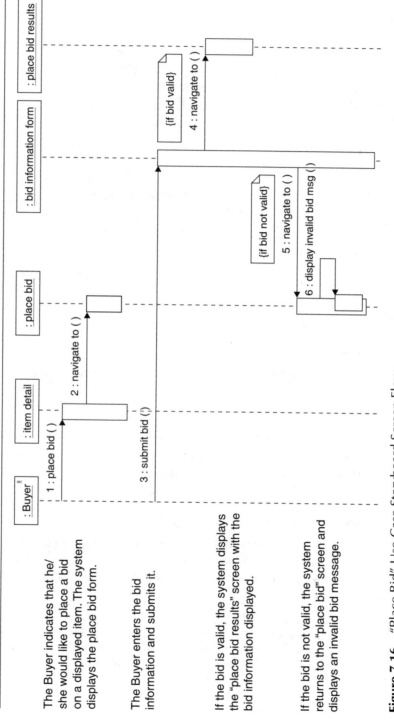

Figure 7.16 "Place Bid" Use-Case Storyboard Screen Flow

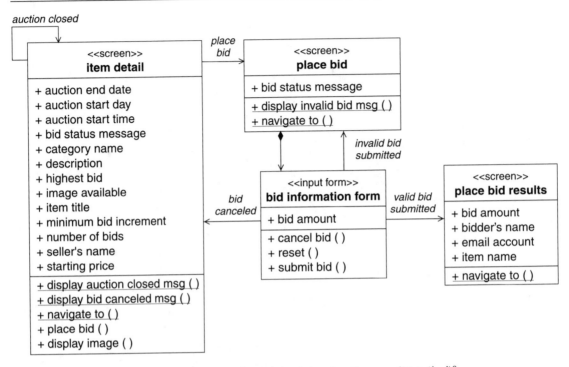

Figure 7.17 "Place Bid" Use-Case Storyboard Participating Screens (Detailed)[8]

Once the user experience for each of the **Use Cases** in the current iteration has been individually analyzed, we perform the following steps looking at the resulting **Use-Case Storyboards** together.

Step: Reconcile the Use-Case Storyboards

At this point we have a **Use-Case Storyboard** for each **Use Case** being addressed in the current iteration. In this step we reconcile these individual **Use-Case Storyboards** and identify a set of **Screens** with consistent content, user

---

8 This "Participants" diagram contains user actions and navigation associations that are not modeled in the interaction diagram shown in Figure 7.16 (for example, canceling a bid, placing a bid on an auction that is closed). However, we have included them here for completeness.

actions, and navigation paths. This reconciliation is important since the analysis of separate **Use Cases** may have resulted in disparate content and user actions being allocated to the same **Screen**. Our goal is to produce a **User-Experience Model** that is consistent across all **Use Cases**.

The result of this reconciliation is the **Navigation Map**. The **Navigation Map** conveys the structure of the **User-Experience Model** by showing the system's **Screens** and the valid navigation paths between them. The **Navigation Map** is essentially the result of combining the "Participants" diagrams of individual **Use-Cases Storyboards**[9]. For most systems, representing the entire **Navigation Map** (all of the **Screens** and their navigation paths) on a single diagram is not practical (the diagram would be too big). Thus, the **Navigation Map** is usually represented using multiple diagrams.

In the Online Auction application, we represent the **Navigation Map** using multiple diagrams, one diagram for each logical grouping of **Screens**. The **Screens** related to auction management and their navigation paths are shown in Figure 7.18. The **User-Experience Model** elements shown on this diagram span **Use-Case Storyboards**. The diagram contains participating **Screens** from the "Create Auction", "Browse Auction Catalog", and "Place Bid" **Use-Case Storyboards**. The location in the **User-Experience Model** of the "Auction Management Navigation Map" diagram (Figure 7.18) is shown in Figure 7.10.

Step: Document Usability Requirements

Usability requirements are concerned with the system properties that make the system easy to use. System-wide usability requirements are documented in the **Supplementary Specification**, whereas usability requirements specific to a **Use Case** are documented in the Special Requirements section of the use-case specification. In any case, the purpose of this step is to make sure that all applicable usability requirements are addressed in the **User-Experience Model**. Where appropriate, traceability can be established between the applicable usability requirements and the user-experience elements. For more information on traceability, see Chapter 10.

---

9 In fact, each **Use-Case Storyboard** "Participants" diagram can be considered a "mini" navigation map whose scope is the associated **Use Case** instead of the whole system.

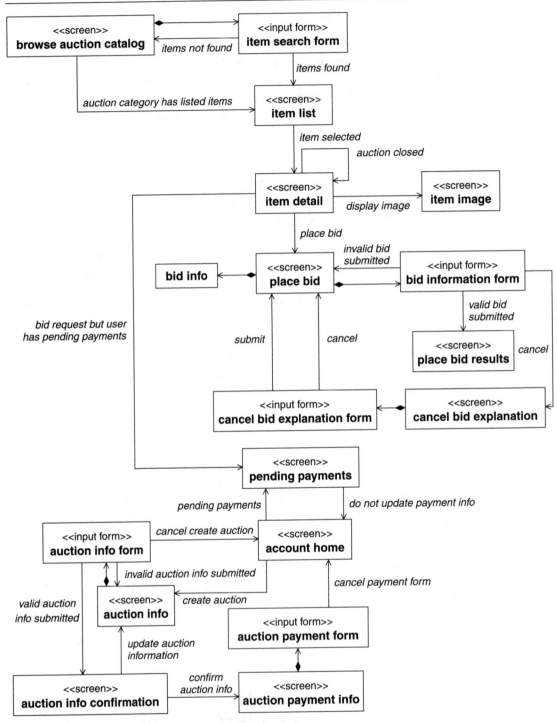

Figure 7.18   Auction Management Navigation Map

Activity: Review the User Experience

OVERVIEW

The purpose of this activity is to review the user-experience artifacts and obtain acceptance of the system's user experience from the system's key stakeholders, especially the end users.

INPUT ARTIFACTS

- ◆ Supplementary Specification
- ◆ Use-Case Model
- ◆ User-Experience Guidelines
- ◆ User-Experience Model (Navigation Map, Screen, Use-Case Storyboard)

RESULTING ARTIFACTS

- ◆ Change Request
- ◆ Review Record

STEPS

- ◆ Conduct the Review

Step: Conduct the Review

In this step, we review the **User-Experience Model**. This review serves as a "quality gate" that ensures that the **User-Experience Model** follows the **User-Experience Guidelines** and is what the user is expecting. It is critical that the user "sign off" on the **User-Experience Model** before the design or implementation of the user interface is performed.

Problems discovered in the **User-Experience Model** or the **User-Experience Guidelines** are documented in **Change Requests**. Once the review is complete, the results of the review, including any action items, are captured in a **Review Record**.

The following checkpoints describe things that should be kept in mind when reviewing the user-experience artifacts.

- ■ There should be one **Use-Case Storyboard** for each **Use Case** being considered in the current iteration.

- ■ The **Screen** flows of the **Use-Case Storyboards** should be consistent with the associated use-case flows of events and with any constraints identified in the **Supplementary Specification**.

- ■ The **Screens** and **Screen** flows should be consistent with the guidelines provided in the **User-Experience Guidelines**.

- ■ For each **Use-Case Storyboard**, the participating **Screens** and the **Screen** flows should be consistent, which means that for every **Screen** instance on the **Screen** flow diagrams, the **Screen** class should appear on the "Participants" diagram, and every message on the **Screen** flow diagrams should correspond to a navigation path that appears on the "Participants" diagram.

■ The dynamic content and user actions defined for each **Screen** should support the **Screen** flows in which the **Screen** participates.

■ The usability requirements should be associated with the appropriate **User-Experience Model** elements.

■ The system's stakeholders, especially the end users, should accept the user experience. The user experience should be what the users expect.

Activity: Use-Case Analysis

OVERVIEW
The purpose of this activity is to define how the behavior of each **Use Case** is provided by the analysis elements of the system.

INPUT ARTIFACTS
◆ Design Guidelines
◆ Design Model (Analysis Class, Use-Case Realization)
◆ Glossary
◆ Use-Case Model (Use Case)
◆ User-Experience Model

RESULTING ARTIFACTS
◆ Design Model (Analysis Class, Use-Case Realization)

STEPS
For each **Use Case** in the current iteration[10]:

◆ Identify the Participating Analysis Classes
◆ Model the Use-Case Flows
◆ Describe the Analysis Classes

The following are performed once per iteration:

◆ Reconcile the Use-Case Realizations
◆ Ensure consistency with the User-Experience Model

---

10 In practice, these steps are performed in parallel (for example, the **Analysis Classes** are identified and described at the same time the use-case flows are modeled). The ability to do this comes with experience. We have chosen to present **Use-Case Analysis** as a series of "passes" through the use-case flows; however, you can minimize the number of "passes" as you become more experienced at applying the process.

In this activity, we populate the **Design Model** with **Analysis Classes** and analysis-level **Use-Case Realizations** that describe the realization of the **Use Cases** of the current iteration at the analysis level. Before we describe the process for identifying and modeling these elements, we briefly describe the structure of the **Design Model**.

In Figure 7.19, we show the structure of the analysis elements in the **Design Model** of the Online Auction application[11].

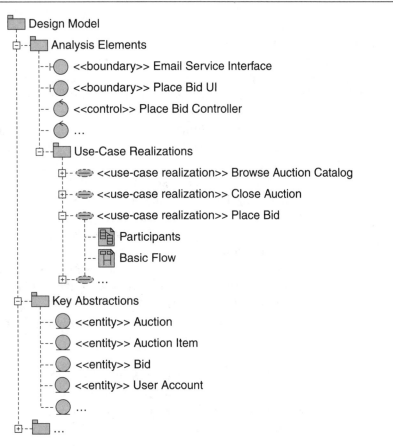

Figure 7.19 Analysis Elements Model Structure

---

11 For a summary of the structures we used for the models of the Online Auction application, see Appendix B, Modeling Guidelines.

The "Use-Case Realizations" package contains an analysis-level **Use-Case Realization** for each **Use Case** in the **Use-Case Model**. Analysis-level **Use-Case Realizations** describe how the **Use Case** is realized in terms of **Analysis Classes**. Like **Analysis Classes** that will have design element counterparts, analysis-level **Use-Case Realizations** will have design-level counterparts that will exist in the **Design Model** (in the "Use-Case Realizations" package directly within the "Design Model" package shown in Figure 7.6). Thus, **Use-Case Realizations** provide the link between the requirements as documented in the **Use Cases** and the software solution that is initially described in terms of **Analysis Classes**, and then later in terms of design elements (see the **Use-Case Design** activity in Chapter 8).

We represent a **Use-Case Realization** as a UML collaboration instance with the stereotype «use-case realization», and give it the same name as the **Use Case** it realizes. If explicit traceability is desired from the **Use-Case Realization** to its associated **Use Case**, a realization relationship can be modeled from the **Use-Case Realization** to its associated **Use Case**, as is shown in Figure 7.20. However, in most cases, using the same name for both the **Use Case** and the **Use-Case Realization** is probably enough. For more information on traceability, see Chapter 10.

Each analysis-level **Use-Case Realization** has a structural view and a dynamic view. The structural view describes the **Analysis Classes** that participate in the **Use-Case Realization** and the relationships between them. It is represented on a class diagram called "Participants". The dynamic view describes the **Analysis Class** interactions that occur during the execution of the **Use Case**. It is represented as a set of interaction diagrams with at least one interaction diagram per use-case flow of events. The location of the diagrams representing these views is shown in Figure 7.19. The development of the structural and dynamic views of the analysis-level **Use-Case Realizations** is what we concentrate on in this activity.

Step: Identify the Participating Analysis Classes

In this step we identify the **Analysis Classes** that perform the behavior described in a **Use Case**, together with their attributes, responsibilities and relationships. The three types of **Analysis Classes** used to represent the system's internal behavior during analysis are summarized in Table 7.2.

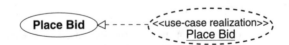

Figure 7.20 Traceability Between a Use-Case Realization and a Use Case

Table 7.2 Analysis Class Types

Analysis Class Type	*UML Representation[12]*	*Description*
Boundary	«boundary»	Boundary classes represent the boundary between the system and its environment.
Control	«control»	Control classes represent the control and coordination logic of the system.
Entity	«entity»	Entity classes encapsulate the information represented in the system.

A *boundary class* is a class used to model the interactions between the system and its surroundings. In general, there is at least one boundary class for each **Actor/Use Case** pair. A system may have several types of boundary classes, representing interactions with a user, an external system, or a device (such as a printer). A boundary class that represents interactions with a user is a placeholder for the detailed user-experience modeling that is performed in the **Model the User Experience** activity. In other words, a single boundary class is a convenient abstraction for a set of **Screens**. The **Screens** and their navigation paths provide a more detailed representation of the user's interaction with the system than the single boundary class. Consistency between the **Analysis Classes** and the **Screens** is discussed later in the step **Ensure Consistency with the User-Experience Model**.

Control classes encapsulate use-case-specific behavior and handle the main control flows. You can start by identifying one control class per **Use Case**, and then refine this as more **Use-Case Realizations** are identified and additional commonality is discovered.

An *entity class* encapsulates information represented within the system, together with any attributes and associated behavior. Entity classes usually represent persistent system elements. As we saw in the **Architectural Analysis** activity, the key abstractions identified in the **Identify Key Abstractions** step were represented as entity classes, and these key abstractions are used as a starting point for identifying the entity classes participating in the **Use Case** being analyzed.

---

12 Table 7.2 contains two UML representations (a stereotype and an icon). The stereotypes and icons are only used during analysis. The design elements that end up realizing these **Analysis Classes** use stereotypes that represent richer design and implementation semantics.

Figure 7.21 is a sequence diagram that shows typical interactions among the different types of **Analysis Classes**. Here we see an **Actor** interacting with a boundary class. The boundary class passes control to a control class that, in turn, coordinates the interactions between two entity classes.

The decoupling of the boundary, control, and entity classes represents the separation of three aspects of the system: interactions with the environment (external interfaces), internal coordination and control flow (business logic) and state management (system information model). This makes the system more tolerant to change. For example, a boundary class decouples the system from its interactions with external elements (such as users, external systems and devices). A control class ensures that use-case-specific behavior is decoupled from entity classes, thus making the entity classes more reusable across **Use Cases**.

While developing the example Online Auction application, we applied a number of the heuristics described in the preceding paragraphs. Specifically, we defined one boundary class for each **Actor/Use Case** pair, one control class for each **Use Case**, and one entity class for system information referenced in the **Use Cases**. When identifying entity classes, we used the key abstractions identified in the **Architectural Analysis** activity (see Figure 7.8) as a starting point, as well as the common terms documented in the **Glossary**.

The **Analysis Classes** identified for the "Place Bid" **Use Case** are shown in Figure 7.22. This diagram represents the initial content of the "Participants" class diagram shown in Figure 7.19. Additional information (for example, relationships between **Analysis Classes**) will be added to this diagram as we perform the remaining steps in this activity (see the **Describe the Analysis Classes** step).

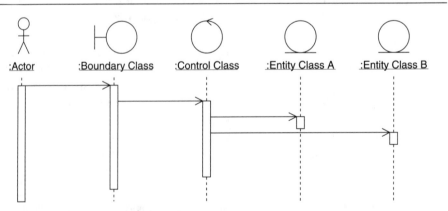

Figure 7.21   Typical Interactions Among Analysis Classes

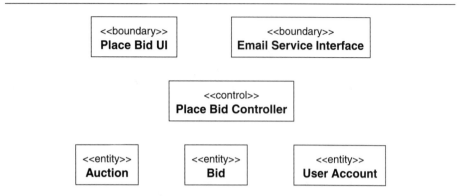

Figure 7.22 "Place Bid" Use-Case Realization Participating Analysis Classes

The location of these **Analysis Classes** and the "Participants" diagram in the **Design Model** is shown in Figure 7.19.

Step: Model the Use-Case Flows

In this step we model the use-case flows of events in terms of the **Analysis Classes** that were identified in the previous step[13]. For each use-case flow of events, we create a UML interaction diagram (either a sequence diagram or a collaboration diagram) that shows how the **Analysis Classes** collaborate to perform the flow of events. In the interaction diagrams, the objects are instances of the **Analysis Classes**, and the messages represent the "responsibilities" of these **Analysis Classes**. A script (a textual annotation) can be added to the interaction diagram to describe the flow if a more detailed description is needed.

When developing the use-case flows for the Online Auction application, we followed the typical interactions between **Analysis Classes** shown in Figure 7.21. The sequence diagram for the "Place Bid" **Use Case** basic flow is shown in Figure 7.23. This "Basic Flow" diagram is placed within the **Use-Case Realization**, as shown in Figure 7.19.

Step: Describe the Analysis Classes

At this point, we have identified the **Analysis Classes** participating in the **Use Case**, and have modeled the flows between them. It is now time to ensure that these classes have the appropriate attributes, responsibilities and relationships required to actually realize that **Use Case**. To do this, we examine the flow diagrams created in the previous step. These interaction diagrams help us determine

---

13 We may even identify new **Analysis Classes**.

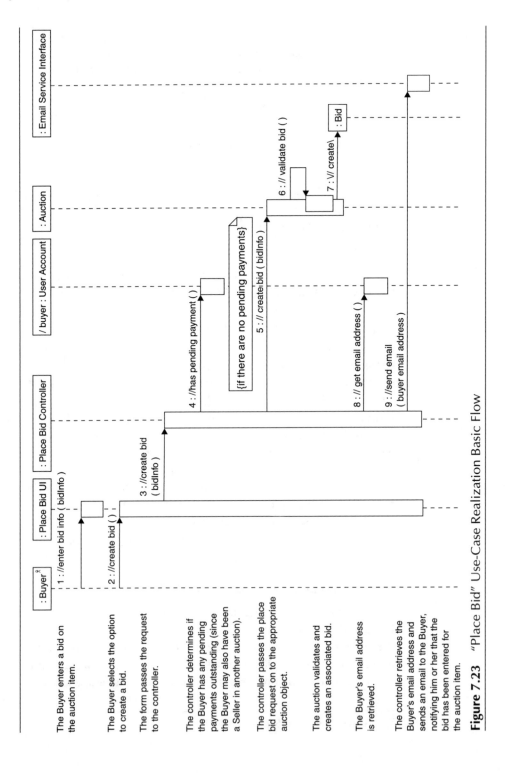

Figure 7.23 "Place Bid" Use-Case Realization Basic Flow

the responsibilities and attributes of the various **Analysis Classes**, as well as help us identify the relationships between the **Analysis Classes**.

As mentioned earlier, the messages on the **Use-Case Realization** flow diagrams represent **Analysis Class** responsibilities. Thus, all of the responsibilities of an **Analysis Class** can be determined by looking at the incoming messages to instances of that **Analysis Class** on the flow diagrams. By convention, each **Analysis Class** responsibility is documented as a UML operation whose name is prefixed with "//". As responsibilities are assigned to each **Analysis Class**, it is also worth considering the attributes that the **Analysis Class** must have in order to fulfill these responsibilities.

The **Analysis Class** relationships are also determined by looking at the **Use-Case Realization** flow diagrams. Each message between **Analysis Class** instances on the diagrams implies some kind of relationship between their respective **Analysis Classes**. Some of these relationships will represent a simple usage of another object (a UML dependency relationship). However, other relationships may imply a particular structural relationship between the respective classes (a UML association or aggregation relationship). Each of these interactions should be examined with the goal of identifying and documenting the nature of these relationships.

For example, in Figure 7.23, to process the user's request to create a bid, the Place Bid Controller must collaborate with the Buyer's User Account to see if the Buyer has any pending payments, and, if not, collaborate with the Auction to create the bid. Thus, the Place Bid Controller class must have a relationship with the User Account class and with the Auction class, as shown in Figure 7.24.

We add the **Analysis Class** relationships, responsibilities and attributes to the **Use-Case Realization** "Participants" diagram created earlier in the **Identify the Participating Analysis Classes** step (Figure 7.22). The resulting "Participants" diagram for the "Place Bid" **Use Case** is shown in Figure 7.24.

Once all of the **Use Cases** in the current iteration have been individually analyzed, we perform the following steps looking at the resulting **Use-Case Realizations** together.

Step: Reconcile the Use-Case Realizations

At this point we have a **Use-Case Realization** for each **Use Case** being addressed in the current iteration. In this step we reconcile these individual **Use-Case Realizations** and identify a set of **Analysis Classes** with consistent responsibilities, attributes and relationships. This reconciliation is important since the analysis of separate **Use Cases** may have resulted in disparate

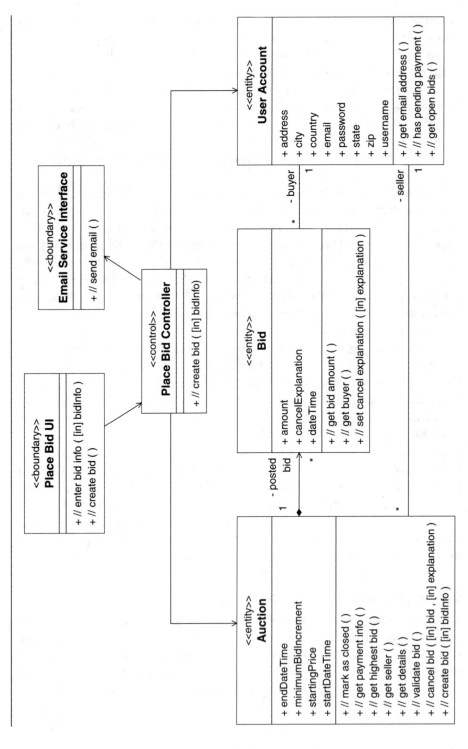

Figure 7.24 "Place Bid" Use-Case Realization Participating Analysis Classes (Detailed)

responsibilities being allocated to the same **Analysis Class**. Our goal is to produce a **Design Model** that is consistent across all **Use Cases**.

Step: Ensure Consistency with the User-Experience Model

As discussed earlier, the **Design Model** and the **User-Experience Model** describe two different aspects of the system, and these two aspects must remain consistent. Before wrapping up the analysis activities for the current iteration, it is important that we "sync up" the **Design Model** and the **User-Experience Model**.

As discussed earlier, boundary classes are used to represent the interactions between the **Actors** and the system, and **Screens** are used to represent the user interface. The **Screens** and their navigation paths provide a user-centric view of the user's interactions with the system, compared with the system's view of those interactions, which is represented by a single boundary class. Thus, there is a relationship between boundary classes representing a user interface and **Screens**. The relationship between the **Use-Case Model**, **Design Model**, and **User-Experience Model** elements is summarized in Figure 7.25.

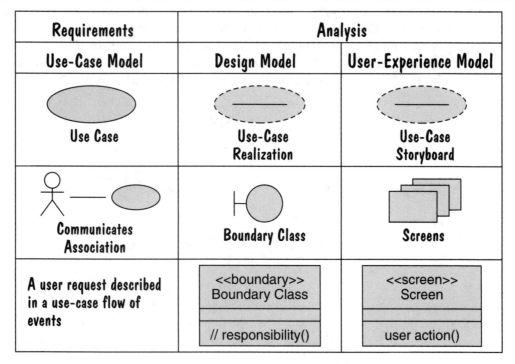

Figure 7.25 Relationships Between Requirements Elements and Analysis Elements

We make the following observations regarding these relationships.

- A **Use Case** in the **Use-Case Model** is realized by a **Use-Case Realization** in the **Design Model**, and by a **Use-Case Storyboard** in the **User-Experience Model**.
- The interactions between an **Actor** and a **Use Case** in the **Use-Case Model** map to a boundary class in the **Design Model** and a set of **Screens** in the **User-Experience Model**.
- Every user request in the use-case description maps to a responsibility defined for a boundary class in the **Design Model**, which maps to a user action defined for a **Screen** in the **User-Experience Model**.

If desired, traceability can be explicitly modeled between the boundary **Analysis Classes** and the **Screens** using a UML dependency relationship with a «trace» stereotype that is drawn from the boundary class to the **Screen**. An example of such traceability is shown for the "Place Bid" **Use Case** in Figure 7.26. However, in many cases, such traceability does not have to be explicitly modeled, but can be derived based on the relationships between the **Use-Case Storyboards** and the **Use-Case Realizations**. For example, there is one **Use-Case Storyboard** and one **Use-Case Realization** for each **Use Case**. For a **Use Case** that has a user interface, there is at least one boundary class representing the user interface in the **Use-Case Realization**. These boundary class(es) map to the **Screens** participating in the associated **Use-Case Storyboard**. For more information on traceability, see Chapter 10.

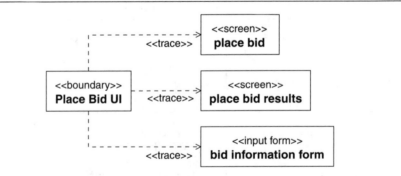

Figure 7.26   Traceability Between Boundary Classes and Screens

Activity: Review the Analysis

OVERVIEW

The purpose of this activity is to review the results of analysis to verify that they accurately represent the system requirements, are consistent with one another, and can serve as a good basis for design.

INPUT ARTIFACTS	RESULTING ARTIFACTS
◆ Design Guidelines	◆ Change Request
◆ Design Model (Analysis Class, Use-Case Realization)	◆ Review Record
◆ Supplementary Specification	
◆ Use-Case Model	
◆ User-Experience Model	

STEPS

◆ Conduct the Review

Step: Conduct the Review

In this step, a review of the analysis artifacts is performed. This review serves as a "quality gate" that ensures that the analysis artifacts are mature enough to support the subsequent design activities. Problems discovered in the artifacts are documented in **Change Requests**. Once the review is complete, the results of the review, including any action items, are captured in a **Review Record**.

The following checkpoints describe things that should be kept in mind when reviewing the analysis artifacts.

- There should be one **Use-Case Realization** for each **Use Case** being considered in the current iteration.
- The **Use-Case Realization** flow diagrams should be consistent with the associated use-case flows of events.
- The allocation of responsibilities across **Analysis Classes** should be balanced and consistent (one **Analysis Class** should not be "doing it all").
- For each **Use-Case Realization**, the participating **Analysis Classes** and flows should be consistent. This means that for every **Analysis Class** instance on the flow diagrams, the **Analysis Class** should appear on the "Participants" diagram, and that every message on the flow diagrams should correspond to a relationship that appears on the "Participants" diagram.

- The attributes and operations defined for each **Analysis Class** should support the flows in which the **Analysis Class** participates.
- The boundary **Analysis Classes** in the **Design Model** and the **Screens** in the **User-Experience Model** should be consistent with each other.
- The flows in the **Use-Case Realizations** should be consistent with the **Screen** flows in the **Use-Case Storyboards**.
- The **Analysis Classes** should provide the dynamic content identified for the **Screens**.
- The **Use-Case Realizations** should be consistent with the guidelines provided in the **Design Guidelines**.

Summary

At the completion of analysis, we have an analysis-level view of the system elements and their interactions in the **Design Model**, as well as a description of the users' interactions with the system in the **User-Experience Model**. In the next chapter, we describe how the results of analysis are used to develop a design that directly supports implementation.

Analysis is a critical part of the overall software development process and, if performed well, will result in a more robust and understandable design, with a clear separation of concerns and a balanced division of responsibility between system elements.

Chapter 8
Design

This chapter describes the design "half" of the Analysis and Design discipline. Analysis, the subject of the previous chapter, Chapter 7, Analysis, takes the system requirements and produces the initial sketch of the solution.

The objective of design is to take the results of analysis and produce a specification that can be efficiently implemented, which is the subject of the next chapter, Chapter 9, Implementation. The design is considered complete, when it is detailed enough to be implemented and tested.

The key inputs to design are the **Design Model** and the **User-Experience Model**. The **Design Model** captures the following results of analysis:

- Key abstractions (modeled as entity **Analysis Classes**) and the relationships between them, which form the foundation of the description of what information must be stored and managed by the system[1]

- Control classes that capture the flow of the system's **Use Cases** and identify the major "business" responsibilities that must be fulfilled by the system's design elements

- Boundary classes that represent the interface between the system and elements that are external to the system

- **Use-Case Realizations** that show how the **Analysis Classes** (boundary, control, and entity classes) interact in realizing the system's **Use Cases**.

---

1 Key abstractions are also referred to as the Business Type Model or System Information Model.

The **User-Experience Model** captures the following results of analysis:

- **Screens** and input forms that represent what information the user will see when working with the system, and
- **Use-Case Storyboards** that show the navigation between **Screens** and represent the interactions between the user and the system, when the system **Use Cases** are performed.

The objective of design is to take these analysis artifacts and produce a set of design artifacts that can be directly implemented with the J2EE platform technologies. The primary output artifacts of design are **Design Subsystems**, **Framework Components**, **Design Classes**, and design-level **Use-Case Realizations**, all captured in the **Design Model**. Design also updates the **Deployment Model**, refines analysis mechanisms into design mechanisms, and converts an initial sketch of the architecture developed during analysis into its final design form.

Design and Iterative Development

As we explained in Chapter 3, An Introduction to the Rational Unified Process, the analysis and design activities vary through the development life cycle as shown in Figure 8.1.

Design activities can start in an iteration of the Inception phase when we may decide, for example, that we will base our solution on a set of existing software elements. These activities then pick up in the early iterations of the Elaboration phase, when we concentrate on designing the major (or as we often call them, architecturally significant) elements of the system. As we move into the iterations of the Construction phase, the design activities taper off and focus on what we could categorize as being peripheral or supporting elements.

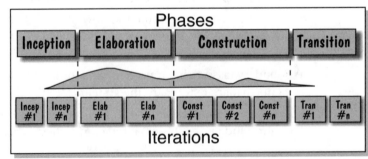

Figure 8.1 Design and Iterative Development

Design Overview

The J2EE Roadmap contains two concurrent workflow details, (1) **Refine the Architecture** and (2) **Detail the Design,** that represent the design aspects of the Analysis and Design discipline, and are shown in Figure 8.2.

The activities of the **Refine the Architecture** workflow detail focus on (1) fine-tuning the architecture that was initially articulated in the **Define an Initial Architecture** workflow detail of analysis and (2) providing a transition from the analysis to design by identifying the major design elements of the system.

The objective of the **Detail the Design** workflow detail is to keep on taking the identified design elements and refining them by working out the details of their content, behavior and relationships. As we have mentioned already, the refinement stops when there is enough detail for the design elements to be implemented.

Workflow Detail: Refine the Architecture

The **Refine the Architecture** workflow detail contains the activities shown in Figure 8.3.

The objectives of these activities are to:

- Identify the design mechanisms of the system (in the **Identify Design Mechanisms** activity)

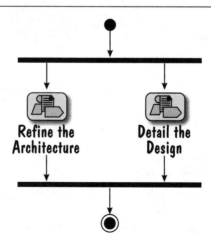

Figure 8.2   Design Overview Diagram

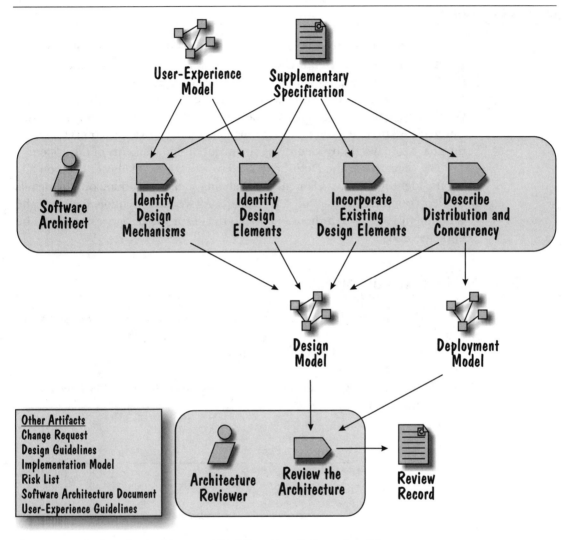

Figure 8.3 Refine the Architecture Workflow Detail Overview Diagram

- Identify major design elements of the system (in the **Identify Design Elements** activity)

- Bring together the user-experience aspects (represented in the **User-Experience Model**) and the business aspects (represented in the **Design Model**) of analysis into a single design of the system (in the **Identify Design Elements** and **Identify Design Mechanisms** activities)

- Identify the opportunity and the impact of incorporating (reusing) existing design (and related implementation) elements (in the **Incorporate Existing Design Elements** activity)

- Consider the impact of concurrency and distribution on the system's architecture (in the **Describe Distribution and Concurrency** activity)

The resulting software architecture is reviewed for consistency in the **Review the Architecture** activity. The consistency and integrity of the architecture is maintained throughout the activities of the **Detail the Design** workflow detail discussed later in this chapter.

The outcome of the activities of this workflow detail is captured in the **Design Model**, the **Software Architecture Document**, the **Design Guidelines** and the **Deployment Model**.

Activity: Identify Design Mechanisms

OVERVIEW

During analysis, we created a list of analysis mechanisms that we thought would improve the consistency and the structure of the J2EE application design. This activity takes that list and identifies design alternatives for each of the mechanisms. The activity should be performed in the early iterations of the project.

INPUT ARTIFACTS

- Design Guidelines
- Design Model
- Software Architecture Document
- Supplementary Specification
- User-Experience Model

RESULTING ARTIFACTS

- Design Guidelines
- Design Model (Design Class, Design Package, Design Subsystem, Framework Component, Interface)
- Software Architecture Document

STEPS

For each identified analysis mechanism:

- Inventory Design and Implementation Mechanisms
- Select Design and Implementation Mechanisms
- Document the Design and Implementation Mechanisms

As you recall from Chapter 7, we use the term "mechanism" broadly to describe a service, an element or a design pattern that can be used repeatedly in our application. We have been using the name of a mechanism and its concise natural-language description as a convenient shorthand for possibly complex behavior or structure. For our Online Auction application, we have identified the mechanisms shown in Table 8.1.

Table 8.1 Analysis Mechanisms

Name	Description
Authentication	Verifies that the user has the credentials to access the system
Authorization	Makes sure that the user requesting specific system services is authorized to access and use those services
Messaging	Sends e-mail messages to the system users
Persistency	Stores system state
Presentation Request Processing	Handles user requests to the system made over the Web interface
System Parameter Management	Handles external parameters

During analysis, the names of the mechanisms and their short descriptions were captured in the **Software Architecture Document**. In this activity, we decide how to realize these mechanisms.

Step: Inventory Design and Implementation Mechanisms

The first step is to examine how a mechanism will be used, and identify the available design and implementation alternatives.

Let's consider two mechanisms from our list–persistency and presentation request processing.

Persistency is a mechanism that is used in two different situations:

1. To store "user session" data that must persist only throughout the execution of a **Use Case** or as long as the user is "signed in" to the J2EE application

2. To store "application" data (states of the business entities managed by the J2EE application) that may persist indefinitely

For both situations, the J2EE platform provides various design and implementation alternatives (or strategies). For short-term (user session) persistency, there are at least two strategies: (1) we can store the data in an HTTP session object that is managed by the Web container or (2) we can store the data in a stateful session EJB managed by the EJB container. For long-term (application data) persistency, we can store the data in a database or in a file. If we decide to use a database, we still have two options: (1) use container-managed persistence (CMP) or (2) use bean-managed persistence (BMP).

Presentation Request Processing is a mechanism that ensures that we handle the user requests coming to the system over the Web in a consistent way.

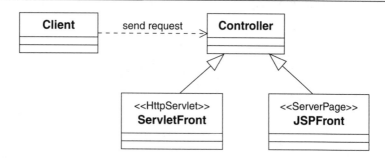

Figure 8.4 Participants in the Front Controller J2EE Pattern

The Front Controller J2EE design pattern (Alur et al. 2001) provides us with a design alternative, which is shown in Figure 8.4[2].

This design alternative recommends that all user requests come to a single element (the Controller). It is the responsibility of the Controller to determine if a request is legal before it is processed. As shown in Figure 8.4, there are two implementation strategies that we need to consider: (1) implement the controller as a servlet («HttpServlet») or (2) implement the controller as a JSP («ServerPage»).

These two examples illustrate that there are usually different alternatives for how we can design and implement a mechanism. In order to choose between those alternatives, we inventory (make a list of) them. RUP refers to the design alternatives as Design Mechanisms and the implementation alternatives as Implementation Mechanisms. Table 8.2 summarizes some of the alternatives we considered for the Online Auction application.

Step: Select Design and Implementation Mechanisms

It is hard to give a general set of rules for selecting a design and an implementation mechanism from those identified in the previous step. Some choices may be obvious, while others may not. Some may be relatively equivalent, while others may have more far-reaching implications. For example, selection of the Front Controller J2EE design pattern to handle Web requests has many implications. One of them illustrates, that design and implementation mechanism choices are not independent. As we briefly discuss in Table 8.3, the choice of how to handle the user's presentation requests in the Web container influences the choice of how to handle user-session persistency. If you are the Software Architect, it is your

---

2 Throughout this book we are using slightly different class stereotypes than the ones used in (Alur et al. 2001). Our stereotypes are consistent with those in "Java Specification Request 26 UML Profile for EJB" (Java Community Process) and those used in RUP. In those cases where stereotype names are different, the differences are small and should not introduce any ambiguities.

Table 8.2 Design and Implementation Mechanisms

Analysis Mechanism	Design Mechanism	Implementation Mechanism
Authentication	Based on password and user ID	The application authenticates the user ID and password against those stored with the relevant user account.
Authorization	Security role-based authorization	J2EE-provided security mechanism.
	Use case-based authorization	The application verifies that a specific user can perform a use case.
Messaging	Mail-based	Java Mail API.
Persistency (user session)	Container-managed session state	HTTP session managed by the Web container.
		Stateful session EJB managed by the EJB container.
Persistency (application)	Container-managed persistence (CMP)	J2EE-provided mechanism.
	Bean-managed persistence (BMP)	JDBC API.
Presentation Request Processing	Front Controller J2EE design pattern	The controller implemented as a servlet.
		The controller implemented as a JSP.
System Parameter Management	Parameters are stored externally and read by the system	Parameters are stored in an XML file and internalized once when the application starts up.
		Parameters are stored in a database and are retrieved when needed.

Table 8.3 Mechanism Choices

Mechanism	*Choice/Justification*
Authorization	We decided to use a simple combination of the use case and security-based authorization. Upon authentication, the user session is assigned a security role. User requests always pass a use-case name as a parameter identifying the use case that is to be executed. If the use case requires authorization, the application checks a list (defined as a system parameter) to see if the security role is permitted to execute the use case.
	This approach supports the addition of new use cases without requiring changes to the authentication code.
Persistency (user session)	We decided to store the user session state in the HTTP session in the Web container.
	This decision requires some explanation, as it is an example of how different design activities influence each other. As we discuss in the **Identify Design Elements** activity, we have chosen to handle the use-case flow of control in the Web container. Since the system element that controls the use-case flow needs access to the session state, for simplicity and performance reasons, the session state is also stored in the Web container.
Persistence (application)	We decided to only use CMP.
	In general, we believe that BMP should only be used when entities cannot be mapped into a database using the container-provided service. In a more complex application, the choice between BMP and CMP may have to be made at the entity level; however, the information model of our example application is not complicated and CMP is both adequate and convenient.
Presentation Request Processing	We decided to adopt the Front Controller J2EE design pattern and implement the controller as a servlet.
	The main function of the controller is to authorize and dispatch user requests. This function is better encoded in a servlet than a JSP.
System Parameter Management	We decided to store system parameters in an XML file and internalize them into an in-memory data structure at application startup.
	The decision was mainly driven by usability concerns; it is much easier to change the content and the structure of an XML file than a database.

responsibility to make these selections. Table 8.3 shows the choices we made for our Online Auction application (we only list the mechanisms for which we identified multiple design and implementation alternatives).

Step: Document the Mechanisms

The results of this activity, such as Table 8.3, which documents the choice of mechanisms, should be captured in the **Software Architecture Document**[3]. Details, such as sample interaction diagrams, usage rules, information about the

---

3 The structure and content of the **Software Architecture Document** are discussed in Appendix A, Describing a Software Architecture.

participants, common parameters, and so on, should be documented in the **Design Guidelines**.

Activity: Identify Design Elements

OVERVIEW

In the activity **Use-Case Analysis**, we identified boundary, control, and entity **Analysis Classes** and the relationships between them. In a parallel activity, **Model the User-Experience**, we also identified the **Screens** supporting user interactions.

Both the **Analysis Classes** and the **Screens** are the first approximation of our solution. The **Identify Design Elements** activity takes this input and identifies **Design Subsystems**, **Framework Components**, **Design Classes**, and **Interfaces** that will become the foundation of the system design.

INPUT ARTIFACTS

- Design Guidelines
- Design Model (Analysis Class)
- Supplementary Specification
- User-Experience Guidelines
- User-Experience Model (Screen)

RESULTING ARTIFACTS

- Design Model (Design Class, Design Package, Design Subsystem, Framework Component, Interface)
- Software Architecture Document

STEPS

- Identify Design Subsystems and their Interfaces
- Identify Framework Components and their Interfaces
- Identify Design Classes

If there is one activity that has the most impact on the system design, this is it. At the completion of this activity we should have identified the core system design elements.

- **Design Classes** (servlets, JSPs and Java classes), whose structure and use are defined by the Java language, HTML and JavaScript
- **Framework Components** (EJBs), whose structure and use are defined by the EJB container specification
- **Design Subsystems**, which represent collections of related elements that should be designed, implemented and deployed as a unit
- **Interfaces**, to represent abstract declarations of responsibilities provided by a **Design Class**, **Framework Component** or **Design Subsystem**

While performing this activity, keep in mind that the objective is to identify the design elements, not to refine their design. The refinement is performed in the activities of the **Detail the Design** workflow detail.

We cannot perform this activity without common principles that guide us through the process of deriving the design elements from the analysis elements. These principles should be identified early in the project's life cycle, captured in the **Design Guidelines,** and continuously refined as the design progresses.

Let's therefore, as an example, begin with an overview of the principles that have guided us through the design of the Online Auction application. These principles, which we believe are general enough to be applicable to a large family of systems, are based on:

- The use of J2EE design patterns (Alur et al. 2001) and the implied separation of the different responsibilities of the application
- Enterprise component design principles described in (Cheesman and Daniels 2001)
- Best practices of developing business components[4] described in (Herzum and Sims 2000)

As we discussed in Chapter 7, we divided the **Design Model** of our Online Auction application into three layers: Presentation, Business, and Integration.

- We organized the Presentation layer following a design refinement of the Presentation Request Processing mechanism discussed earlier. This refinement is based on the Service to Worker J2EE pattern (Alur et al. 2001). The pattern integrates two other patterns, the Front Controller and the Composite View, and adds dispatcher classes, view classes, and helper classes to the front controller class. The structure and participants of the refined mechanism are shown in the class diagram in Figure 8.5.

We summarize the roles of the participants in the following list.

- All requests from a user (represented by the Client element) are handled by the FrontController servlet.
- The FrontController delegates the processing of a request to a particular UseCaseDispatcher Java class. Each UseCaseDispatcher is responsible for handling all steps of a **Use Case** and hence understands the use-case flow of events.

---

4 Two authors of this book, Peter Eeles and Wojtek Kozaczynski, were members of SSA's DOCA development team where the business component concepts were refined and tested. Peter was the architect of the deployment infrastructure and Wojtek was the chief architect of the team.

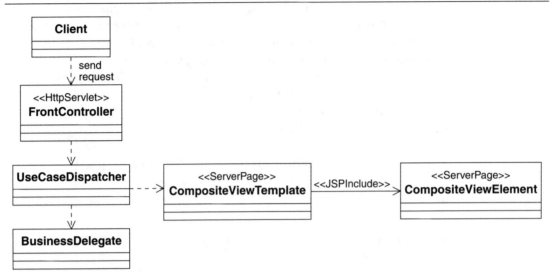

Figure 8.5   The Implementation Strategy for the Presentation Layer

- A UseCaseDispatcher delegates the tasks of screen building to views that are implemented as JSPs (CompositeViewTemplate and CompositeView-Element). The views are organized by following the Composite View pattern, which we discuss in more detail in the step **Identify Design Classes**.

- Views don't communicate directly with elements in the Business layer—this is the responsibility of each UseCaseDispatcher. If business data needs be displayed to the user, the data is obtained by a UseCaseDispatcher, through the use of a BusinessDelegate helper Java class, and then passed to views that build screens.

We decided to organize the Business layer of the system as a set of **Design Subsystems** that we stereotype «EnterpriseComponent»s. An enterprise component is similar to a "business component" as described by Peter Herzum and Oliver Sims (Herzum and Sims 2000) and a "component" as described by John Cheesman and John Daniels (Cheesman and Daniels 2001). It is a software implementation of a business concept or business process. It is a collection of related elements that should be a unit of design, implementation and deployment. We represent enterprise components as **Design Subsystems** for the following reasons.

- An enterprise component's elements and the internal collaborations of those elements are completely hidden behind one or more **Interfaces.**

- From the outside, an enterprise component is a single model element that collaborates with other model elements to fulfill its responsibilities. The description of an enterprise component's externally visible **Interfaces** and dependencies form its *specification*.

- On the inside, an enterprise component is implemented by the design elements that realize the enterprise component's specification.

Well-designed enterprise components have one more important property, which is that each enterprise component should manage a disjoint part of the system's state. This property greatly improves system maintainability and ease of testing.

We will discuss shortly how we have identified the enterprise components shown in Figure 8.6. In the meantime, the figure is an example of the external perspective of the Auction Manager enterprise component from our Online Auction application. The specification of the Auction Manager enterprise component states that it provides the Auction Manager **Interface** and requires the User Account Manager **Interface**. We can also see that the User Account Manager **Interface** is provided by the User Account Manager enterprise component.

We decided to organize the internal structure and control access to our enterprise components, following a combination of four Sun J2EE design patterns (Alur et al. 2001): Business Delegate, Service Locator, Session Façade and Value Object. We show the participants of this composite pattern in Figure 8.7. To provide a more complete picture of the patterns used in the Online Auction application, we also included the elements of the presentation request processing mechanism in the figure.

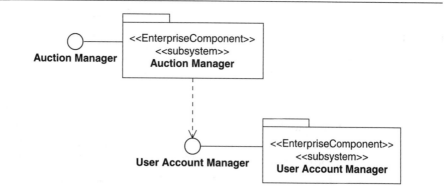

Figure 8.6 An External Perspective of an Enterprise Component

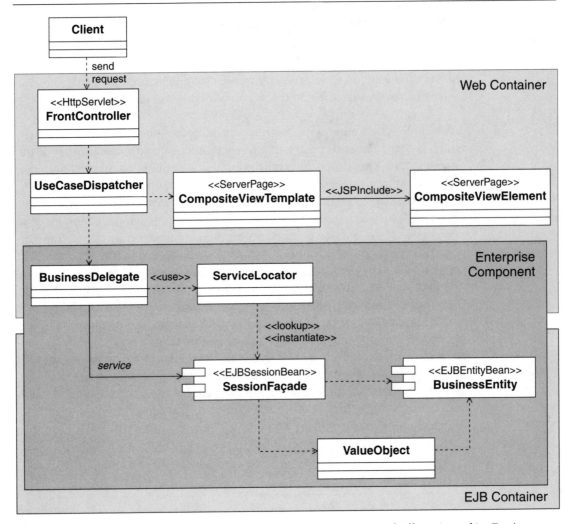

Figure 8.7   An Internal Perspective of an Enterprise Component and Allocation of Its Design Elements to Containers

It is interesting to notice, that although all design elements of an enterprise component belong to the Business layer of the system, some of them (Business-Delegate and ServiceLocator in Figure 8.7) execute in a Web container, whereas the others execute in an EJB container. Also, from an internal perspective, a business delegate is a client's proxy for the enterprise component. We shall discuss business delegates in more detail shortly.

The design structure in Figure 8.7 implies a number of important design decisions:

- The central element of an enterprise component is a façade session EJB (SessionFaçade in the figure). The façade realizes the **Interface** of the enterprise component, supports container-managed transactions, and prevents direct access to system resources.

- Clients access an enterprise component via one or more business delegate(s)[5] (BusinessDelegate in the figure). Business delegates use service locators (ServiceLocator in the figure) to find and instantiate session façades. We use the service locator to hide platform and technology-specific details such as the use of JNDI and object creation.

- An enterprise component manages a collection of entity EJBs (Business-Entity in the figure).

- Enterprise components don't pass references to the entity EJBs they manage. They only pass the state of the EJBs using value objects (ValueObject in the figure).

As you can see from looking at Figure 8.7, we use business delegates as the "connection points" between the Presentation and the Business layers of the system. When a use-case dispatcher creates an instance of a business delegate, it is essentially creating a proxy of an instance of an enterprise component.

The design structures of the Presentation and Business layers described above are the architectural foundation of our Online Auction application. Each project needs an architecture that guides us through the steps of the **Identify Design Elements** activity. If you are the Software Architect, it is your responsibility to define that architecture and to capture the design mechanisms and implied design principles in the **Design Guidelines** (see previous activity, **Identify Design Mechanisms**). Before we move to the discussion of the steps of the **Identify Design Elements** activity, we need to make one more important point about different granularities of design elements. We will be identifying design elements at three levels of granularity described in the following list and shown in Figure 8.8.

---

5 There is no guideline that states that an enterprise component should have only one associated business delegate. Usually a component must support a number of **Use Cases** and hence may have groups of responsibilities that it performs. It is up to the architect to decide if the groups should be "assigned" to multiple business delegates or one business delegate.

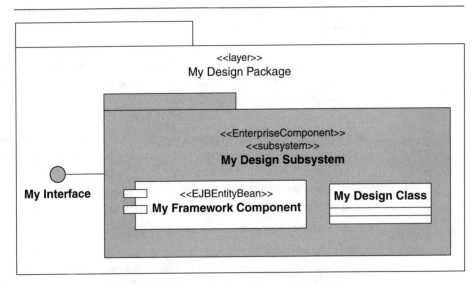

Figure 8.8   The Different Granularities of Design Elements[6]

- The largest element is a **Design Subsystem** that exposes one or more
  Interfaces. We use **Design Subsystems** to represent enterprise components. A **Design Subsystem** is represented in UML as a subsystem.
- The next smaller element is a **Framework Component**, which we use to
  represent EJBs. A **Framework Component** is represented in UML as a
  component.
- The smallest design element we consider is a **Design Class** (together with
  its attributes, operations and relationships), which is used to represent
  servlets, JSPs, and Java classes. A **Design Class** is represented in UML as
  a class.

To manage the design elements, we group them in **Design Packages** as
shown in Figure 8.8. The top-level packages in the **Design Model** are stereotyped as «layer». We discussed layers in Chapter 7.

We are now ready to discuss the steps of the **Identify Design Elements**
activity and illustrate them with examples. We will start by identifying the
largest granularity elements first (the **Design Subsystems**) because they define

6 This diagram is a slight simplification as the enterprise component **Design Subsystem** contains subpackages
that contain the **Framework Components** and **Design Classes**.

the core of the logical structure of the system and they are composed of the smaller granularity elements (the **Framework Components** and the **Design Classes**).

Step: Identify Design Subsystems and Their Interfaces

Within our architecture, **Design Subsystems** are used to represent enterprise components. We use enterprise components to encapsulate business behavior as well as access to, and the management of, system data. The best place to start looking for the application's enterprise components is the set of **Analysis Classes** (control, boundary, and entity classes) that were identified during the **Use-Case Analysis** activity.

Some general guidelines for identifying enterprise components are as follows.

- Divide the entity classes into groups such that members of a group can be managed together by a separate enterprise component.

- Look at analysis-level realizations of interrelated **Use Cases.** In particular, look for and group similar responsibilities of the control **Analysis Classes** participating in those realizations. There is a good chance that similar (or related) responsibilities should belong to the same enterprise component.

- Group related responsibilities that involve the same group of entity classes identified in the first bullet. If an enterprise component is to manage a set of entities, the responsibilities involving manipulating those entities should belong to that component.

Each group of responsibilities that we identify by following the above guidelines becomes a base from which we can derive the **Interface** of an enterprise component. As we work through the above steps, we should start putting information into the **Design Model**, as described here.

- For each group of identified responsibilities, create a subsystem stereotyped as «EnterpriseComponent» in the Business layer of the **Design Model**.

- In each subsystem, create a package named "Design". This package will contain the design elements that will compose the enterprise component.

- In each subsystem, create a package named "Specification". This package will contain a description of the enterprise component **Interface**.

- Then, create an **Interface** in the Specification package of each enterprise component that has the same name as the enterprise component.

- Finally, capture the identified responsibilities of the enterprise components as operations on their **Interfaces**.

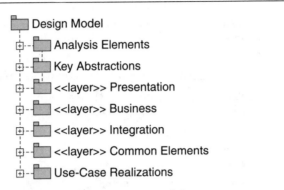

Figure 8.9 Root-level Packages of the Design Model

Let's illustrate the process with an example. During the **Architectural Analysis** activity, we defined the key abstractions of our Online Auction application, and we put them in the "Key Abstractions" package of the **Design Model** as shown in Figure 8.9. Unlike other **Analysis Classes** that we don't intend to maintain after they have been used to identify and define the design elements, we will keep the key abstractions as the base of the system's information model.

The key abstractions we have identified are shown in Figure 8.10.

We have divided the entities into two groups:

1. A group that has to do with user account, credit, and payment information. This group includes User Account, Credit Card, and Pending Payment entities.

2. A group that has to do with auctions and bidding. This group includes Auction, Auction Item, Bid, and Category entities.

Our initial design assumption is that we will have an enterprise component that manages each group. We name these components User Account Manager and Auction Manager as we show in Figure 8.11. We will discuss the other two components, Credit Service and Sign In Logger, shortly.

We show the resulting organization of the **Design Model**[7] in Figure 8.12. The newly identified enterprise components reside in the Business layer of the model.

---

7 See Appendix B, Modeling Conventions for a summary of the model organization guidelines we follow in the book.

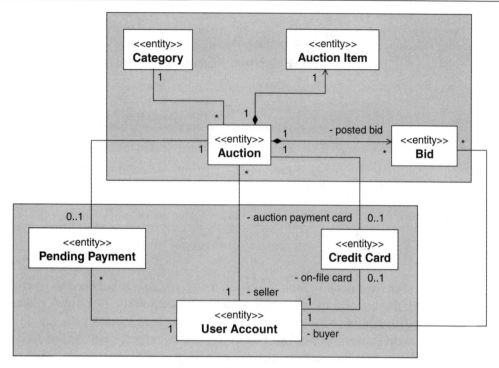

Figure 8.10 The Key Abstractions Identified During Analysis

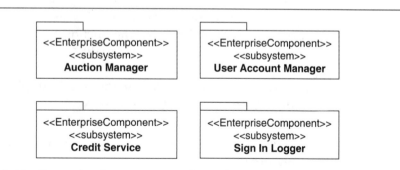

Figure 8.11 Enterprise Components in the Online Auction Application

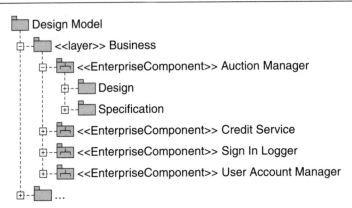

Figure 8.12 The Business Layer in the Design Model Structure

Now we need to look at the analysis **Use-Case Realizations** to come up with groups of responsibilities, which will become the first approximation of the **Interfaces** of the enterprise components. Let's consider the Auction Manager enterprise component. This enterprise component will be involved in the realization of the auction-related **Use Cases** (Create Auction, Browse Auction Catalog, Place Bid and Close Auction). In Figure 8.13 we show a sequence diagram of the Create Auction **Use Case** basic flow of events. We captured the sequence during analysis.

The place to look for the responsibilities of enterprise components, is the methods of the controller **Analysis Classes**. The sequence in Figure 8.13 shows two responsibilities that the Auction Manager enterprise component will have to fulfill (see the messages to the CreateAuctionController instance):

1. Obtain all auction categories so they can be displayed to the user (the *//get auction categories* message)
2. Create the auction and its associated auction item information (the *//create auction* message) which includes validating the auction information

It is important to notice that the CreateAuctionController communicates with the User Account entity to see if the seller has pending payments. Since the entity is not in the group of entities managed by the Auction Manager enterprise component (see Figure 8.10), we assume that the *//has pending payment* message in Figure 8.13 represents a responsibility of the User Account Manager enterprise component.

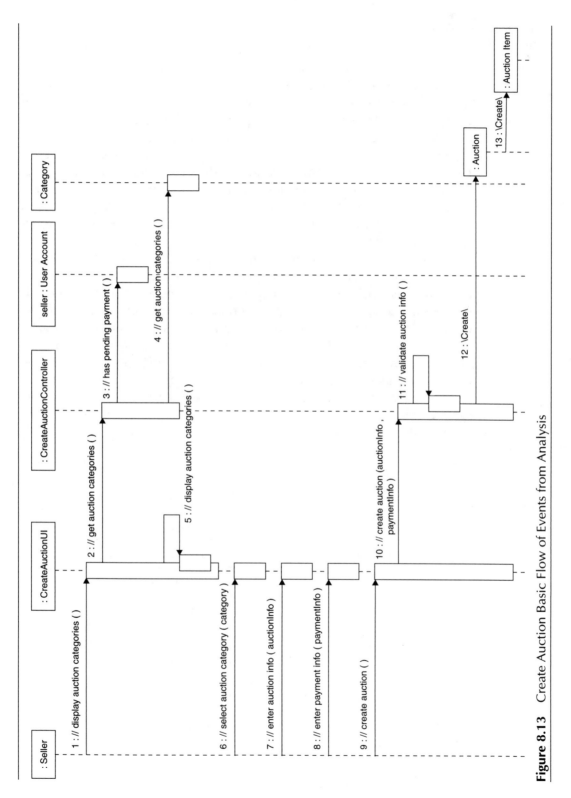

Figure 8.13 Create Auction Basic Flow of Events from Analysis

157

After looking at the basic and alternative flows of the Create Auction, Browse Auction Catalog, Place Bid, and Close Auction **Use Cases**, and also at the requests to the Auction Manager from other **Use Cases**, we have arrived at the initial set of Auction Manager enterprise component responsibilities shown in Table 8.4. For clarity, we have grouped similar responsibilities.

The last step of identifying an enterprise component is placing its initial **Interface** description in the **Design Model**. The result is shown in Figure 8.14. We have created an **Interface** that has the same name as the enterprise component, and that has an operation defined for each responsibility of the enterprise component. These operations are revisited in the **Detail the Design** workflow detail.

There are two other enterprise components in Figure 8.11. The Credit Service component is an example of a boundary analysis class representing an external system that evolved into an enterprise component during design. This happens if a boundary class handles nontrivial connection logic. For example, elements of our system may issue concurrent requests to an external system, but that system may be able to process them only sequentially. In such a case, it will be the responsibility of such a "boundary" enterprise component to queue the requests, invoke the service sequentially and then return the results to the appropriate clients. The Credit Service component is used by the Auction Manager enterprise component to charge the Seller a transaction fee when his or her auction is closed with a winning bid.

Table 8.4 Responsibilities of the Auction Manager Enterprise Component

Group	Responsibility
Auction-related responsibilities	create auction set auction values close expired auctions get open auction for category get open auctions for user
Bid-related responsibilities	add bid cancel bid get highest auction bid get auction bids
Auction item-related responsibilities	get item get minimum bid value set item values
Auction category-related responsibilities	get auction categories get categories with open auctions

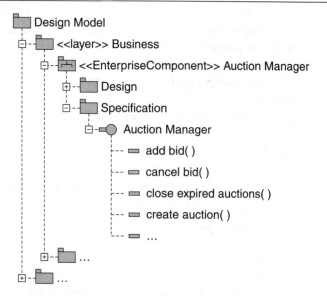

Figure 8.14 Auction Manager Interface Description

The Sign In Logger enterprise component, also shown in Figure 8.11, is used by the User Account Manager component during the sign-in process to log who has signed into the system and when they signed in.

The following list gives a few simple and useful checkpoints for evaluating the result of the **Identify Design Subsystems and Their Interfaces** step.

- Enterprise components should have balanced responsibilities. A single enterprise component should not be "doing it all."

- An enterprise component should have consistent responsibilities. When an enterprise component's responsibilities are disjoint, it should be split into two or more enterprise components.

- An enterprise component should manage a disjoint section of the system's information model (should be responsible for managing a subset of the system state).

- There should not be two enterprise components with identical or very similar responsibilities.

Looking at the above checkpoints and at the Table 8.4, you may be asking if we should have one Auction Manager enterprise component or four smaller components each responsible for one identified group of responsibilities. We have decided to have one component mainly because of its relatively small size.

Step: Identify Framework Components and Their Interfaces

As we explained earlier when discussing the granularity of the design elements, in our architecture, **Framework Components** represent EJBs.

Our architecture provides heuristics for identifying entity and session EJBs associated with enterprise components. The heuristics we used are summarized below.

For each enterprise component:

- Create a session EJB that will fulfill the role of the component's session façade (SessionFaçade in Figure 8.7).

- Create entity EJBs to represent the key abstractions managed by the component. Recall that we used groupings of key abstractions to identify the enterprise components and their responsibilities. Now we simply create entity EJBs to represent those key abstractions. Although we could consider representing each entity class in our key abstractions model as an entity EJB, we should consider grouping multiple entities into a single EJB to increase their granularity (see the example below).

- Populate each entity EJB's implementation class and remote (or local) **Interface** with the attributes identified during analysis and define its primary key class.

Let's illustrate the process using the Auction Manager enterprise component as an example. For this component, we create a façade session EJB called AuctionManagerEJB. Figure 8.15 shows the UML representation of this EJB. We

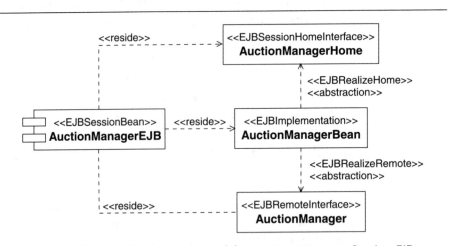

Figure 8.15 The UML Representation of the Auction Manager Session EJB

represent EJBs as UML components with an appropriate stereotype (such as «EJBEntityBean» or «EJBSessionBean»)[8]. Entity and Session EJBs expose both a home and a remote **Interface,** which we represent as UML classes[9] with the appropriate stereotypes applied. The bean implementation class has the stereotype «EJBImplementation». The «reside» dependency is drawn between the UML component and the classes that comprise the EJB.

If you go back to Figure 8.10, you will see that we decided that the Auction Manager enterprise component should manage four entities: Auction, Auction Item, Bid, and Category. We could represent each entity as a separate entity EJB, but we know that each Auction always contains one and only one Auction Item. Hence we have decided to put both entities into one entity EJB (AuctionEJB) that will store both auction and auction item information. The EJBs we have identified are shown in Figure 8.16.

Let's also make an assumption that the Auction, Bid and Category entity EJBs will always run in the same container as the associated AuctionManager session EJB. As a result, the EJBs provide local (rather than remote) EJB interfaces, as described in Chapter 2, An Introduction to the Java 2 Platform, Enterprise Edition.

The resulting **Design Model** structure we use to capture the identified **Framework Components** is shown in Figure 8.17. As you can see, we place all elements associated with a particular EJB in the same package.

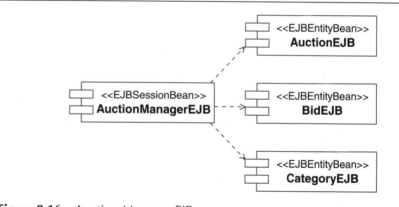

Figure 8.16   Auction Manager EJBs

---

8 The EJB UML representation is defined in "Java Specification Request 26 UML Profile for EJB" (Java Community Process).

9 A Java interface is not modeled as a UML interface since it is not semantically equivalent. For example, a Java interface can have fields, whereas a UML interface cannot.

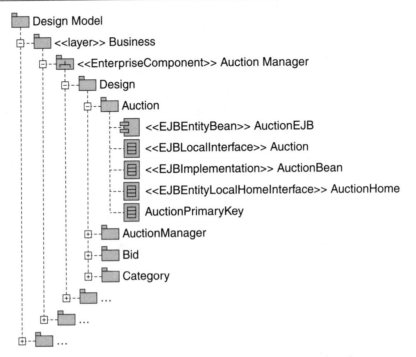

Figure 8.17 The Auction Manager Enterprise Component-Related EJBs

Step: Identify Design Classes

This is the last step of the **Identify Design Elements** activity. We showed how to identify the **Design Subsystems** (the enterprise components) and the **Framework Components** (the EJBs). What is left is to identify **Design Classes**. As before, our architecture greatly simplifies that task. If you look at Figure 8.7, you can see that there are only a few kinds of **Design Classes** in our architecture:

- A front controller servlet
- Use-case dispatcher Java classes
- View JSPs
- Business delegate Java classes
- Service locator Java classes
- Value object Java classes

We can defer the discovery of any other classes, such as additional "helpers," until detailed design and implementation.

Let's start from the Presentation layer. We know that we have only one front controller in the system, so we create a class PresentationRequestController, stereotyped as «HttpServlet». We place it in a "Common Elements" package in the Presentation layer package of the **Design Model.** Now, for each **Use Case** we do the following (see Figure 8.7 for reference):

- Create a Java class for the use-case dispatcher.

- Create a class stereotyped «ServerPage» for each unique **Screen** in the associated **Use-Case Storyboard** of the **User-Experience Model**.

- Place these classes in the Presentation layer package of the **Design Model.** We recommend dividing the Presentation layer package into subpackages to group elements that belong to related sets of **Use Cases**. In the case of our Online Auction application, we created two such subpackages; one for Auction Management and the other for User Account Management. We placed elements that are not specific to a **Use Case** in the Common Elements package (as we did for the PresentationRequestController servlet).

The results of applying the above rules for the Create Auction **Use Case** are shown in a fragment of the **Design Model** shown in Figure 8.18.

The CreateAuctionDispatcher class is the use-case dispatcher, and the auction_create_success, auction_info, and auction_info_confirmation server pages are associated with the **Screens** from the Create Auction **Use-Case Storyboard**.

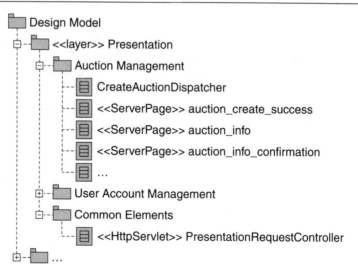

Figure 8.18 Design Model Structure Showing Design Classes in the Presentation Layer

We now consider the **Design Classes** in the Business layer. Following our architectural guidelines we can identify some of the key classes that will be part of the identified enterprise components. For each enterprise component we do the following (see Figure 8.7 as a reference):

- Create a Java class for the enterprise component business delegate[10]
- Create a Java class for the service locator that provides access to the session façade EJB of the component
- For each entity EJB managed by the component:
  - ◆ Create a Java class to pass entity attributes by value (that is, a class that conforms to the Value Object J2EE design pattern).
  - ◆ If the entity EJB represents a composition, such as the Auction and Auction Item, you may need to create a Java class to pass the values of the composition as well as classes to pass the values of its individual parts.

The results of applying the above rules to the Auction Manager enterprise component are shown in a fragment of the **Design Model** in Figure 8.19. The AuctionManagerDelegate and the AuctionManagerHomeLocator classes are the component's business delegate and service locator classes, respectively. The AuctionValues and ItemValues classes are used to pass the entity EJB values to the clients of the enterprise component.

In Figure 8.20 we show another view of the identified classes. It is a view from the perspective of a particular **Use Case** and can be thought of as an instantiation of the patterns shown in Figure 8.7. All classes in Figure 8.20 participate in the Create Auction **Use Case**. We will discuss use-case participants and interactions between them in more detail in the **Use Case Design** activity of the **Detail the Design** workflow detail.

At that beginning of describing this activity, we mentioned that we decided to use the Composite View pattern to organize the view classes (see Figure 8.5). We can now explain this in more detail. The essence of the pattern is that use-case dispatchers always call the same JSP (the CompositeView Template in Figure 8.5 and the template JSP in Figure 8.20). This JSP provides the overall look and feel of the site[11] and includes other JSPs such as menus and use-case-specific pages. Some of these view classes are included statically, such as the menu JSP in Figure 8.20 to build the "standard" page elements such as the

---

10 As we noted earlier, for more complicated enterprise components we may create multiple business delegates.

11 This is why sometimes the composite view template JSP is referred to as the "skin" server page of the site.

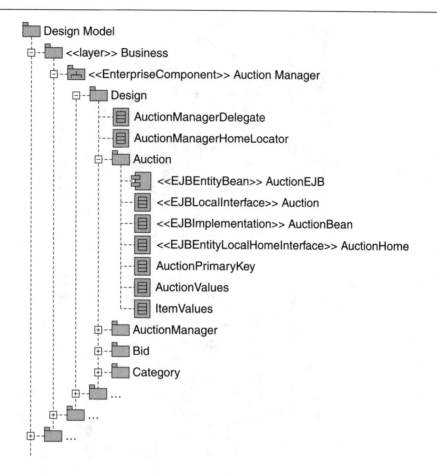

Figure 8.19 Design Model Structure Showing Design Classes in the Business Layer

menus, header, and footer. Others JSPs can be included at runtime, like all other JSPs in Figure 8.20. These view classes build the "dynamic" elements of pages.

This concludes the steps of the **Identify Design Elements** activity. We have spent a disproportionate amount of time describing this activity, but we believe we have done that for some very good reasons, which we summarize here.

- This activity, together with the mechanisms and guidelines provided by the **Identify Design Mechanisms** activity, forms a "bridge" between analysis and design.
- The quality of the results of this activity determines the quality of the system design.

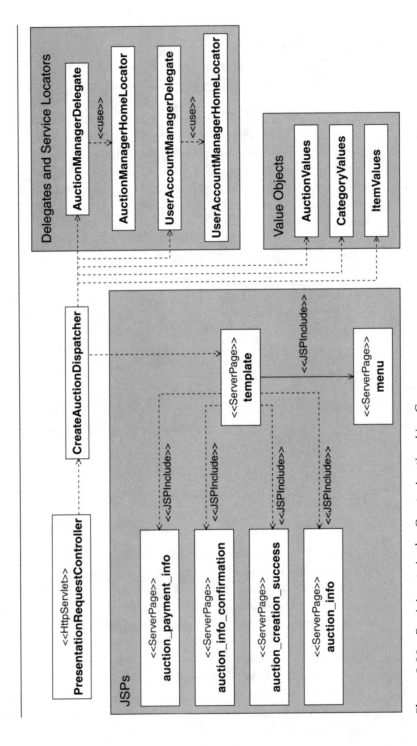

Figure 8.20 Participants in the Create Auction Use Case

■ At the conclusion of this activity, we should have identified and described all key design elements of the system and the relationships between them. Any additional design elements should be of a secondary, or supportive, nature and should be discovered during detailed design and implementation. Discovery of major design elements late in the project's life cycle indicates a flaw in requirements, analysis, or the discussed aspects of design.

Before we move on, we would like to make a couple of important points. While performing this activity, it is important to maintain a delicate balance between identifying design elements and refining their design. This activity should focus on identifying the elements. The activities of the **Detail the Design** workflow detail focus on refining their design.

We would also like to emphasize that, in reality, the steps for identifying the design elements are performed concurrently. There is no rule that enterprise components must be identified before Presentation layer classes are identified. On the other hand, there are obvious sequential dependencies. For example, we cannot identify facade session EJBs until we know what enterprise components we have in the system.

Activity: Incorporate Existing Design Elements

OVERVIEW

The objective of this activity is to compare the already identified design elements with existing assets and determine which of them, if any, can be incorporated (reused) in the design.

INPUT ARTIFACTS

◆ Design Guidelines
◆ Design Model

RESULTING ARTIFACTS

◆ Design Model (Design Class, Design Package, Design Subsystem, Framework Component, Interface)
◆ Software Architecture Document

STEPS

◆ Identify Reuse Opportunities
◆ Reverse-Engineer Assets
◆ Incorporate Existing Design Elements into the Design Model

Organizations that build similar systems often have software assets that can be reused during development of a new system. There may also exist assets that can be purchased or obtained from sources such as tools or infrastructure providers, community Web sites, public exchanges, and so on.

An asset is an artifact or a set of artifacts that have been developed with an explicit purpose of being reused on multiple projects. Assets can range from requirements statements through patterns and mechanisms to finished components.

Reuse is a tricky business. We all practice what is referred to as "ad hoc reuse." We reuse classes that have worked for us before, we reuse design structures and parts of examples we find in books and on the Internet, and so on. Very few of us, however, practice "systematic reuse," which is the development and reuse of assets that have been systematically designed, built and packaged for use on multiple projects.

As we mentioned, the concept of assets covers a potentially broad spectrum of artifacts. In this activity, we concentrate on the identification of reusable **Design Subsystems** (enterprise components) and **Framework Components** (EJBs). We assume that reuse of mechanisms has been considered in the previously discussed **Identify Design Mechanisms** activity. We also assume that use of large-granularity external subsystems, like the credit service enterprise component in our case, have been captured in the form of boundary classes during analysis and have already evolved into **Design Subsystems**, **Frameworks Components**, or **Design Classes**.

By presenting this activity after the **Identify Design Elements** activity, we may be giving a wrong impression that these two activities should be performed sequentially. In reality, these two activities are quite interconnected and should be performed concurrently. For example, if one of the non-functional requirements of the system is that it be based on a set of existing assets, then the **Incorporate Existing Design Elements** activity is performed in the early iterations of the project, possibly as early as in the Inception phase, in order to incorporate those assets.

Step: Identify Reuse Opportunities

We start by looking for design elements, such as enterprise components and EJBs, that offer **Interfaces** similar to the candidate **Interfaces** identified in the design. We should look for similar responsibilities, attributes, parameters and return values. Even if there is not an exact match, there may be opportunities to make minor changes to the design of the system that will allow the reuse of an identified component. Simple changes include rearranging or adding parameters to an **Interface** or refactoring the **Interface** by splitting it into several **Interfaces**, one or more of which match those of the existing component. When we identify a reuse candidate, we need to consider its non-functional properties, as well as its functionality. For example performance, security or cost of a component may disqualify it from being reused despite an otherwise perfect match of its **Interfaces**.

In our Online Auction application, the User Account Management enterprise component would be a good candidate for being implemented by an existing reusable component. User account management is a rather common function and there are commercially available components that could be considered as candidates. Were we building a commercial auction system, we would have seriously considered acquiring the User Account Management enterprise component from a third party rather than building it ourselves.

Step: Reverse-Engineer Assets

If reuse of an existing **Design Subsystem** or **Framework Component** in its entirety is not possible, we may still consider reusing one or more of its parts. This is more ad hoc than systematic reuse, but is a viable option as software round-trip-engineering tools have become quite sophisticated. Some of these tools can reverse-engineer Java classes, JSPs, deployment descriptors and database schemas. They can also generate the implementation from the design elements.

Databases, and the data residing in them, represent an important source of reusable assets. For example, reverse-engineering a database schema is an excellent first step in identifying what information used by the application already resides in existing databases. The set of **Design Classes** that result from such reengineering can be then mapped into the entity EJBs and/or types identified in the **Identify Design Elements** activity.

Step: Incorporate Existing Design Elements into the Design Model

As we decide to incorporate existing elements in our design, we need to account for them in the **Design Model**. The extent of the model changes may vary. On the one hand we may modify a candidate **Interface** of a **Design Subsystem** to allow for reuse of an existing, functionally similar component. This will not result in changes to the overall **Design Model** structure. On the other hand, we may refactor an identified **Design Subsystem** into two **Design Subsystems**, one that will be reused and another that will still have to be developed. This will add a new **Design Subsystem** to the model structure.

Activity: Describe Distribution and Concurrency

OVERVIEW

The purpose of this activity is to analyze the system distribution and concurrency requirements and describe how they are realized in the implementation environment.

INPUT ARTIFACTS

◆ Deployment Model

◆ Design Model

◆ Implementation Model

◆ Supplementary Specification

RESULTING ARTIFACTS

◆ Deployment Model

◆ Design Model

◆ Software Architecture Document

STEPS

◆ Define the Network Configuration

◆ Distribute Elements to Containers and Nodes

◆ Analyze Application Concurrency

◆ Identify Concurrency Mechanisms

Some systems are inherently distributed in that different physical nodes provide different services, which may give rise to concurrency. The J2EE platform has evolved to support distributed enterprise computing. The commercial implementations of the J2EE technologies not only provide interprocess communication, load balancing, and distributed resource management, but they also hide a lot of the gory details of using those capabilities. Leading implementations provide scalability and load balancing out of the box. This means we don't have to do anything special to a system design to execute it on a cluster of nodes. The same modules are deployed to a load-balancing container that can run on multiple processes and nodes in a fashion that is transparent to the logic of the application.

However, "application concurrency" can also be introduced in systems that are not distributed for scalability and performance reasons. *Application concurrency* is a "designed-in" separation of the system's logic into concurrent threads of computation. Application concurrency goes hand in hand with application distribution. If a system runs on multiple nodes providing independent computational resources, the nodes can lend themselves to concurrently executing components. Addressing the concerns of application concurrency and distribution is the focus of this activity.

It is not our intention to provide an exhaustive or even thorough coverage of concurrency and distribution in J2EE. However, the steps described below should provide useful guidance on how to address the main concurrency and distribution issues encountered when designing a J2EE application.

Step: Define the Network Configuration

In the context of J2EE, the concept of a "node" can be confusing. In RUP, a node represents a processing device, such as a server computer, to which elements can be deployed. However, as described in Chapter 2, we do not deploy elements directly to nodes for two reasons. The first is that we physically deploy J2EE modules, not the elements contained in those modules. The second is that we deploy to a container that executes on a particular node (a server), not to the node directly (containers can be considered "virtual nodes").

It can be argued that describing the deployment of J2EE modules to containers is of little value because it is obvious that a WAR is deployed to a Web container, an EJB-JAR to an EJB container, and so on. However, there is value in describing the deployment of a system when there are explicit requirements that certain elements of the system reside on a node with specific characteristics (for example, a node that supports a database, or a node supporting a legacy system).

In cases like this, where there is value in articulating the physical distribution of the system, the first step is to show the distributed configuration of the nodes (and, optionally, the system resources allocated to each node[12]) in the **Deployment Model**. An example of a deployment diagram is shown in Figure 8.21. In this example, which is a refinement of the initial **Deployment Model** diagram from the **Architectural Analysis** activity, the database with

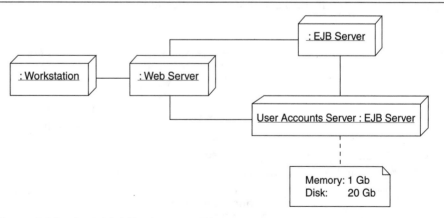

Figure 8.21   An Initial Deployment Diagram

12 See the UML note attached to the node in Figure 8.21.

user accounts and the components that access that data run on a specialized node (EJB server) identified as the "User Accounts Server."

Step: Distribute Elements to Containers and Nodes

This step is a complement to the previous step. Having identified the nodes, we now need to decide which elements to deploy on them.

As described in Chapter 2, J2EE elements are packaged within J2EE modules, which are then deployed. Elements that need to run on a specific node must be packaged together in a separate J2EE module, and then that module is deployed only to that node.

For example, if we know that the elements that access the user accounts database must be deployed to a separate node (the User Accounts Server shown in Figure 8.21), then these elements must be packaged in a separate J2EE module that is then deployed to the User Accounts Server. We illustrate such situation in Figure 8.22, where the useraccountmanager.jar file (which will contain the UserAccountManager EJB) is only deployed to the User Accounts Server node. We discuss J2EE modules in some more detail in Chapter 9.

Step: Analyze Application Concurrency

Application concurrency is a term used to refer to the splitting of application logic into concurrent threads of execution in order to initiate multiple parallel activities. This is usually done for performance reasons. For example, this might allow an application to do useful work while waiting for a response from a slower legacy system. The purpose of this step is to analyze the application and identify opportunities for application concurrency.

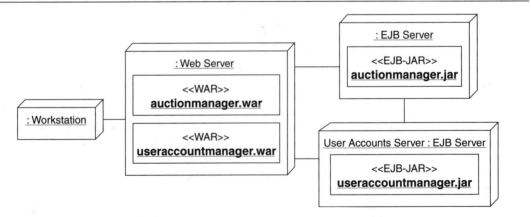

Figure 8.22 Elements Deployed on Separate Physical Nodes

The Online Auction application does not present many opportunities for application concurrency, because most of its operations are relatively simple and naturally sequential. However, the Close Auction **Use Case** presents some interesting possibilities. As first presented in Chapter 6, Requirements, the basic flow of the Close Auction **Use Case** is detailed in the following list.

1. The use case starts when the time for an auction to close has been reached.
2. The auction is marked as closed, so that no more bids are accepted.
3. The system collects the transaction fee from the Seller's account by submitting a payment request to the Credit Service Bureau.
4. The system sends an e-mail to the Buyer, notifying the Buyer that he or she is the auction winner.
5. The system sends an e-mail to the Seller, notifying the Seller that the auction has been closed and that a transaction fee has been debited from his or her account.
6. The use case ends.

Let's assume that auctions are closed on the hour. In a large auction system, many auctions may have to be closed at the same time. As we see from the **Use Case** flow, there are quite a number of bookkeeping operations that must be performed on each closed auction. On the other hand, we would like to close auctions instantaneously so we can stop the bidding. We can leverage concurrency to help us with this by following the algorithm described here.

- Find the auctions that must be closed.
- Mark each of these auctions as closed (by, for example, changing the value of their Status attribute to "closed"). This will make these auctions inaccessible for bidding.
- Distribute the account charging and mailing operations on the closed auctions among a set of concurrently executing "bookkeeping" components (we briefly discuss one design strategy in the next step **Identify Concurrency Mechanisms**).

Step: Identify Concurrency Mechanisms

As we mentioned earlier, the concurrency associated with load balancing is supported by most J2EE platform implementations. However, application concurrency has to be supported by the application logic and hence needs to be designed. The objective of this step is to identify the mechanisms that will support application concurrency.

Application concurrency mechanisms are somewhat limited in the J2EE platform. In general, any Java class can create a new thread of execution. An EJB, however, cannot start, stop, suspend or resume a thread. This restriction is due to the fact that an EJB container must provide a predictable environment in which an EJB executes.

We can, however, make use of message-driven EJBs that can execute concurrently. Following our Close Auction processing example discussed in the previous step, we can create a queue that is processed by a number of concurrently executing message-driven EJBs. In this design the AuctionManager EJB is responsible for populating the queue (using the Java Messaging Service, JMS), and each of the message-driven EJBs is responsible for processing items on the queue by charging the Seller's account and e-mailing both the Buyer and the Seller.

Activity: Review the Architecture

OVERVIEW

The purpose of this activity is to formally review the results of the refined architecture before moving on to detailed design.

INPUT ARTIFACTS

- Design Guidelines
- Risk List
- Software Architecture Document
- Supplementary Specification
- User-Experience Guidelines

RESULTING ARTIFACTS

- Change Request
- Review Record

STEPS

- Conduct the Review

Architectural flaws are known to be the hardest to fix and the most damaging in the long run. Detecting and fixing them early can save a lot of time later in the project. Detecting these flaws is a key objective of this activity.

Step: Conduct the Review

We strongly advise that someone external to the project participate in the review of the architecture. A good review should examine multiple aspects of the system and include aspects often neglected such as system operations, administration and maintenance.

There are three major areas that the review should concentrate on:

- The system artifacts, in particular the **Software Architecture Document**, the **Design Guidelines** and the **Design Model**. The reviewer should concentrate on the mechanisms, logical system structure, key design elements and their interactions, and the quality of the artifacts. The objective is to ensure that the architecture fits the system requirements, that it is not overdone or oversimplified, and that it addresses the recognized development risks. Additional potential design and requirements mismatches include unrealistic requirements or missing requirements.

- The nonfunctional properties (or quality attributes) of the system. Architectural quality attributes, such as performance, reliability, ease of modification, security, or safety, are hard to measure. Only a few of them can be objectively measured. Performance is an example of an attribute where measurement is possible. Other attributes are more qualitative or subjective. The reviewer should start by making a list of the important properties, such as performance or security, together with the expected or desired values of these properties (both qualitative and quantitative). Next the reviewer should gather information about how the proposed architecture meets the described nonfunctional requirement. The very exercise of precisely specifying the system attributes and asking questions like "How have you achieved the response time below three seconds?" usually quickly reveals weak points of the architecture.

- The exceptional or boundary conditions. The reviewer should start from preparing a list of questions that exemplify those exceptional situations such as "What happens with a user transaction when the user is disconnected from the system in the middle of the transaction?" or "How do you recover from the EJB server failure?" Then the reviewer should ask the Software Architect to walk him or her through scenarios, illustrating how the system architecture addresses these exceptional situations.

Workflow Detail: Detail the Design

The **Detail the Design** workflow detail contains the activities shown in the Figure 8.23.

The objective of these activities is to refine the identified design elements by working out the details of their content, behavior and relationships. The refinement of a design stops when the element can be handed off for implementation[13].

---

13 The hand-off should not be interpreted as passing the artifacts to another team or person, because in many cases the same person will do both the design and the implementation.

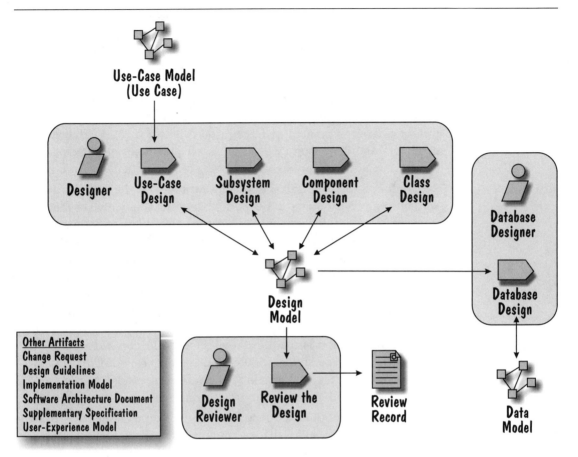

Figure 8.23 Detail the Design Workflow Detail Overview Diagram

The design activities of this workflow detail are organized around the type of design element they focus on.

- **Subsystem Design** focuses on a **Design Subsystem** (enterprise components).
- **Component Design** focuses on a **Framework Component** (EJB).
- **Class Design** works on a **Design Class** (servlet, JSP, or Java class).
- **Database Design** focuses on the **Data Model** elements (the database schema in particular).

These activities are highly interrelated and are often performed concurrently. For example, we cannot refine the design of an enterprise component without considering the design of the entity EJBs it manages. Similarly, we cannot finish the design of a use-case dispatcher class before we have fully defined the **Interfaces** of the enterprise components it uses.

The **Use-Case Design** activity brings all design elements together by analyzing how they collaborate to realize the system **Use Cases**.

As always, the workflow detail culminates with a review of the produced results.

The activities of this workflow detail don't have an implied sequence. For example, one could ask if **Use-Case Design** should happen first to make sure that the specifications of the design elements support the **Use Cases** before they are detailed or if **Use-Case Design** be done last to make sure that we did not miss anything. In reality, both of these approaches have some validity; however, we will start our discussion from the **Use-Case Design** activity because it unifies the other activities.

Activity: Use-Case Design

OVERVIEW

The primary purpose of this activity is to demonstrate that the system's **Use Cases** can be realized through collaborations of the identified design elements. The other purpose is to help refine the design of the elements by considering all contexts in which they will work.

INPUT ARTIFACTS

- ◆ Design Guidelines
- ◆ Design Model (Design Class, Design Subsystem, Framework Component, Interface, Use-Case Realization)
- ◆ Software Architecture Document
- ◆ Supplementary Specification
- ◆ Use Case

RESULTING ARTIFACTS

- ◆ Design Model (Use-Case Realization)

STEPS

For each **Use Case** in the current iteration:

- ◆ Realize Each Flow of Events

Once per iteration:

- ◆ Reconcile the **Use-Case Realizations**

This activity is the design corollary of the **Use-Case Analysis** activity described in Chapter 7. The main difference is that in this activity we show how design elements, rather than **Analysis Classes**, collaborate to realize a **Use Case**. This activity therefore discusses the refinement of the analysis-level **Use-Case Realizations** created during analysis and results in design-level **Use-Case Realizations**.

Step: Realize Each Flow of Events

In analysis we developed a **Use-Case Realization** that shows how **Analysis Classes** realize the **Use Case**. We represented the participants in the analysis-level **Use-Case Realization** on a class diagram. We also represented the realization of each flow of events on an interaction diagram (such as a sequence diagram). For example, the basic flow interaction diagram of the analysis-level Create Auction **Use-Case Realization** is shown in Figure 8.13.

In design, we describe the realization of the **Use Case** in terms of the design elements identified in the **Identify Design Elements** activity. For example, Figure 8.20 depicts the participants of the Create Auction **Use Case**. In Figure 8.24, we describe how some of these participants interact to realize the **Use Case** functionality.

We have simplified both diagrams for readability without, we hope, obscuring the **Use Case** description. In the Participants diagram (shown in the model structure in Figure 8.20) we only show business delegates and locators of the enterprise components. As noted earlier, a business delegate provides a convenient representation of an enterprise component in that it exposes the interface to the enterprise component, but completely encapsulates its internals (a business delegate is a "smart proxy" for an enterprise component). Business delegates, therefore, allow us to create greatly simplified interaction diagrams when describing the realization of the flow of events of a **Use Case**. For example, in the sequence diagram shown in Figure 8.24, we don't describe the details of how the use-case dispatcher obtains an instance of the business delegates using the enterprise component service locator. We only show the use-case dispatcher communicating with the business delegate.

As we work through each analysis-level **Use-Case Realization**, we refine the design of the participating design elements and, in particular, we fully describe their operations.

The architecture and the mechanisms developed in the **Refine the Architecture** workflow greatly simplify the development of **Use-Case Realizations**. Because most of the **Use-Case Realizations** follow the same set of patterns and use a common set of mechanisms, their structure is similar to the one shown in Figure 8.24 and Figure 8.20.

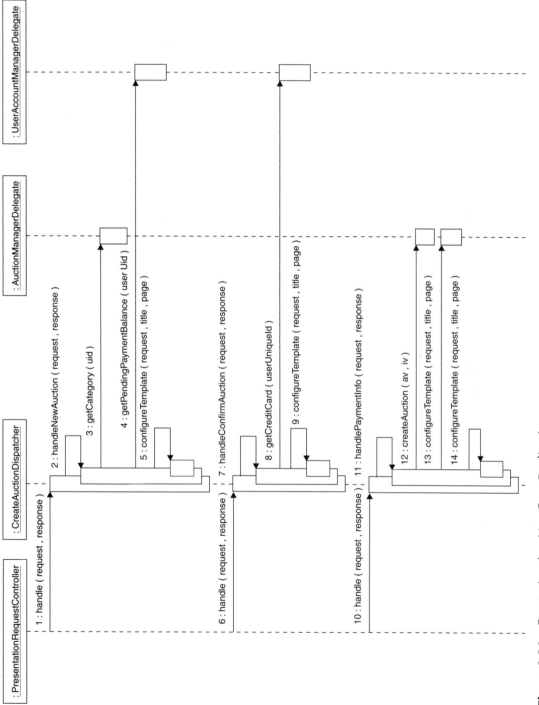

Figure 8.24 Create Auction Use-Case Realization

Step: Reconcile the Use-Case Realizations

By now we should have a design-level **Use-Case Realization** for each **Use Case** addressed in the current iteration. In this step, we reconcile the individual **Use-Case Realizations** and unify design elements by identifying:

- Opportunities to unify design elements; that is, opportunities to replace a set of elements with overlapping responsibilities with one element that unifies all of them
- Opportunities to abstract common behavior using inheritance or delegation between design elements

For example, in the Online Auction application, we recognized that all use-case dispatchers were performing integrity checks on the data input by the user. After closer examination, we decided to develop a generic input field validation mechanism. In order to simplify the code of the use-case dispatchers, we implemented the logic of the mechanism as a method on a *DefaultDispatcher* class, from which all of the use-case dispatchers inherit.

Activity: Subsystem Design

OVERVIEW
The purpose of this activity is to "look inside" each subsystem and define its internal structure and the collaborations of its elements.

INPUT ARTIFACTS
- Design Model (Design Subsystem, Interface)
- Design Guidelines

RESULTING ARTIFACTS
- Design Model (Design Class, Design Subsystem, Framework Component, Interface)

STEPS
- Distribute Subsystem Behavior to Subsystem Elements
- Describe Subsystem Dependencies

A **Design Subsystem** is a part of a system that encapsulates behavior, exposes its services through a set of **Interfaces**, and packages other model elements. In our architecture, we use **Design Subsystems** to represent enterprise components, which implement a business concept or a set of business responsibilities and manage a disjoint portion of the system state.

The initial description of an enterprise component includes a candidate **Interface**, a number of **Framework Components** (a façade session EJB and a set of entity EJBs), and a number of **Design Classes** (candidate value objects, a business delegate and a service locator). The detailed design of these design elements must be completed before we can implement the enterprise component (see Chapter 9).

We have identified candidate **Interfaces** of the enterprise components in the **Identify Design Elements** activity (see Table 8.4). Now, during detailed design of the enterprise component, these initial candidate **Interfaces** are refined into concrete **Interfaces**. The consistency and completeness of these **Interfaces** is verified in the **Use-Case Design** activity, where the enterprise component interactions with other system elements are put together and reviewed.

The key property of an enterprise component is that it is fully described by its **Interface**. In our architecture, the enterprise component's business delegate class realizes this **Interface**. In most cases, the same **Interface** is also realized by the session façade of the enterprise component and the business delegate simply exposes the business methods to the client (in this respect, it is a smart proxy of the session façade).

Each enterprise component **Interface** exposes a view of the system state that can be inspected and/or modified via that **Interface**. This view is referred to as the interface information model in (Cheesman and Daniels 2001). This information model does not have to be exactly equal to the sum of the entity EJBs managed by the enterprise component. This is because there may be information in the entities never exposed to the enterprise component clients directly. Conversely, the enterprise component may expose computed information that is not directly stored in its entities.

Step: Distribute Subsystem Behavior to Subsystem Elements

Given the discussion in the **Identify Design Elements** activity described earlier, we already have an initial draft of the elements of the **Design Subsystems** representing our enterprise component. We will now concentrate on the refinement of these design elements.

Consider, for example, the Auction Manager enterprise component shown in Figure 8.25. Following the pattern names discussed at the start of this chapter, the AuctionManagerDelegate Java class is the business delegate, the AuctionManagerHomeLocator class is the service locator, the AuctionManagerEJB component is the session façade, and the CategoryEJB, AuctionEJB and BidEJB components are business entities. From an "internal" perspective, we should expect to see these elements used when describing the subsystem's behavior.

From an "external" perspective, the subsystem behavior is described by its **Interface**, which is realized in our architecture by the business delegate and the session façade. The operations that a business delegate must support were first identified during the **Identify Design Elements** activity as the business operations of an enterprise component's **Interface**. During the **Use-Case Design**

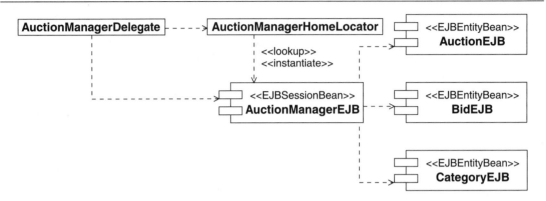

Figure 8.25 Design Elements of the Auction Manager Enterprise Component

activity these operations were further refined. Because business delegates realize their enterprise component's **Interfaces**, they can be conveniently used as an enterprise component proxy.

The business delegate of the Auction Manager enterprise component is shown in Figure 8.26.

Each business service listed in an enterprise component's **Interface** is realized by a collaboration of its elements. Descriptions of these collaborations can be represented in the same way as the design element collaborations documented within the **Use-Case Realizations** in the **Use-Case Design** activity—as UML collaboration instances. If you choose to model the realization of an enterprise component's operation in terms of the interactions of its elements, define a collaboration instance for the operation, using the operation name as the collaboration instance name, and stereotype the collaboration instance «InterfaceRealization». Then define a sequence diagram that describes the collaboration among the subsystem elements when performing the operation. An example is shown in the sequence diagram in Figure 8.27. This diagram represents a collaboration of the elements of the Auction Manager enterprise component realizing the addBid operation. The UserTransaction object represents a transaction context and the two methods *begin()* and *commit()* demarcate the transaction boundaries. This object is a low-level helper class that we have included for completeness.

The **Interface** operation realizations are placed within the "Interface Realizations" subpackage of the enterprise component, as shown in Figure 8.28.

Step: Describe Subsystem Dependencies

During the **Subsystem Design** activity, we make sure that all subsystem external dependencies are identified. Dependencies between enterprise components

AuctionManagerDelegate
+ addBid ( )
+ AuctionManagerDelegate ( )
+ cancelBid ( )
+ closeExpiredAuctions ( )
+ createAuction ( )
+ getActiveBids ( )
+ getAllCategories ( )
+ getAuction ( )
+ getBid ( )
+ getBids ( )
+ getCategoriesWithOpenAuctions ( )
+ getCategory ( )
+ getHighestBid ( )
+ getItem ( )
+ getMinimumBid ( )
+ getOpenAuctionsForCategory ( )
+ getOpenAuctionsForUserAccount ( )
+ searchOpenAuctions ( )
+ setAuction ( )
+ setItem ( )

Figure 8.26   Auction Manager Business Delegate

can be represented as dependencies between the **Design Subsystems** that represent the enterprise components and the **Interfaces** of the other enterprise components that the enterprise components are dependent on. An example from our Online Auction system is shown in Figure 8.29.

Design Subsystems should only depend on the **Interfaces** of other **Design Subsystems** and not on their internals. In the architecture of the Online Auction application, this means that an enterprise component should only depend on the business delegates of the enterprise components it depends on. This approach ensures that a subsystem is treated as a "black box" and, while its internal implementation may change, other components don't see that change as long as its external **Interface** stays the same.

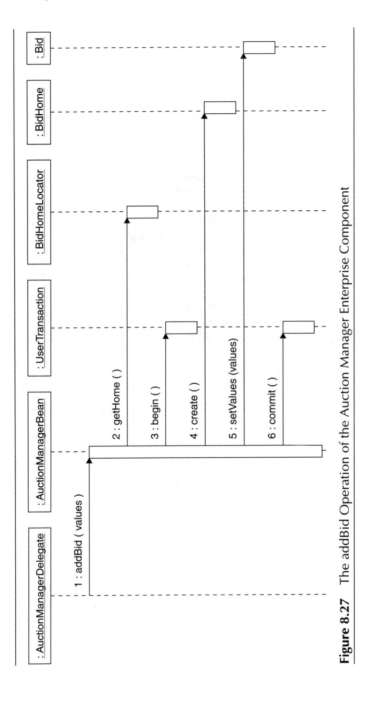

Figure 8.27 The addBid Operation of the Auction Manager Enterprise Component

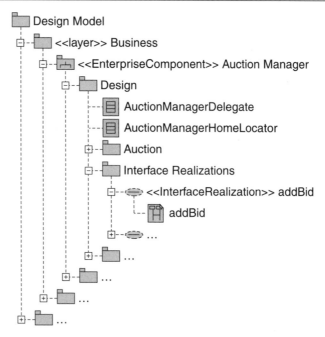

Figure 8.28 Interface Realization in the Design Model

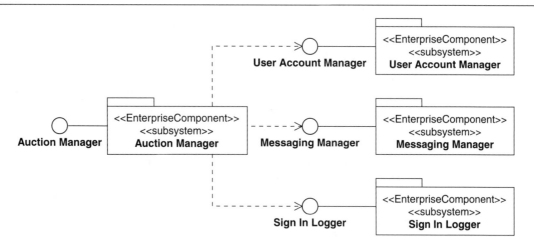

Figure 8.29 Design Subsystem Dependencies in the Design Model

Activity: Component Design

OVERVIEW

The purpose of this activity is to refine and document the behavior, structure, and dependencies of the **Framework Components**.

INPUT ARTIFACTS

◆ Design Model (Framework Component, Interface)

RESULTING ARTIFACTS

◆ Design Model (Design Class, Framework Component, Interface)

STEPS

◆ Distribute Component Behavior to Component Elements
◆ Describe Component Dependencies

As we discussed earlier, we use **Framework Components** to represent EJBs. We identified the EJBs in the **Identify Design Elements** activity. Then, in the **Subsystem Design** activity, we distributed the enterprise component responsibilities between its session and entity EJBs. In this activity, we refine the design of those EJBs to the point where they can be implemented.

Step: Distribute Component Behavior to Component Elements

As described in Chapter 2, an EJB comprises a number of elements. Specifically, all EJBs (with the exception of message-driven EJBs) have a home and remote **Interface** (or local home and local **Interface**), and an implementation class. Entity EJBs also have an associated primary key class.

The behavior of an EJB is characterized by the operations on its home and remote **Interfaces**. The purpose of this step is to specify how the EJB implementation class, and the elements it depends on, realizes these operations. We also need to specify any operations that the EJBs must implement in order to be managed by the container. For example, BMP entity EJBs must implement operations that store and restore their state.

In this step, we should also define the transactional properties of the EJBs.

We have already seen in Figure 8.15 how to model the structure of an EJB in UML. The elements that comprise an EJB are also grouped in a **Design Package** in the **Design Model** structure. We show a recommended model structure in Figure 8.17.

Step: Describe Component Dependencies

In the previous step, by defining the interactions of the EJB implementation classes, we may have identified specific dependencies of the EJB implementation classes on other design elements. In this step, we simply describe and document these dependencies for the team members that will be using and implementing them.

Activity: Class Design

OVERVIEW

Key **Design Classes** were identified during the **Identify Design Elements** activity. Additional classes may also have been identified during the **Subsystem Design** and **Component Design** activities. In this activity, we concentrate on the detailed design of these **Design Classes**.

INPUT ARTIFACTS

◆ Design Guidelines

◆ Design Model (Design Class)

◆ Supplementary Specification

RESULTING ARTIFACTS

◆ Design Model (Design Class)

STEPS

◆ Define Class Visibility

◆ Define Class Operations

◆ Define Class Attributes

◆ Define Class Dependencies and Relationships

In this activity we refine the design of servlets, JSPs[14], and other Java classes. The objective of the activity is to ensure that the **Design Classes** provide the required behavior and that sufficient information is provided to unambiguously implement them.

Step: Define Class Visibility

Classes can be assigned a visibility with respect to the **Design Package** in which they reside. For example, a particular class may be considered "private" to the **Design Package** in which it resides, if it is only ever used by other elements inside that **Design Package**. Keep in mind that elements within a **Design Subsystem** are implicitly private and therefore don't need to be declared as having private visibility. In our architecture, the only public class shown in the enterprise component structure is the business delegate.

---

14 Although JSPs are not Java classes, they can contain an arbitrary logic and we consider them in this activity.

Step: Define Class Operations

The majority of operations on classes are identified during the **Use-Case Design**, **Subsystem Design** and **Component Design** activities. However, we may not have identified all operations. For example, we may need additional operations to support:

- Object creation
- Object deletion
- Object comparison (to test to see if two instances of a class are the same)
- Object copy
- Interaction with a supporting mechanism (such as garbage collection or "serialization" of an object into a data stream)

The naming conventions of the implementation language should be used when naming operations, return types, and parameters and their types. This naming convention should be described in the **Design Guidelines**.

We also identify the visibility of each operation as either public (the operation is visible outside of this class), protected (the operation is visible only to the class itself, or to its subclasses), or private (the operation is only visible to the class itself).

Finally, we may also identify operations that apply to the class as a whole, rather than each instance. In the Java programming language, these operations are identified using the "static" keyword. An example of such an operation is one that returns all instances of the class.

Step: Define Attributes

At this point, some of the attributes of the major design classes, especially those representing the key abstractions, may already be defined. However, this is where their signatures are refined. Also, during the definition of operations, we may identify additional attributes needed by the class in order to carry out the operations. For each attribute, we define characteristics such as its name, its type, any initial value, and its visibility (in terms of being private, protected, or public).

A class can also move through a number of states that affect the behavior of its operations. It is useful to consider representing these states using one or more attributes.

Step: Define Dependencies and Relationships

In this step we describe dependencies, associations and generalizations between classes.

A dependency should be added between two classes when one class needs to "use" the other. Dependencies are transient, existing only for a limited duration, and do not represent a structural relationship between classes. Class A depends on class B for reasons such as those in the following list.

- An instance of class B is passed as a parameter in an operation of class A.
- An instance of class B is passed as a return value from an operation of class A.
- An instance of class B is used in the implementation of one of the operations of class A.

An association is a relationship between two classes that implies that instances of these classes have a structural relationship. We may also choose to refine an association and make it an aggregation relationship. An association between two classes can also be given a number of attributes such as:

- Navigability (to show the direction of the association)
- Multiplicity (to show how many instances of one class can be associated with one instance of the other class)
- Association name
- Role name (to name the role of the instances of a class in the association)

Classes may be organized into a generalization hierarchy to reflect common behavior and common structure. A common superclass can be defined, from which subclasses can inherit both behavior and structure.

When we find a generalization for two or more subclasses, we create a superclass to contain the common attributes, associations, aggregations, and operations. We then remove the common structure and behavior from the subclasses.

Activity: Database Design

OVERVIEW

The objectives of this activity are twofold: (1) to ensure proper mappings between the entity EJBs and the underlying database and (2) to define behavior that is best implemented in the database rather than in the application code.

INPUT ARTIFACTS

- Data Model
- Design Guidelines
- Design Model
- Supplementary Specification

RESULTING ARTIFACTS

- Change Request[15]
- Data Model
- Implementation Model

STEPS

- Map Entity EJBs to the Data Model
- Distribute Class Behavior to the Database

The entity EJBs are the primary means of realizing persistency in J2EE applications. However, those EJBs must use an underlying persistency technology to store their state. In the majority of cases, it is relational database technology. As shown in the **Detail the Design** workflow detail diagram in Figure 8.21, the design of the database is the responsibility of the Database Designer, not the Application Designer. However, the entity EJBs cannot be designed in isolation from the database design because these activities may affect each other.

Step: Map Entity EJBs to the Data Model

If you remember from our earlier discussion, there are two options for persistency for entity EJBs: container-managed persistence (CMP) and bean-managed persistence (BMP). In this step, we consider each of these two cases.

The EJB container persists CMP entity EJBs in the tables of a relational database. In order to store the state of an entity EJB, the container has to be given a mapping between the EJB and a table, and between the bean attributes and the rows in the table. The Application Designer and the Database Designer have to ensure that these mappings are both type-compatible and semantically correct.

---

15 A **Change Request** is necessary because the design of the database may result in request for changes to the **Design Model**.

They have to ensure that the database types can be properly converted to and from the Java types and that the table columns and entity attributes represent the same information. In the process of defining the table-to-EJB mapping, the design of both the tables and the EJBs may have to be adjusted.

Also, an entity EJB can provide any number of custom finder methods that are exposed on its home **Interface**. For each such method, there must be a query statement that is executed when the method is called. The finder query statements must be consistent with the schema of the underlying database. The mappings for CMP entity EJBs and the finder query statements are captured in the EJB deployment descriptors that were introduced in Chapter 2.

BMP entity EJBs store and retrieve their state themselves, and hence, they can use any storage mechanism. In practice, however, we most often use a relational database and then use JDBC to access it.

In general, you should use BMP entity EJBs only when the deployment tools cannot map the bean to a database table. This is because BMP entity EJBs are harder to maintain and are coupled to the underlying database schema.

If you are using a BMP entity EJB, you must provide:

- Implementations of methods for loading, storing, and removing the EJB that will be called by the container
- Implementations for the finder methods and create methods on the home interface that return instances of the primary key class

Because of their tight coupling with the underlying database, BMP entity EJB design cannot be done in isolation from the database design, even more so than the design of CMP entity EJBs.

Step: Distribute Class Behavior in the Database

Most databases support a stored procedure capability. A stored procedure runs within the process space of the database management system, and provides the ability to perform database-related actions on the server without having to transfer data across a network. Stored procedures usually come in two flavors: actual procedures and triggers.

Procedures are executed explicitly by an application and can return values. Triggers are invoked implicitly when some database event occurs (insert a row, update a row, delete a row, and so on), have no parameters (since they are invoked implicitly), and do not provide return values.

Because of their explicit invocation, procedures can only be used by BMP entity EJBs. Triggers, on the other hand, have general applicability. The use of stored procedures should be considered for performance reasons and carefully examined with the Database Designer. It is the responsibility of the Database Designer to write them and store them in the database system.

Activity: Review the Design

OVERVIEW

The purpose of this activity is to formally review the detailed design before starting implementation.

INPUT ARTIFACTS	RESULTING ARTIFACTS
◆ Design Guidelines	◆ Change Request
◆ Design Model	◆ Review Record
◆ Supplementary Specification	
◆ Use-Case Model	
◆ User-Experience Model	

STEPS

◆ Conduct the Review

Step: Conduct the Review

With each successive iteration more and more of the system design is detailed. However, before we proceed to implementation, we should review the detailed design to ensure that it meets the following criteria:

- It fulfills the system's requirements.
- It is consistent with the design guidelines.
- It is detailed enough for implementation.

The review should concentrate on:

- The design-level **Use-Case Realizations** developed in the iteration. Evaluate each **Use-Case Realization** to make sure that it implements the required system behavior and that the behavior has been distributed to the appropriate design elements.
- The design elements detailed in the iteration. Examine the **Interfaces** of the **Design Subsystems** and **Framework Components** to make sure they provide the required services. For the **Design Subsystems** and **Framework Components** also make sure that the behavior they expose is realized by the collaboration of their elements.

As always, any defects identified during the review should be documented in **Change Requests,** and the responsibility for finding a resolution should be assigned to a member of the team.

Summary

In this chapter we discussed how to produce a detailed design of a system from the results of analysis that support the requirements. We began by identifying common design mechanisms that provide part of the architectural foundation of the system.

With architectural guidelines in hand, we proceeded to identify the design elements. We classified the elements according to their granularity from enterprise components, to EJBs to classes. We described an approach to identifying the enterprise components and their services using the key abstractions and the analysis-level **Use-Case Realizations**. Then we proceeded to identify the EJBs and classes, still closely following our architectural guidelines.

After identifying the design elements, we proceeded to refine their design. As in analysis, the **Use Cases** provided us with the convenient instrument for looking at and refining related sets of design elements to make sure that they collaborate to deliver the required system functionality.

We completed the design activities by refining and documenting the detailed designs of the individual elements.

Although we used our Online Auction application as an example throughout the chapter, we believe that the design process we described and the elements of the architecture we used are applicable to a large family of online enterprise systems.

Before we move on to discussing the implementation of the design, we want to emphasize again the iterative nature of the process we are presenting. The design is produced over a number of iterations. Design may start very early in the Inception phase with the selection of reusable components. It intensifies in the Elaboration phase, when the key system elements are designed, and may even be a part of late iterations of the Construction phase when peripheral system elements are completed.

Chapter 9

Implementation

This chapter continues on from Chapter 8, Design and discusses the refinement of design elements into implementation elements. The key objectives of the implementation activities of the J2EE Developer Roadmap are as follows:

- To define the organization of the implementation elements (including both source and executable code)
- To produce and unit test the implementation elements

The **Design Model** elements we will refine during implementation include **Design Subsystems** (that represent enterprise components), **Interfaces**, **Framework Components** (that represent EJBs), and **Design Classes** (that represent servlets, JSPs, and Java classes).

The result of the implementation activities is the **Implementation Model**. The model contains representations of the implementation elements of a J2EE application, including both source code and executable code. Specifically, the **Implementation Model** contains **Implementation Directories** and **Implementation Files**. An **Implementation Directory** represents a physical directory on disk, and is represented in UML as a package. An **Implementation File** represents a physical file on disk, and is represented as a UML artifact[1].

---

1 The representation of a physical file as a UML artifact was introduced in UML 1.4.

We would like to point out that we do not have to represent the implementation visually. In fact, we recommend only creating a UML representation of the implementation (or an aspect of it) when it adds value. We discuss a number of optimizations that mitigate the need for a UML representation later in this chapter.

In this chapter, we specifically discuss the implementation of JSPs, servlets, EJBs and other design elements. We find it useful to characterize these elements by the manner in which they are both deployed and organized as shown in Table 9.1.

The first category shown in Table 9.1 represents implementation elements that are deployed in an EJB container (such as the classes that implement an EJB). These elements are organized within Java packages, a concept that is part of the Java programming language. This concept is discussed in more detail later in this chapter.

The second category represents Java implementation elements that are deployed in a Web container (such as servlets). These elements are also organized within Java packages. However, it is useful to distinguish these implementation elements from those deployed in an EJB container because they are deployed to a different container (a web container as opposed to an EJB container).

The third category represents implementation elements that are deployed in a Web container (such as JSPs, image files, and static HTML files) but that are organized within physical directories that are accessed relative to a "virtual directory." A *virtual directory* is a logical name that is understood by the Web server, and that the Web server (through configuration information) maps to a physical directory. For example, the URL http://www.pearlcircle.com/auctions/auctionmanagement/auction_info.jsp refers to the file auction_info.jsp

Table 9.1   Three Categories of Elements Considered in Implementation

Category	Deployment Location	Organization
EJB	EJB Container	Java package
Servlet	Web Container	Java package
JSP, image file, static HTML file	Web Container	Directory[2]

---

2 The "root" directory is known as a "virtual directory" as discussed in this chapter.

that resides in the directory auctionmanagement that itself resides in the virtual directory "auctions."

In this chapter, we are also concerned with the implementation of J2EE modules (JAR files)[3] and their associated deployment descriptors (though these elements have no direct counterpart in the **Design Model**).

Implementation and Iterative Development

As shown in Chapter 3, An Introduction to the Rational Unified Process, the implementation activities vary through time as shown in Figure 9.1.

Each iteration results in a release (internal or external) of an executable product and so implementation activities are performed throughout the project's life cycle. Implementation activities are most visible during the construction phase, when all of the major risks have been addressed, the architecture has been baselined, and the project is focused on delivering the functionality of the system.

Implementation Overview

The J2EE Developer Roadmap describes two implementation workflow details, as shown in Figure 9.2.

The **Structure the Implementation Model** workflow detail is typically performed early in the project's life cycle since it is concerned with the overall

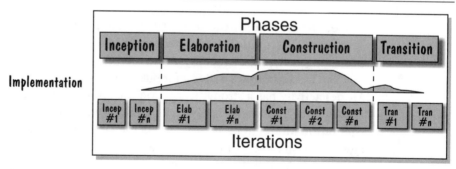

Figure 9.1　Implementation and Iterative Development

---

3 Including the J2EE application as a whole.

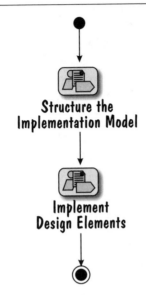

Figure 9.2 Implementation Overview Diagram

organization of the implementation elements. The **Implement Design Elements** workflow detail, on the other hand, occurs throughout the project's life cycle, and is concerned with the actual construction of the implementation elements such as JSPs, servlets, EJBs, and J2EE modules.

Workflow Detail: Structure the Implementation Model

The **Structure the Implementation Model** workflow detail contains two activities: (1) **Structure the Implementation Model** and (2) **Review the Implementation**, as shown in Figure 9.3.

The **Design Model** that is an input to the **Structure the Implementation Model** activity has a strong bearing on the structure of the **Implementation Model** since, as we shall see, we can largely derive the structure of the **Implementation Model** from the structure of the **Design Model**. However, we should always bear in mind that these two model structures address different concerns. The **Design Model** structure provides a logical system partitioning that manages the complexity of the design, while the **Implementation Model** structure provides a physical system partitioning that manages the complexity of the implementation (in terms of directories and files) and supports team development.

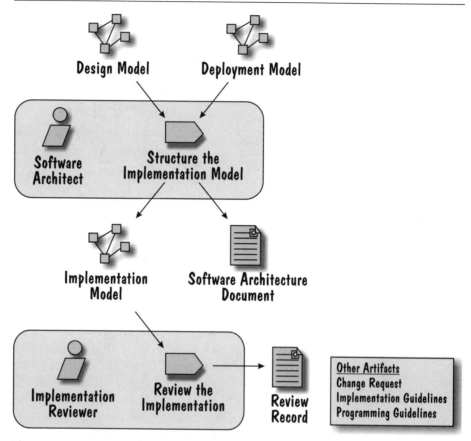

Figure 9.3   Structure the Implementation Model Workflow Detail Overview Diagram

One difference between the **Design Model** structure and the **Implementation Model** structure is that the **Implementation Model** is constrained by the implementation environment and any conventions we choose to apply. For example, Java class names cannot contain spaces. We acknowledge these constraints in this chapter. The **Structure the Implementation Model** activity is followed by the **Review the Implementation** activity.

Activity: Structure the Implementation Model

OVERVIEW

This activity is typically the first activity that refines the **Design Model** into an **Implementation Model**. It establishes the structure of the **Implementation Model** in which implementation elements will reside. Subsequent activities contribute to the population of the **Implementation Model**.

INPUT ARTIFACTS

◆ Deployment Model

◆ Design Model (Design Package, Design Subsystem)

◆ Implementation Guidelines

RESULTING ARTIFACTS

◆ Implementation Model (Implementation Directory)

◆ Software Architecture Document

STEPS

◆ Establish the Implementation Model Structure

◆ Update the Software Architecture Document

The structure of the **Implementation Model** should acknowledge the different categories of implementation elements described in Table 9.1, as well as address integration and testing concerns. For example, it should be possible to create a J2EE application as a succession of **Builds**[4] that are individually integrated and tested. A well-structured **Implementation Model** also supports concurrent development, whereby different elements of the system can be implemented in parallel by different developers (or teams of developers). Concurrent development requires consideration of configuration management concerns that are discussed in more detail in Chapter 10, Additional Topics. All of these concerns have been taken into account in the **Implementation Model** structure of the Online Auction application discussed in this chapter.

An important benefit of the **Implementation Model** is that it allows the organization and content of the implementation to be documented and communicated visually (possibly before any code has actually been written). For example, we can communicate the directory structures (**Implementation Directories**) that will be used to hold the various implementation elements (**Implementation Files**) and also give an indication of how these implementation elements trace to elements in the **Design Model**. Given an appropriate modeling toolset, this traceability can lend itself to round-trip engineering of

---

4 Integration activities and the **Build** artifact are out of scope of the J2EE Developer Roadmap. For more information on integration, see Chapter 10, Additional Topics.

the elements represented in the **Implementation Model** to code and back, thereby keeping the visual and physical elements "in sync."

Step: Establish the Implementation Model Structure

This step considers three facets of the **Implementation Model**, each of which is considered separately since each requires its own physical organization within the **Implementation Model**:

- The Java packaging structure
- The virtual directory structure
- The organization of J2EE modules and their associated deployment descriptors

We start by establishing the Java packaging structure. This structure can be derived from the structure of the **Design Model**, whereby we create an **Implementation Directory**, representing a Java package, for each **Design Subsystem** (that represents an enterprise component) and each **Design Package** whose contents will be implemented in Java. Consider the **Design Model** structure shown in Figure 9.4.

The corresponding **Implementation Model** structure is shown in Figure 9.5.

As we can see from Figure 9.5, the structure of the **Design Model** is replicated below a package named "pearlcircle"[5] (the packages "com" and "pearlcircle" are derived from the domain name "www.pearlcircle.com"). All Java elements defined within the "pearlcircle" package will, as a result, have a fully qualified name that is prefixed with "com.pearlcircle". For example, the fully qualified name of the "bid" package is "com.pearlcircle.business.auctionmanager.bid". The convention of using a Web domain name as the initial Java package name guarantees that Java class names will be unique, even if a third-party Java class library is incorporated.

We now consider the virtual directory structure. A virtual directory is represented as an **Implementation Directory** (a package with the stereotype «VirtualDirectory»). An example from the Online Auction application is shown in Figure 9.6. Once again, we can derive the structure of this aspect of the **Implementation Model** from the structure of the **Design Model**[6]. In this

---

5 Since the Java programming language does not allow spaces in package names, a Java package name might not be identical to the name of the equivalent **Design Package**.

6 Due to the constraints imposed by the naming of directories accessed by the Web server, the names of the directories under the virtual directory are not always identical to those in the **Design Model**.

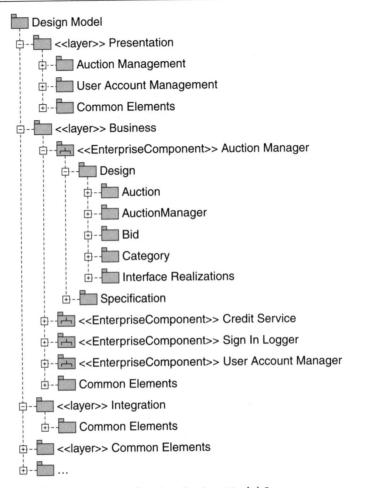

Figure 9.4 Online Auction Application Design Model Structure

case, we create an **Implementation Directory** for each **Design Subsystem** and each **Design Package** whose content will be implemented by elements accessed via a virtual directory (such as JSPs). In our architecture, these elements reside in the Presentation layer of the **Design Model**. We therefore create an **Implementation Directory** for each **Design Package** in the Presentation layer.

Finally, in establishing the **Implementation Model** structure, we also need to account for the J2EE application and J2EE modules (and their associated deployment descriptors) that will be created. These elements have no counterparts in the **Design Model**. However, it is possible to determine an initial set of

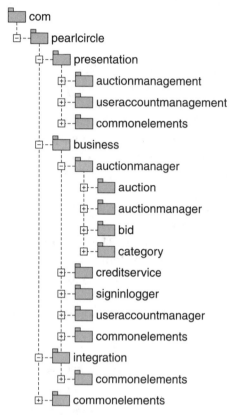

Figure 9.5 Java Packaging in the Online Auction Application

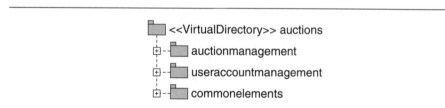

Figure 9.6 Virtual Directory Structure in the Online Auction Application

J2EE modules based on the structure of the **Design Model** and the intended distribution of the system represented in the **Deployment Model**.

Consider the **Design Model** structure shown in Figure 9.4. We can infer the J2EE modules (and their associated deployment descriptors) by assuming that we will have one EJB-JAR for each enterprise component in the Business layer (each of these EJB-JARs may contain many EJBs) and one WAR for each package in the Presentation layer. Such assumptions and conventions concerning the transition from design to implementation should be documented in the **Implementation Guidelines**.

When identifying the J2EE modules, we must take into consideration the **Deployment Model**. For example, if a subset of EJBs needs to reside in a particular EJB container, then this subset needs to be placed in its own EJB-JAR file so that it can be separately deployed.

To represent the J2EE modules in the **Implementation Model**, we create an **Implementation Directory** with the name "Deployment Support," as shown in Figure 9.7. We partition the J2EE modules into their own **Implementation Model** package hierarchy because J2EE modules can contain elements from more than one of the other hierarchies. For example, a Web archive file may contain virtual directory elements (JSPs, for example) and Java elements (servlets, for example). The "Deployment Support" **Implementation Directory** contains an **Implementation Directory** for each J2EE module, and the **Implementation Directory** has the same name as the J2EE module it contains. This allows us to group related elements (specifically the JAR file and its associated deployment descriptor). The figure also shows an **Implementation**

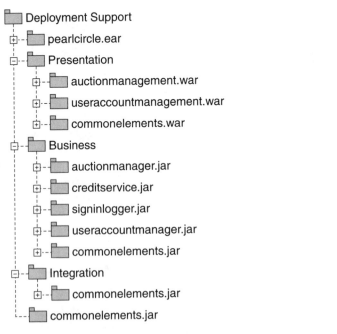

Figure 9.7 Deployment Elements Structure

Directory that will contain the EAR file that represents the J2EE application as a whole.

Even though deployment is considered outside the scope of the J2EE Developer Roadmap, we would like to review how each of these J2EE modules will be deployed. All of the WAR files will be deployed to the Web container only, since their content (such as JSPs and servlets) are only required in the Web container. However, a J2EE module associated with an enterprise component (for example) contains not only elements that need to be deployed in an EJB container, but also elements that need to be deployed in the Web container (such as the business delegates and service locators). In our example, we have chosen to deploy these J2EE modules to both the EJB container and the Web container, even though some of the elements are redundant since they may never be accessed within that container.

We could have chosen to provide finer-grained J2EE modules that ensure that only those elements required by a particular container are deployed to that container, but we have chosen not to take this approach in our example.

At this point, we consider the basic structure of the **Implementation Model** to be established.

The **Implementation Model** structure is documented in the **Software Architecture Document**. For more information on documenting the software architecture, see Appendix A, Describing a Software Architecture.

Activity: Review the Implementation

OVERVIEW

The purpose of this activity is to formally review the structure of the **Implementation Model**.

INPUT ARTIFACTS

- Implementation Guidelines
- Implementation Model
- Programming Guidelines

RESULTING ARTIFACTS

- Change Request
- Review Record

STEPS

- Conduct the Review

Step: Conduct the Review

In this step, we perform a formal review of the **Implementation Model** structure. This review serves as a "quality gate" that ensures that the reviewed artifacts are mature enough to support subsequent development activities. Problems discovered in the artifacts should be documented in **Change Requests**. Once the review is complete, the results of the review, including any action items, are captured in a **Review Record**.

The following checkpoints describe things that should be kept in mind when reviewing the structure of the **Implementation Model**.

- The **Implementation Model** structure should be comprehensive and support all required implementation elements (Java, virtual directory, and deployment support elements).

- The **Implementation Model** structure should acknowledge the constraints imposed by the implementation environment.

- The **Implementation Model** structure should conform to the appropriate **Implementation Guidelines** and **Programming Guidelines** used on the project.

- The **Implementation Model** structure should support concerns such as integration, testing, and concurrent development.

Workflow Detail: Implement Design Elements

The **Implement Design Elements** workflow detail contains three activities: **Implement Design Elements**, **Perform Unit Tests**, and **Review the Implementation**, as shown in Figure 9.8.

The workflow detail contains activities performed when we write and compile the source code and unit test the results. The same person often undertakes the **Implement Design Elements** and **Perform Unit Tests** activities, leading to a quick turnaround of simple fixes to problems. More significant problems (that have possibly resulted from defects in dependent software, or the design) are handled more formally by opening a **Change Request** that is subject to the change control process.

This workflow detail concludes with a review in the activity **Review the Implementation**.

Activity: Implement Design Elements

OVERVIEW

The purpose of this activity is to implement a specific design element, which may result in the implementation of multiple design elements since some design elements contain other design elements (for example, implementing a **Design Subsystem** may involve implementing multiple **Interfaces**, **Framework Components** and **Design Classes**).

INPUT ARTIFACTS

◆ Data Model

◆ Design Model (Design Class, Framework Component, Design Subsystem, Interface)

◆ Implementation Guidelines

◆ Implementation Model

◆ Programming Guidelines

STEPS

◆ Implement Design Subsystems

◆ Implement Framework Components

◆ Implement Design Classes and Interfaces

◆ Implement Deployment Elements

RESULTING ARTIFACTS

◆ Change Request

◆ Implementation Model (Implementation Directory, Implementation File)

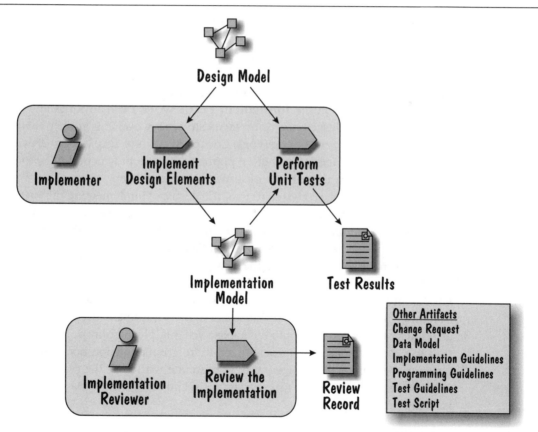

Figure 9.8   Implement Design Elements Workflow Detail Overview Diagram

The **Implement Design Elements** activity focuses on the implementation of **Design Subsystems** (that represent enterprise components), **Framework Components** (that represent EJBs), **Interfaces** (that represent EJB **Interfaces** and other Java **Interfaces**) and **Design Classes** (that represent servlets, JSPs, and Java classes), together with J2EE modules and their associated deployment descriptors. This activity results in the production of one or more **Implementation Files** that implement these design elements. In implementing these design elements, we may also create additional **Implementation Directories**. For J2EE applications, the following **Implementation Files** may be produced:

- Source files (such as JSPs, static HTML files, image files, Java files)
- Compiled files (Java bytecode files)
- J2EE modules (WAR, EJB-JAR, JAR and EAR files)
- Deployment descriptors (XML files)

There is not a strict sequencing of steps in this activity, since the implementation of the various design elements can occur in parallel. The sequence in which elements are implemented is often driven by the dependencies between the implementation elements. For example, an appropriate deployment descriptor may be created in the **Implement Deployment Elements** step before its content is populated in the **Implement Framework Components** and **Implement Design Classes and Interfaces** steps. However, it is equally valid to execute the **Implement Framework Components** and **Implement Design Classes and Interfaces** steps before populating the deployment descriptor in its entirety in the **Implement Deployment Elements** step.

In this book, we have chosen to treat the details of implementing the various design elements very lightly since there are many excellent books on both Java and Web programming. Rather, we have concentrated on describing a process within which such activities occur. In the J2EE Developer Roadmap, all programming conventions are specified in the **Programming Guidelines** artifact[7].

We have also chosen to leave the implementation of any required persistence as an exercise for the reader, primarily because the J2EE platform provides a number of transparencies in this area (such as automatically mapping the attributes of CMP entity EJBs to a database schema, given appropriate information in a deployment descriptor). Again, there are many good books that discuss the mechanics of implementing persistence with the J2EE platform. The implementation of such persistence should acknowledge the **Data Model** that is an input to this activity.

---

7 Whereas the **Implementation Guidelines** artifact is concerned with issues such as the structure of the **Implementation Model**.

Step: Implement Design Subsystems

In this step, we consider the implementation of **Design Subsystems**. As discussed in Chapter 8, in our architecture a **Design Subsystem** represents an enterprise component that may contain a number of finer-grained design elements, **Framework Components** (that represent EJBs), and **Design Classes** (that represent servlets, JSPs, and Java classes). Thus, the implementation of an enterprise component can be considered to be the sum of the implementation of its constituent parts. The implementation of these design elements is discussed in subsequent steps. Although not discussed in any detail in this book, we also recognize the need to implement build utilities, such as makefiles. The build order of the elements that compose an enterprise component can be derived from the dependencies specified between these elements in the **Design Model**.

Step: Implement Framework Components

Again, as we discussed in Chapter 8, a **Framework Component** represents an EJB and contains a number of **Design Classes** (such as the bean implementation class and, if the bean is an entity EJB, a primary key class) and **Interfaces** (such as the home and remote **Interfaces**). Thus, the implementation of an EJB, like the implementation of an enterprise component, can be considered to be the sum of the implementation of its constituent parts. The implementation of these design elements is discussed in the next step.

The creation of the deployment descriptor that describes an EJB is discussed later in this activity, in the step **Implement Deployment Elements**. However, since this deployment descriptor will contain a description of the EJB that is considered in this step, this aspect of its content may be populated in this step.

Again, we may also implement a makefile associated with each EJB. The build order of the elements that compose an EJB can also be derived from the dependencies specified between these elements in the **Design Model**.

Step: Implement Design Classes and Interfaces

In this step we implement the **Design Classes** and **Interfaces** that have been defined in the **Design Model**. In our architecture, discussed in Chapter 8, a **Design Class** is used to represent:

- The presentation request controller (a servlet)
- A use-case dispatcher (a Java class)
- A view class (a JSP)
- A business delegate (a Java class)
- A service locator (a Java class)

- An EJB implementation class (a Java class)
- An EJB primary key class (a Java class)
- A value object (a Java class)

An **Interface** is used to represent:

- An EJB home interface (a Java interface)
- An EJB remote interface (a Java interface)
- An EJB local home (a Java interface)
- An EJB local interface (a Java interface)

We saw earlier, in the activity **Structure the Implementation Model**, that we can derive the **Implementation Model** structure from the structure of the **Design Model**. In addition, we can also derive the required **Implementation Files** from the design elements.

Let's start by considering the design elements that are implemented as Java classes or Java interfaces. Consider the **Design Model** structure shown in Figure 9.9. Here we can see various design elements, including a **Design Subsystem** (Auction Manager enterprise component), a **Framework Component** (Auction EJB), a **Design Class** (AuctionManagerDelegate) and an **Interface** (Auction).

Since, in the Java programming language, there is a one-to-one mapping between a Java class (or Java interface) and its associated source file and Java bytecode file, we can derive the **Implementation Files** we need as shown in Figure 9.10. The **Implementation Files** are accommodated within the **Implementation Model** structure defined in the **Structure the Implementation Model** activity. Although not shown in this example, this mapping also holds true for other design elements (such as the PresentationRequestController servlet) that are implemented as Java elements.

We now consider the design elements that are implemented as virtual directory elements, such as JSPs, image files and static HTML pages. Consider the **Design Model** structure shown in Figure 9.11. Here we can see various Auction Management-related virtual directory elements (specifically, the JSPs).

Again, we can derive the corresponding **Implementation Files** as shown in Figure 9.12.

As with the implementation of EJBs discussed earlier, the execution of this step may result in the population of certain aspects of the deployment descriptor that describes the elements implemented in this step.

Step: Implement Deployment Elements

The implementation of deployment elements refers specifically to the implementation of J2EE modules and their associated deployment descriptors. As

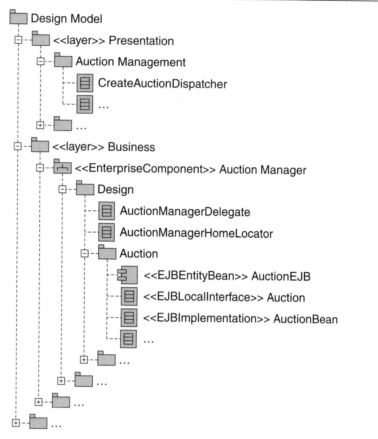

Figure 9.9 Java Elements in the Design Model

noted earlier, the population of the deployment descriptors may occur at the same time as the creation of the implementation elements.

The names of the deployment descriptors, and the directories in which they reside, are defined by the J2EE platform specification (as described in Chapter 2, An Introduction to the J2EE Platform, Enterprise Edition). Given this constraint, and the structure of the **Implementation Model** described earlier, we can define the implementation elements shown in Figure 9.13.

An important aspect of implementing deployment elements is to specify the content of each J2EE module. This can be shown on a UML component diagram. An example is shown in Figure 9.14, where we see a subset of the **Implementation Files** contained in the auctionmanager.jar file. An **Implementation File** is represented as a UML artifact.

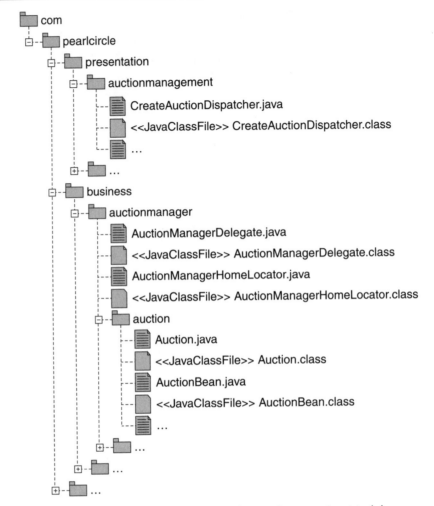

Figure 9.10 Java Implementation Files in the Implementation Model

During assembly (which is outside the scope of the J2EE Developer Road-map), the content of an EAR file could be represented in a similar manner. In this case, we would see the J2EE modules contained within an EAR file as being resident within the file.

Implementation Optimizations

Before leaving this activity, it is worth discussing two optimizations that can help us during implementation.

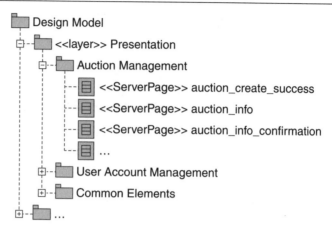

Figure 9.11 Virtual Directory Elements in the Design Model

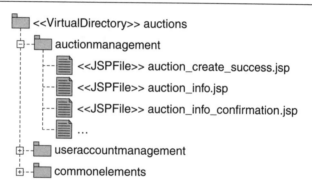

Figure 9.12 Virtual Directory Implementation Files in the Implementation Model

The first of these optimizations is the concept of "round-trip engineering" (RTE) from model to code and back. This capability is often provided with a UML modeling tool, and can help ensure that the **Implementation Model** and the code are kept in step. For example, we may add an operation to a **Design Class** or **Interface** that should be reflected in the corresponding source code. Conversely, we may add an operation in the source code that should be reflected in the corresponding design element.

When we perform round-trip engineering using a modeling tool, there must be a means for defining the relationship between a design element and its associated implementation element. One obvious solution is for the modeling tool to support the explicit assignment of the design element to its associated

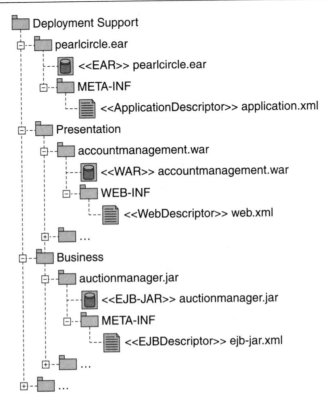

Figure 9.13 Deployment Elements

implementation element. However, this assignment may also be provided implicitly. For example, we can derive the name of a Java source code file from the design element it implements.

The second optimization is to only model when it adds value. For example, we have described how to model J2EE modules and their associated deployment descriptors in UML. It can be argued that the visualization provided by simply looking at the content of the deployment descriptors is sufficient to understand the composition of the J2EE application in terms of deployment elements, and that the use of UML adds little value. In any case, the decision as to what should or should not be modeled should be described in the **Implementation Guidelines**.

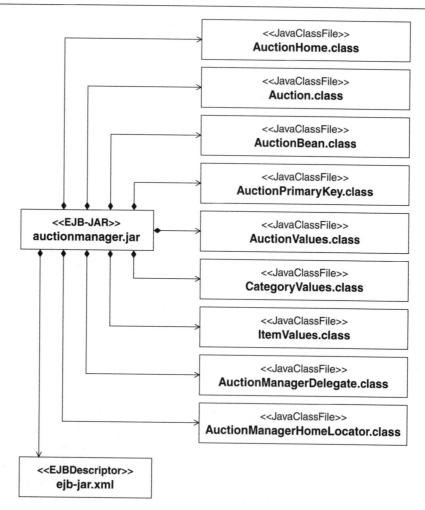

Figure 9.14   The Content of the Auction Manager EJB JAR

Activity: Perform Unit Tests

OVERVIEW

The purpose of this activity is to verify that the behavior of a unit conforms to its specification, as well as to verify the internal structure of a unit.

In the context of this activity, a "unit" refers to the smallest testable element (unit) of the software. A unit is usually the responsibility of a single developer.

INPUT ARTIFACTS

◆ Design Model

◆ Implementation Guidelines

◆ Implementation Model (Implementation File)

◆ Programming Guidelines

◆ Test Guidelines

◆ Test Script

RESULTING ARTIFACTS

◆ Change Request

◆ Test Results

◆ Test Script

STEPS

◆ Implement Unit Tests

◆ Execute Unit Tests

◆ Evaluate the Execution of Unit Tests

◆ Verify Unit Test Results

◆ Recover from Halted Unit Tests

This activity is concerned solely with the unit testing of the elements (typically, **Implementation Files)** that are produced by a single developer. However, the Test discipline of RUP covers broader testing activities than just the unit testing performed by a single developer. For example, RUP covers the various forms of integration, system and acceptance testing. This is discussed further in Chapter 10.

Step: Implement Unit Tests

The purpose of this step is to create or refine any **Test Scripts** that are required to test a unit[8]. In order to verify the specification of the unit under consideration, when developing the **Test Scripts** we take into account the **Implementation Guidelines** (which provide guidance on transforming design

---

8 We consider an aspect of a **Test Script** to be the data that is used to execute the test and the data that is used to verify the test output.

elements into implementation elements) and the **Programming Guidelines** (which provide guidance on the content of source code). The **Test Scripts** should adhere to any **Test Guidelines** that have been defined.

Step: Execute Unit Tests

In this step, we execute the **Test Scripts** produced in the previous step. In executing a unit test, the following tasks are typically performed.

- The test environment is setup to ensure that all required elements, such as hardware, software, tools, data, and so on, have been implemented and are in the test environment.
- The test environment is initialized to ensure that all implementation elements are in the correct initial state for the start of testing.
- The **Test Scripts** are executed and the **Test Results** captured.

Step: Evaluate the Execution of Unit Tests

In this step, we determine whether the unit tests have executed normally (the **Test Results** constitute a "pass" or "fail") or abnormally (the unit tests did not complete).

If the tests executed normally, we then verify the **Test Results**, as described in the step **Verify Unit Test Results**. If the tests executed abnormally (for example, if there was a hardware failure on the machine executing the tests), then we determine why this occurred, as described in the step **Recover from Halted Unit Tests**.

Step: Verify Unit Test Results

If the unit tests have executed as expected, we first need to ensure that the **Test Results** are reliable and reflect the appropriate execution of the target-of-test. For unexpected **Test Results**, we make sure that the test errors are not caused by an error in the unit test itself (for example, missing or corrupt test data).

If any reported failures are due to errors identified in the test artifacts or due to problems with the test environment, then the appropriate corrective action should be taken and the unit tests executed again. If the **Test Results** indicate the failures are genuinely due to the target-of-test then, depending on the scope of the failure, we can either fix the problem (by executing the **Implement Design Elements** activity, as required) and retesting the target-of-test, or we can open a **Change Request** with an indication of the appropriate corrective actions that could be taken.

Step: Recover from Halted Unit Tests

If the unit tests have terminated abnormally, then we determine the cause of the termination, correct the problem, and re-execute the unit tests as defined in the step **Execute Unit Tests**.

Activity: Review the Implementation

OVERVIEW

The purpose of this activity is to verify the implementation elements.

INPUT ARTIFACTS

- Implementation Guidelines
- Implementation Model
- Programming Guidelines

RESULTING ARTIFACTS

- Change Request
- Review Record

STEPS

- Conduct the Review

Step: Conduct the Review

In this step, a formal review of the input artifacts is performed. Problems discovered in the artifacts should be documented in **Change Requests**. Once the review is complete, the results of the review, including any action items, are captured in a **Review Record**.

The following checkpoints describe things that should be kept in mind when reviewing the implementation artifacts.

- The implementation elements should conform to the appropriate **Implementation Guidelines** and **Programming Guidelines**.
- The code should be self-documenting. It should be possible to understand the code by reading it.
- The code should be straightforward and avoid "clever" solutions.
- All implementation errors (such as compilation or execution errors) should have been addressed or **Change Requests** opened, as appropriate.

Summary

In this chapter, we have described the implementation of the various design elements. We have also described how to represent these elements in an **Implementation Model** that contains **Implementation Directories** and **Implementation Files** that together represent the developed system. This chapter concludes our tour through the J2EE Developer Roadmap. In the next chapter, Chapter 10, we conclude the book with a discussion of topics not covered in any detail in the preceding chapters.

Chapter 10
Additional Topics

This chapter contains a brief discussion of those topics that have been post-poned (or treated very lightly) in other chapters.

This book has concentrated on the RUP disciplines that are of most interest to a J2EE developer: Requirements, Analysis and Design, and Implementation. This section briefly discusses the remaining RUP disciplines and, in particular, focuses on the relevance of each of these disciplines to the J2EE developer.

Business Modeling

Business Modeling may be undertaken for a number of reasons. For example, we may wish to undertake Business Modeling in order to *gain an understanding of current problems in the organization* and identify areas of potential im-provement. This improvement may be provided through the implementation of applications that automate aspects of the business. Such automation may address problems such as poor performance or excessive human error.

Business Modeling may also be undertaken to ensure that customers, end users, and developers have a common *understanding of the structure of the target organization*. This understanding may be communicated as precise def-initions of roles, responsibilities and interactions between elements of the organization.

Business Modeling can also be undertaken when *deriving requirements for applications* that are built to support the organization. For example, a par-ticular application may be required to interoperate with other applications that automate other aspects of the business, and may be required to be accessed by certain roles within the organization, which might result in a requirement to access the application through certain devices, such as a WAP phone for mobile users.

Business Modeling can be very important because it puts the system to be developed in the business context. Business Modeling provides an input to the Requirements activities, as well as to the Analysis and Design activities, since business entities can be used as an input to identifying entity classes.

Testing

The scope of testing discussed in Chapter 9, Implementation is confined to unit testing. However, RUP contains an extensive Test discipline that supports testing concerns beyond those of the individual developer.

In particular, RUP acknowledges the need to integrate the work of a number of developers and discusses *integration testing, system testing* and *acceptance testing*. Integration is a software development activity in which separate software components are combined into an executable whole. Integration testing is concerned with testing this whole. System testing is traditionally performed when the software is functioning as a whole, and the target of testing is the end-to-end functioning of the system. The goal of acceptance testing is to verify that the software can be used by the end-users to execute the functionality of the system.

From the perspective of the J2EE Developer Roadmap, the Requirements artifacts (such as the **Use-Case Model** and **Supplementary Specification**) and Implementation artifacts (such as **Implementation Directories, Implementation Files** and **Test Scripts**) are a significant input to the activities of the Test discipline.

Deployment

The Deployment discipline of RUP is focused on ensuring that the software product is available for its end users, and it defines a number of artifacts as a result (such as **Release Notes, Installation Artifacts** and **Training Materials**). From a J2EE perspective, the Deployment discipline emphasizes that solely producing the software product is not sufficient to transition a product to its end users, and that other concerns, such as installation and training, must be considered.

A key artifact of the Deployment discipline is a **Deployment Unit**. A **Deployment Unit** consists of a **Build** (a collection of executable elements, such as a J2EE application or J2EE modules), documents (**End-User Support Material** and **Release Notes**) and **Installation Artifacts**.

Configuration and Change Management

Most of the artifacts that the developer produces are subject to configuration and change management. RUP describes a comprehensive Configuration and Change Management discipline that addresses:

- *Configuration Management (CM)*, which is concerned with the versioning of project artifacts, the production of a **Build** from the correct versions of the constituent parts, the management of workspaces[1], and the production of measurements, such as those that allow the rate of change of artifacts (which may provide an indication of stability) to be measured.
- *Software Manufacturing*, which is concerned with the automation of steps to compile, test, and package software for distribution.
- *Change Request Management (CRM)*, which addresses the organizational infrastructure (such as a Change Control Board), required to assess the cost, schedule, and impact of a change to existing artifacts.
- *Change Tracking*, which provides a history of, and rationale for, changes made to the artifacts.
- *Configuration Status Accounting (Measurement)*, which is concerned with measuring the current state of artifacts based on the type, number, rate, and severity of defects found and fixed during the course of product development.

Certain artifacts, such as documents and source code files, can be configured and change managed in their entirety. This is not the case with other artifacts such as the **Design Model**. Multiple developers must work concurrently on different parts of the model, and these parts must be individually configured and change managed. Concurrent access to the same model requires that the model be structured to support this way of working (see the **Structure the Implementation Model** activity in Chapter 9).

---

1 A *workspace* is a private area in which changes to artifacts are made, but are not immediately visible to other team members.

Project Management

The Project Management discipline of RUP provides a framework for managing software-intensive projects. It provides practical guidelines for planning, staffing, executing, and monitoring projects, as well as providing a framework for managing risk.

It is interesting to note that a number of artifacts produced by the J2EE developer influence the planning aspects of Project Management. For example, the **Use-Case Priority List**, **Use Cases**, **Design Subsystems**, **Design Packages**, and **Framework Components** are all inputs to the planning of the development of a J2EE application.

As has been mentioned several times throughout this book, RUP is iterative in nature. This aspect is of particular significance to the Project Manager who must plan the iterations of the project. Planning is essentially performed at two levels. The first is at the level of phases. This planning is captured in a phase plan[2], which provides a holistic perspective of the project's phases and iterations. For example, the phase plan provides an indication of the anticipated number and duration of iterations of the project. An extract from an example phase plan is shown in Table 10.1.

The second level of planning occurs at the level of iterations. This planning is captured in an **Iteration Plan**, which provides a detailed fine-grained view of the tasks, resources, resource dependencies, and durations for the iteration. As the project progresses, there are always two **Iteration Plans** being considered. The first **Iteration Plan** is associated with the current iteration. The second **Iteration Plan** is associated with the next iteration. One aspect of an **Iteration Plan** is often a Gantt chart, which shows the timeline of the iteration. An example of an Elaboration **Iteration Plan** is shown in Figure 10.1.

Table 10.1   An Extract from a Phase Plan

Phase	*Number of Iterations*	*Start*	*End*
Inception	1	Week 1	Week 4
Elaboration	2	Week 5	Week 12
Construction	2	Week 13	Week 20
Transition	1	Week 21	Week 24

---

2 The phase plan is part of the RUP **Software Development Plan** artifact.

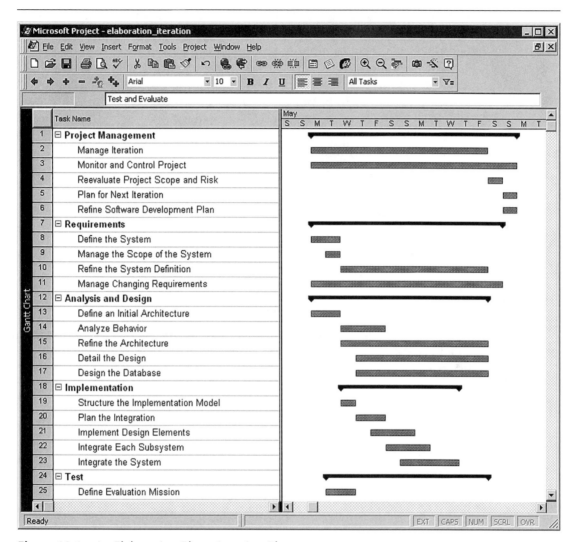

Figure 10.1 An Elaboration Phase Iteration Plan

Environment

The Environment discipline of RUP defines activities that are focused on providing a process and toolset for use on a project. This may involve configuring RUP in some way, as well as integrating a set of tools. For example, in defining the

J2EE Developer Roadmap, we followed the activities described in the Environment discipline of RUP. In RUP terms, the J2EE Developer Roadmap constitutes one aspect of a **Development Case** artifact.

The Environment discipline also contains activities and artifacts explicitly aimed at defining the guidelines to be used on the project. For example, the activities of the Environment discipline produce the following guidelines, which we reference in the J2EE Developer Roadmap.

- **Use-Case Modeling Guidelines**
- **User-Experience Guidelines**
- **Design Guidelines**
- **Implementation Guidelines**
- **Programming Guidelines**

Other Considerations

There are also a number of considerations that apply across disciplines that should be mentioned. One of the most significant of these is the development of a traceability strategy. *Traceability* is the ability to trace a project element to other related project elements. For example, we could explicitly model the traceability from an EJB to the key abstraction(s) that it was derived from. Traceabilities may be set up to:

- Allow the source of requirements to be determined
- Ensure that all requirements have been implemented
- Allow the impact of making requirement changes to be assessed
- Verify that the application does only what it was intended to do

Implementing a traceability strategy requires careful thought, since there is a cost involved in creating and maintaining any traceability. However, given appropriate conventions and tool automation, much of this cost can be reduced. For more information on developing a traceability strategy, see RUP.

In Conclusion—A Note from the Authors

While writing this book, we kept a number of objectives in mind. The most obvious of these was to present a useful subset of the RUP, the J2EE Developer Roadmap, which effectively addresses the complexities of developing J2EE applications, and can be immediately applied. In addition, we deliberately placed an emphasis on exemplifying this process through the development of an Online Auction application, from requirements through to implementation.

When we first considered bringing our experiences together on paper, we were concerned about the longevity of such a publication. We were concerned with the continuing evolution of the J2EE platform. We were asking ourselves and our colleagues: will our book still be relevant in 12 months' time? Will initiatives such as Web services dramatically affect the J2EE Developer Roadmap that we advocate?

Of course, we would not have written the book if we had concluded that the material would age rapidly. This book is about how to build a specific kind of application (an enterprise application), with specific technologies (J2EE), and is not about the technologies themselves. We strongly believe that even though the J2EE technologies will improve and include more services, our process roadmap for building J2EE applications will stay fundamentally the same. Of course, we may have to add, or possibly remove steps and change their details, but nothing will remove the need to do good requirements, analysis, design, and implementation, or reduce the benefits of developing iteratively.

The framework on which the roadmap has been built, the Rational Unified Process itself, demonstrates the longevity of a good process. RUP has been constructed with longevity in mind and has been successfully applied to many software development projects—projects that differ dramatically in terms of size[3], complexity and domain. While the technologies that underpin the J2EE platform may evolve, we are confident that the roadmap we have presented in this book for "Building J2EE Applications with the Rational Unified Process" will prove useful to you for some time to come.

In closing, we strongly encourage you to make your own improvements to the roadmap. Although we like to think of the J2EE Developer Roadmap as a cookbook for J2EE developers, even the best recipe can be improved by a good cook.

---

3 RUP has been successfully applied to projects that range from one person, to hundreds of people.

Appendix A

Describing a Software Architecture

Introduction

Although we all often use the term "architecture," and we certainly use it in the book, there is no commonly accepted agreement on what architecture is and how it is described. As a result, if we ask to see the architecture of a system, we are usually given a set of diagrams and possibly documents that describe some, usually structural, aspects of that system. The purpose of this appendix is to explain what we mean when we say "architecture" and how we recommend describing it.

What Is Architecture?

To define architecture, it is easier to start from its role, rather than to look at it as a set of artifacts. The following definition was derived from Mary Shaw and David Garlan (Shaw and Garlan 1996) and then refined by Philippe Kruchten, Grady Booch, Kurt Bittner, and Rich Reitman from Rational.

"Software architecture encompasses the set of significant decisions about the organization of a software system including:

- Selection of the structural elements and their interfaces by which the system is composed

- Behavior as specified in collaborations among those elements
- Composition of these structural and behavioral elements into larger subsystems
- Architectural style that guides this organization

Software architecture also involves functionality, usability, resilience, performance, reuse, comprehensibility, economic and technology constraints and tradeoffs and aesthetic concerns."

This definition emphasizes the fact that architecture involves a set of key design decisions, rules and patterns (a set of constraints) that define a framework in which the design and implementation of the system take place. Architectural decisions are the most fundamental decisions, and changing them late in the development of a system may have significant ripple effects on the system itself and on the project that is delivering the system.

Communicating the Architecture of a System

It is impossible to describe any system from only a single perspective. The more complicated a system, the more aspects we need to consider and describe. Software systems are no exception, and describing them is particularly difficult because of software's invisibility.

To describe software systems, we use models. Each model captures a particular aspect of the system or is a projection of the system from what we call a *viewpoint*. A viewpoint describes:

- One or more system model(s) and view(s) (projections) of those models
- The stakeholders interested in the view(s)
- The stakeholders' concerns that should be addressed through the view(s)

According to our definition, an architecture description is a subset of the system description, in that it addresses the critical design decisions made by the architect. Hence, an architecture is also represented through a set of views defined by viewpoints. As described in IEEE-1471-2000 (IEEE 2000) an architect can define his or her own viewpoints and views to communicate the architecture of the system. However, we recommend the following set of commonly used views:

- The Requirements View, describing both functional and non-functional significant architectural requirements (commonly referred to as SARs)

- The Logical View, which describes key design mechanisms, architecturally important design elements, their interdependencies and the organization of these elements into subsystems and layers

- The Implementation View, which describes the key implementation elements such as code artifacts, executables, and modules

- The Process View, which describes processes and threads, and the allocation of the logical and/or the implementation elements to these processes and threads

- The Deployment View, which contains a description of various system nodes such as computers or routers, and the allocation of the logical, implementation, or process elements to these nodes

This set of views is known as the "4 + 1 architecture view model" and was first proposed by Philippe Kruchten (Kruchten 1995)[1]. It is easy to see that the views are consistent with the process artifacts discussed throughout this book. In other words, we can think of an architecture view as containing selected elements (those most relevant to the architecture) from the described process artifacts. The correspondence between the views and the major artifacts of the J2EE Developer Roadmap is shown in the Table A.1.

Table A.1 Correspondence Between Architecture Views and J2EE Developer Roadmap Artifacts

View	*J2EE Developer Roadmap Artifacts*
Requirements View	Use-Case Model Supplementary Specification
Logical View	Design Model User-Experience Model Data Model Design Guidelines
Implementation View	Implementation Model
Process View	Design Model[2]
Deployment View	Deployment Model Implementation Model[3] (deployment support)

---

1 In the paper Philippe Kruchten calls the Requirements View the Use-Case View.

2 The **Design Model** is the main source of information for both Logical and Process Views. Its elements are sometimes also used in the Deployment View to show allocation of design elements to nodes.

3 The **Deployment Model** shows the allocation of implementation elements to system nodes.

The Software Architecture Document

The **Software Architecture Document**, commonly referred to as the SAD, is an artifact that is used in a number of activities discussed in the book. It is the primary artifact where the architecture of a system is described, and it contains references to all other architecturally significant artifacts. In other words, if someone wants to understand the architecture of a system, then the SAD is the place from which to start.

The SAD should show how the key architectural concerns are addressed, and so it is best organized along the architectural views discussed above. The following is a brief description of a commonly used SAD structure, with a short description of the content of its sections.

1. Introduction   This section describes the scope of the architecture and lists references to all supporting documents and artifacts. Artifacts that are usually referenced are the **Glossary**, the **Supplementary Specification**, the system models, and any standards and stakeholder documents that pertain to the system.

2. Architecture Representation   This section describes how the architecture is represented. We recommend the 4 + 1 view model as the base of the representation. However, the architect may want to add additional views or notations, and these should be described in this section.

The rest of this SAD structure description assumes that the 4 + 1 view model is followed.

3. Requirements View   This section is usually broken up into two subsections. The first subsection discusses the architecturally significant **Use Cases**.

The architecturally significant **Use Cases** are those that are developed in iterations of the Elaboration phase to:

- Exercise and test the main system elements and their collaborations
- Investigate identified areas of risk to assist with the definition of risk elimination and mitigation strategies.

The second subsection discusses system-wide architectural goals and constraints that are not associated with any **Use Case** in particular. It refers to the **Supplementary Specification** and describes the system-wide requirements and objectives that have significant impact on the architecture. This subsection should also describe requirements for system properties such as performance, size, scalability, security, and privacy. It may also capture special constraints such as use of off-the-shelf products, integration with legacy software, a reuse strategy, required development tools, and team structure and schedule.

4. Logical View   This section describes the architecturally significant parts of the **Design Model**, and the **User-Experience Model**, and may also reference the **Design Guidelines**. It should start with a discussion of the significant design mechanisms and patterns that shape the system structure. It should then discuss system decomposition into layers and **Design Subsystems**, as well as any other architecturally significant design elements (such as **Framework Components** and **Design Classes**). The key abstractions of the system are also considered architecturally significant and should be described in this section. The descriptions of the architecturally significant design elements should reference specific parts of the **Design Model**, where the element's responsibilities and relationships are specified.

In cases of a complicated or unusual user experience, the description of the architecturally significant design elements should also reference parts of the **User-Experience Model** and explain dependencies between those design elements and user-experience elements (**Screens** and input forms) and the **Screen** flows, as documented in the **Use-Case Storyboards**.

This section should illustrate how the architecturally significant design elements work together. This is best done by showing a few selected **Use-Case Realizations** of the architecturally significant **Use Cases** and by explaining how the design elements contribute to their functionality.

5. Process View   This section is particularly important in systems that manage operating system processes and threads. The J2EE technologies support computing resource management. Hence, in the case of J2EE-based systems the Process View is usually only used to describe any desired application concurrency (application concurrency is discussed in more detail in Chapter 8, Design). In such cases, the Process View can describe:

- The servlets used to create and manage multiple threads of control
- Any Java applications that the system integrates with that manage their own threads of control, and the design elements with which those Java applications communicate
- The use of JMS or message-driven EJBs to manage the application concurrency

6. Implementation View   This section is a view of the **Implementation Model**, with the emphasis on the structure of the model (the Java packages and virtual directories). This view is important because the structure of the **Implementation Model** has a major impact on, for example, concurrent development and testing.

7. Deployment View   This section is a view of the **Deployment Model** and the **Implementation Model**. It shows one or more network (hardware) configurations on which the system is deployed and runs. It also shows the allocation of containers to nodes and the allocation of J2EE modules (**Implementation Model** elements) to the containers.

It is also possible and sometimes informative to show how design elements (such as **Design Subsystems** and **Framework Components**) are allocated to nodes.

8. System Properties   The SAD should conclude with a discussion of how the software architecture contributes to achieving the architectural goals and constraints described in the Requirements section. The System Properties section is where this discussion should take place.

This section usually includes a discussion of key system properties such as performance and portability.

Appendix B

Modeling Conventions

This appendix provides a summary of the modeling conventions used in this book. In particular, we focus on the use of the UML, and on the model structures that have been recommended and described in Chapters 6-9.

UML Representation of J2EE Developer Roadmap Elements

In this section, we provide a summary of the UML representation of the elements in the J2EE Developer Roadmap. The content of this section is derived from a number of sources. In particular, the conventions for modeling EJBs have been derived from Java Specification Request 26 (JSR 26), which has been defined by the Java Community Process. The conventions for modeling other J2EE elements, such as JSPs and servlets, have been derived from the work of Jim Conallen (Conallen 2000) and internal initiatives within Rational Software.

Requirements Artifacts

Artifact	UML Representation	Examples	Stereotype(s)
Actor	Actor		None
Glossary	None	N/A	N/A
Software Architecture Document	None	N/A	N/A
Supplementary Specification	None	N/A	N/A
Use-Case Model[1]	Model		«use-case model»
➤Use Case	Use Case		None
➤Use-Case Package	Package		None
Use-Case Priority List	None	N/A	N/A

Analysis Artifacts

Artifact	UML Representation	Examples	Stereotype(s)
Deployment Model	Model		«deployment model»
Design Model	Model		«design model»
➤Analysis Class	Class	Boundary Class	«boundary»
		Control Class	«control»
		Entity Class	«entity»
➤Design Package	Package		None
		Layer	«layer»
➤Use-Case Realization	Collaboration Instance		«use-case realization»
Software Architecture Document	None	N/A	N/A
User-Experience Model	Model		«user-experience model»
➤Navigation Map	Class Diagram(s)		None
➤Screen	Class		«screen»
➤Use-Case Storyboard	Collaboration Instance		«use-case storyboard»

---

1 The tables containing artifacts show subartifacts (artifacts contained within another artifact) after the parent artifact with their name preceded by a "➤".

Design Artifacts

Artifact	UML Representation	Examples	Stereotype(s)
Data Model	Model		«data model»
Deployment Model	Model		«deployment model»
Design Model	Model		«design model»
➤Design Class	Class		None
		EJB Implementation Class	«EJBImplementation»
		EJB Primary Key Class	None
		HTML Form	«HTMLForm»
		HTML Page	«ClientPage»
		JSP	«ServerPage»
		Servlet	«HttpServlet» «GenericServlet»
➤Design Package	Package		None
		Layer	«Layer»
➤Design Subsystem	Subsystem		None
		Enterprise Component	«EnterpriseComponent»
➤Framework Component	Component		None
		EJB	«EJBSessionBean» «EJBEntityBean» «EJBMessageDrivenBean»
➤Interface	Interface		None
	Class[2]	EJB Interface	«EJBRemoteInterface» «EJBSessionHomeInterface» «EJBEntityHomeInterface» «EJBLocalInterface» «EJBSessionLocalHomeInterface» «EJBEntityLocalHomeInterface»
		Java Interface	«JavaInterface»
➤Use-Case Realization	Collaboration Instance		«use-case realization»
Software Architecture Document	None	N/A	N/A

---

2 A UML Class is used to represent a Java Interface since a Java interface is not the same as a UML interface (for example, a Java interface may have attributes).

Implementation Artifacts

Artifact	UML Representation	Examples	Stereotype(s)
Implementation Model	Model		«implementation model»
➤Implementation File	Artifact		None
		Deployment Descriptor	«ApplicationDescriptor» «ApplicationClientDescriptor» «EJBDescriptor» «WebDescriptor»
		HTML file	None
		Java Bytecode File	«JavaClassFile»
		Java Source File	None
		J2EE Module	«EAR» «EJB-JAR» «JAR» «WAR»
		JSP File	«JSPFile»
➤Implementation Directory	Package		None
		Java Package	None
		Virtual Directory	«VirtualDirectory»
Software Architecture Document	None	N/A	N/A

Design Relationships

The following table summarizes the J2EE-specific relationships that may occur between **Design Model** elements.

UML Representation	*Examples*		*Stereotype(s)*
	Between	*And*	
Association	HTML page	HTML page or JSP	«HTMLLink»
	JSP	HTML page	«Build»
	HTML form	JSP	«Submit»
	JSP	JSP	«JSPInclude» «JSPForward»
Aggregation	HTML page	HTML form	«Build»
Dependency	EJB	EJB element	«reside»
	EJB implementation class	EJB home interface	«EJBRealizeHome»
	EJB implementation class	EJB remote interface	«EJBRealizeRemote»
	EJB implementation class	EJB local interface	«EJBRealizeLocal»
	EJB implementation class	EJB local home interface	«EJBRealizeLocalHome»

Design Class Attributes and Operations

The following table summarizes the J2EE-specific stereotypes that can be applied to the attributes and operations of a **Design Class**.

UML Representation	*Element*	*Stereotype*
Attribute	EJB CMP field	«EJBCmpField»
	EJB primary key field	«EJBPrimaryKeyField»
	HTML input field	«HTMLInput»
	HTML select field	«HTMLSelect»
	HTML submit button	«HTMLSubmit»
	HTML text area	«HTMLTextArea»
Operation	EJB business method	«EJBBusinessMethod»
	EJB create method	«EJBCreateMethod»
	EJB finder method	«EJBFinderMethod»
	EJB home method	«EJBHomeMethod»
	EJB select method	«EJBSelectMethod»

J2EE Developer Roadmap Model Structure Guidelines

In this section, we describe some recommendations for structuring the content of the J2EE Developer Roadmap models. For more information on how to define the content of these models, and the rationale for this structure, see the process chapters (Chapters 6–9).

The model structures described in this section have been used throughout the book and in the sample application. They can be replaced by any number of equally valid structures without affecting the process.

Use-Case Model

The recommended structure of the **Use-Case Model** is shown in Figure B.1. This structure is described in Chapter 6, Requirements.

User-Experience Model

The recommended structure for the **User-Experience Model** is shown in Figure B.2. This structure is described in Chapter 7, Analysis.

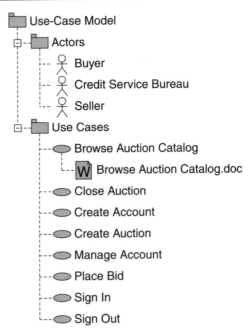

Figure B.1   Use-Case Model Structure

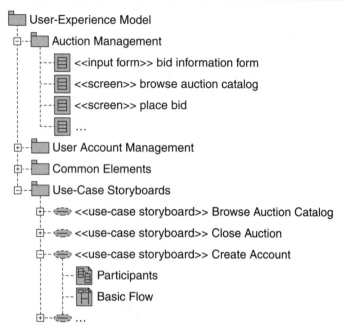

Figure B.2 User-Experience Model Structure

Design Model

The recommended structure of the **Design Model** is shown in Figure B.3. This structure is initially described in Chapter 7, and is then refined in Chapter 8, Design.

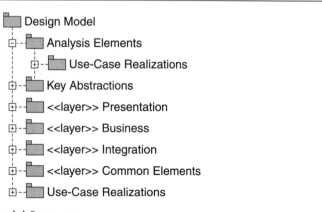

Figure B.3 Design Model Structure

The analysis activities result in the population of the "Analysis Elements" and "Key Abstractions" packages. The structure of these packages is shown in Figure B.4. This structure is described in Chapter 7.

The structure of the "Presentation" layer is shown in Figure B.5. This structure is described in Chapter 8.

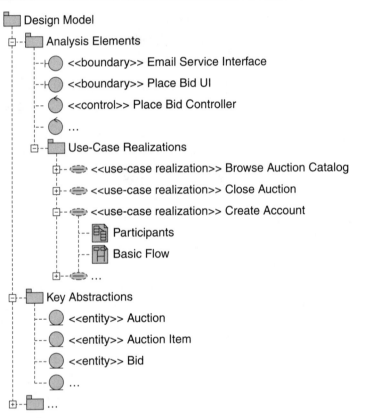

Figure B.4 Structure of the Analysis Aspects of the Design Model

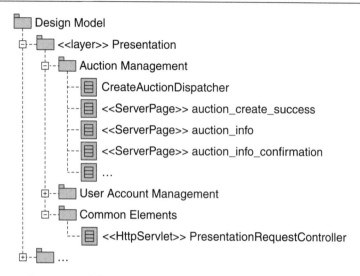

Figure B.5   Structure of the Presentation Layer in the Design Model

The structure of the "Business" layer is shown Figure B.6. This structure is described in Chapter 8.

The structure of the "Use-Case Realizations" package is shown in Figure B.7. This structure is described in Chapter 8.

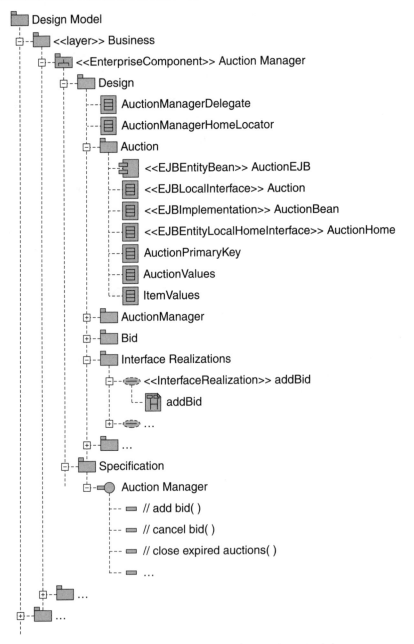

Figure B.6 Structure of the Business Layer in the Design Model

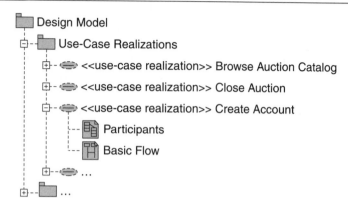

Figure B.7   Structure of the Use-Case Realizations Package in the Design Model

Implementation Model

The **Implementation Model** comprises a number of structures that are discussed in Chapter 9, Implementation, namely:

- A structure to describe elements that are organized by Java package (see Figure B.8)
- A structure to describe elements that are organized within a virtual directory (see Figure B.9)
- A structure to describe deployment elements (see Figure B.10)

Java Packaging Structure   The Java packaging structure is shown in Figure B.8. This structure is described in Chapter 9.

Virtual Directory Structure   The virtual directory structure is shown in Figure B.9. This structure is described in Chapter 9.

Deployment Elements Structure   The structure to support deployment elements is shown in Figure B.10. This structure is described in Chapter 9.

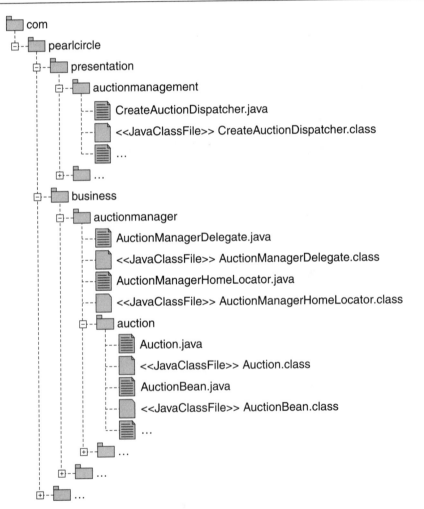

Figure B.8   Java Packaging Structure in the Implementation Model

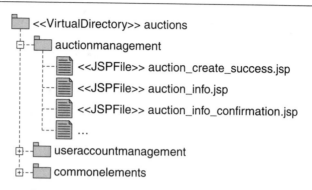

Figure B.9   Virtual Directory Structure in the Implementation Model

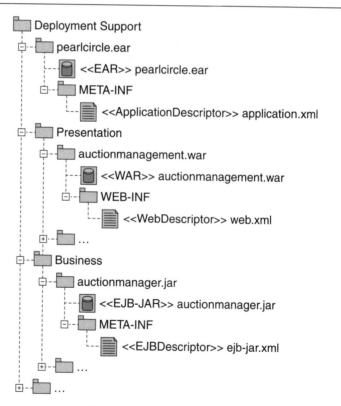

Figure B.10   Deployment Elements Structure in the Implementation Model

Appendix C
Glossary

This glossary defines the terms and acronyms used in this book.

Terms

This section lists the concepts, artifacts and roles of the J2EE Developer Roadmap.

Activity   An activity is a unit of work that provides a meaningful result in the context of the project.

Actor (artifact)   An Actor defines a coherent set of roles that users of the system can play when interacting with it. An Actor instance can be played by an individual, an external system, or an external device. An Actor is contained within the Use-Case Model.

Analysis Class (artifact)   An Analysis Class represents an early conceptual model of an element of the system that has responsibility and behavior. In the J2EE Developer Roadmap, an Analysis Class is contained within the Design Model because the roadmap does not include a separate Analysis Model.

Application Component Provider   The application component provider is a J2EE-defined role that encompasses a number of responsibilities, such as EJB developer and HTML document designer. These roles are responsible for producing the J2EE application components and for packaging these into appropriate J2EE modules.

Application Concurrency Application concurrency is a "designed-in" separation of the system's logic into concurrent threads of computation. The developer, using defined mechanisms, must explicitly implement application concurrency.

Architecture Reviewer (role) The Architecture Reviewer plans and conducts the formal reviews of the overall software architecture.

Artifact An artifact is a physical piece of information that (1) is produced, modified, or used by a process, (2) defines an area of responsibility, and (3) is subject to version control. An artifact can be a model, a model element, or a document.

Change Request (artifact) Changes to development artifacts are proposed through Change Requests (CRs). Change Requests are used to document and track defects, enhancement requests and any other type of request for a change to the product. The benefit of Change Requests is that they provide a record of decisions and, due to their assessment process, ensure that the impact of the changes is understood across the project.

Component A component is a nontrivial, nearly independent, and replaceable part of a system that fulfills a clear function in the context of a well-defined architecture. A Component conforms to and provides the physical realization of a set of interfaces.

Configuration A configuration is the set of system artifacts that define a particular version of a system or part of a system.

Configuration Item A configuration item is an element that should be placed under configuration management. A Configuration Item is individually versioned and, thus, can be uniquely identified at a given point in time. A Configuration Item is part of a configuration.

Data Model (artifact) The Data Model describes the logical and physical representation of persistent data in the system. It also includes any behavior defined in the database, such as stored procedures, triggers, constraints, and so forth.

Database Designer (role) The Database Designer defines the tables, indexes, views, constraints, triggers, stored procedures, tablespaces or storage parameters, and other database-specific constructs needed to store, retrieve, and delete persistent objects.

Deployment Model (artifact) The Deployment Model shows the configuration of processing nodes at runtime, the communication links between them, and the elements that reside on them.

Design Class (artifact)   A Design Class is a description of a set of objects that share the same responsibilities, relationships, operations, attributes, and semantics. A Design Class is contained within the Design Model.

Design Guidelines (artifact)   The Design Guidelines contain project-specific guidance on how to create the system's design.

Design Model (artifact)   The Design Model describes the realization of Use Cases in terms of design elements, and is used as an essential input to activities in Implementation and Test. It contains Design Packages, Design Classes, Design Subsystems, Framework Components, Interfaces, and Use-Case Realizations.

Design Package (artifact)   A Design Package is a collection of Design Classes, relationships, Use-Case Realizations, diagrams, and other Design Packages. It is used to structure the Design Model by dividing it into smaller parts. A Design Package is contained within the Design Model.

Design Reviewer (role)   The Design Reviewer plans and conducts the formal design reviews.

Design Subsystem (artifact)   A Design Subsystem is a model element which has the semantics of a package (it can contain other model elements) and a class (it has behavior). The behavior of the subsystem is provided by classes or other subsystems it contains. A subsystem realizes one or more Interfaces, which define the behavior it can perform. A Design Subsystem is contained within the Design Model.

Designer (role)   The Designer defines the responsibilities, operations, attributes, and relationships of one or several design elements, and determines how they should be implemented.

Discipline   A discipline is a collection of activities that are related to a major "area of concern" within the overall project

Framework Component (artifact)   A Framework Component is a part of a system that encapsulates behavior, exposes a set of interfaces, has semantics defined by a component framework, and whose instances are deployable to a node (such as an individual computer), or a container (as defined by the component framework). A Framework Component is contained within the Design Model.

Glossary (artifact)   The Glossary defines important terms used by the project.

Implementation Directory (artifact)   An Implementation Directory is a physical directory (folder) in the file system that is used to organize files. An Implementation Directory is contained within the Implementation Model.

Implementation File (artifact)   An Implementation File represents a physical file that results from implementing and integrating design elements. Implementation Files include both deliverable files, such as executables, and files from which the deliverables are produced, such as source code files. An Implementation File is contained within the Implementation Model.

Implementation Guidelines (artifact)   The Implementation Guidelines contain project-specific guidance on how to create the system's implementation.

Implementation Model (artifact)   The Implementation Model is a composite, comprehensive artifact that encompasses all of the artifacts needed to build and manage the system in the runtime environment. The Implementation Model contains Implementation Directories and Implementation Files.

Implementation Reviewer (role)   The Implementation Reviewer plans and conducts the formal reviews of the implementation.

Implementer (role)   The Implementer is responsible for implementing and testing design elements, in accordance with the project's adopted standards.

Interface (artifact)   An Interface defines a set of behaviors (a set of operations). An Interface is contained within the Design Model.

Iteration   An Iteration is a distinct sequence of activities that results in a release (internal or external) of an executable product.

Iteration Plan (artifact)   An Iteration Plan is a time-sequenced set of activities and tasks, with assigned resources and task dependencies, for a given iteration.

Model   A model is a complete description of a system from a particular perspective ("complete" meaning that you don't need any additional information to understand the system from that perspective).

Navigation Map (artifact)   The Navigation Map expresses the structure of the screens in a system, along with their potential navigation pathways. The Navigation Map is contained within the User-Experience Model.

Phase   A phase is the time between two business milestones, during which a well-defined set of objectives is met, artifacts are completed, and decisions are made to move or not move into the next phase.

Programming Guidelines (artifact)   The Programming Guidelines describe the conventions to be used when working with a programming language.

Reference Architecture (artifact)   A Reference Architecture is, in essence, a predefined architectural pattern, or set of patterns, possibly partially or completely instantiated, designed and proven for use in particular business and technical contexts, together with supporting artifacts to enable their use. Often, these artifacts are harvested from previous projects.

Requirement   A requirement describes a condition or capability to which a system must conform, either derived directly from user needs, or stated in a contract, standard, specification, or other formally imposed document.

Requirements Reviewer (role)   The Requirements Reviewer plans and conducts the formal review of the requirements.

Requirements Specifier (role)   The Requirements Specifier details the requirements.

Review Record (artifact)   A Review Record is created to capture the results of the review of a project artifact.

Risk List (artifact)   A Risk List is a list of known and open risks to the project, sorted in decreasing order of importance and associated with specific mitigation or contingency actions.

Roadmap   A RUP roadmap provides a tour through RUP, with some viewpoint in mind. For example, that viewpoint may be a specific development context (for example, J2EE online enterprise systems), or a specific role (for example, software developer). A roadmap describes the elements of the process that are relevant to that viewpoint, and ignores the elements that are not relevant. A roadmap is intended to be a directed reading and learning aid and can be thought of as a customized view of the process.

Role   A role defines the behavior and responsibilities of an individual, or a set of individuals working together as a team, within the context of a software development organization. A role is responsible for one or more artifacts and performs a set of activities.

Screen (artifact)   A Screen is a user interface abstraction that is used to represent a completed user interface instance with which the actor works. A Screen is contained within the User-Experience Model.

Software Architect (role)   The Software Architect leads and coordinates technical activities that establish the overall structure of the system, the key system elements, and the interfaces between these elements.

Software Architecture Document (artifact)   The Software Architecture Document provides a comprehensive architectural overview of the system, using a number of different architectural views to depict different aspects of the system.

Stakeholder   A stakeholder is an individual who is materially affected by the outcome of the system.

Supplementary Specification (artifact)   The Supplementary Specification captures the system requirements that are not readily captured in the Use Cases. Such requirements include legal and regulatory requirements (and application standards), quality attributes of the system to be built (including usability, reliability, performance, and supportability requirements), and other requirements such as operating systems and environments, compatibility requirements, and design constraints.

System Analyst (role)   The System Analyst leads and coordinates requirements elicitation by outlining the system's functionality and by scoping the system.

Test Guidelines (artifact)   Test Guidelines are used to record policies such as standards to be adhered to by a project or practices to be followed by the practitioners on a given project.

Test Results (artifact)   Test Results are a collection of summary information determined from the raw output captured during the execution of one or more tests.

Test Script (artifact)   A Test Script is the step-by-step instructions that realize a test, enabling its execution. Test Scripts may take the form of either documented textual instructions that are executed manually or computer-readable instructions that enable automated test execution.

Use Case (artifact)   A Use Case is a sequence of actions a system performs that yields an observable result of value to a particular Actor. A Use Case is contained within the Use-Case Model.

Use-Case Model (artifact)   A Use-Case Model is a model of the system's intended functions and its environment, and serves as a contract between the customer and the developers. It contains Actors, Use Cases, and Use-Case Packages. The Use-Case Model is used as an essential input to activities in analysis, design, and test.

Use-Case Modeling Guidelines (artifact)   The Use-Case Modeling Guidelines contain project-specific guidance on how to create the system's Use-Case Model.

Use-Case Package (artifact)   A Use-Case Package is a collection of Use Cases, Actors, relationships, diagrams, and other Use-Case Packages. It is used to structure the Use-Case Model by dividing it into smaller parts. A Use-Case Package is contained within the Use-Case Model.

Use-Case Priority List (artifact)   The Use-Case Priority List contains a list of Use Cases and/or use-case scenarios in priority order.

Use-Case Realization (artifact)   A Use-Case Realization describes how a particular Use Case is realized within the Design Model, in terms of collaborating design elements. A Use-Case Realization is contained within the Design Model.

Use-Case Storyboard (artifact)   A Use-Case Storyboard is a logical and conceptual description of how a Use Case is realized in the user interface, including the interaction required between the Actor(s) and the system. A Use-Case Storyboard is contained within the User-Experience Model.

User-Experience Designer (role)   The User-Experience Designer defines the user actions, dynamic content, and navigation paths of one or several Screens, and determines how they should be implemented.

User-Experience Guidelines (artifact)   The User-Experience Guidelines contain project-specific guidance on how to create the system's user-experience.

User-Experience Model (artifact)   The User-Experience Model provides an abstraction of the user interface elements and the user's interaction with the system. It contains Screens, Use-Case Storyboards, and a Navigation Map. The User-Experience Model defines the contract between the presentation and business aspects of the system. A separate User-Experience Model is not needed if the system does not have a user-experience aspect (for example, a user-interface), or if that aspect is very well known, or of minor importance.

User-Experience Reviewer (role)   The User-Experience Reviewer plans and conducts the formal reviews of the system's user experience.

Viewpoint   A viewpoint is used to describe an architecture. A viewpoint describes one or more system model(s) and view(s) (projections) of those models, the stakeholders interested in the view(s), and the stakeholders' concerns that should be addressed through the view(s).

Virtual Directory   A virtual directory is a logical name that is understood by the Web server, and that the Web server (through configuration information) can map to a physical directory.

Vision (artifact)   The Vision defines the problem being solved, and the stakeholders' view of the product to be developed, specified in terms of the stakeholders' key needs and features.

Workflow Detail   A Workflow Detail is a grouping of activities that are often performed "together" to produce a specific result.

Workspace   A workspace is a private area in which changes to artifacts are made, but are not immediately visible to other team members.

Acronyms

Acronym	*Description*
BMP	Bean-Managed Persistence
CMP	Container-Managed Persistence
CORBA	Common Object Request Broker Architecture
DOM	Document Object Model
EAR	Enterprise ARchive
EIS	Enterprise Information System
EJB	Enterprise JavaBean
HTML	HyperText Markup Language
HTTP	HyperText Transfer Protocol
IIOP	Internet Inter-ORB Protocol
J2EE	Java 2 Platform, Enterprise Edition
J2ME	Java 2 Platform, Micro Edition
J2SE	Java 2 Platform, Standard Edition
JAAS	Java Authentication and Authorization Service
JAR	Java ARchive
JAXP	Java API for XML Parsing
JCA	J2EE Connector Architecture
JDBC	Java DataBase Connectivity
JMS	Java Message Service
JNDI	Java Naming and Directory Interface
JSP	JavaServer Pages
JTA	Java Transaction API
JVM	Java Virtual Machine
MTS	Microsoft Transaction Server
OMG	Object Management Group
RAR	Resource ARchive
RMI	Remote Method Invocation
RUP	Rational Unified Process
SAX	Simple API for XML Parsing
SSL	Secure Socket Layer
WAP	Wireless Access Protocol
WAR	Web ARchive
WML	Wireless Markup Language
WORA	Write Once, Run Anywhere
XML	eXtensible Markup Language
XSLT	eXtensible Stylesheet Language Transformations

Bibliography

Alur, Deepak, Crupi, John, and Malks, Dan. (2001) *Core J2EE Patterns: Best Practices and Design Strategies*, Upper Saddle River, New Jersey: Prentice Hall.

Cheesman, John and Daniels, John. (2001) *UML Components: A Simple Process for Specifying Component-Based Software*, Reading, MA: Addison-Wesley.

Conallen, Jim. (2000) *Building Web Applications with UML*, Reading, MA: Addison-Wesley.

Herzum, Peter and Sims, Oliver. (2000) *Business Component Factory: A Comprehensive Overview of Component-Based Development for the Enterprise*, New York: John Wiley & Sons.

Institute of Electrical and Electronics Engineers (IEEE). (2000) "IEEE-Std-1371-2000 Recommended Practice for Architectural Description of Software Intensive Systems."

Java Community Process. "Java Specification Request 26 UML Profile for EJB," available at: www.jcp.org.

Kruchten, Philippe. (2000) *The Rational Unified Process, An Introduction*, Second Edition, Reading, MA: Addison-Wesley.

Kruchten, Philippe. (November 1995). "The 4 + 1 View Model of Architectures," *IEEE Software*, 12:6.

Rational Software Corporation. (2002) "Rational Unified Process 2002.05," available at: www.rational.com.

Shaw, Mary and Garlan, David. (1996) *Software Architecture: Perspectives on an Emerging Discipline*, Upper Saddle River, New Jersey: Prentice Hall.

Index

Rational Minds and Addison-Wesley Authors—
What a Combination!

0-201-73829-5

0-201-70913-9

0-8053-5340-2

0-8053-0594-7

0-201-57168-4

0-201-70044-1

0-201-73038-3

0-201-79166-8

0-201-42289-1

0-201-54435-0

0-201-92476-5

0-201-57169-2

0-201-70710-1

0-321-12247-X

0-201-72163-5

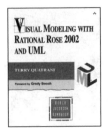

0-201-72932-6

0-201-30958-0

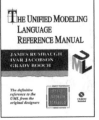

0-201-30998-X

0-201-60478-7

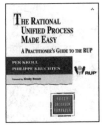

0-321-16609-4

 For more information on these books by Rational Software Corporation employees, please go to **www.awprofessional.com**

informIT